SOUTH ASIAN FEMINISMS IN DIASPORA

SOUTH ASIAN FEMINISMS IN DIASPORA

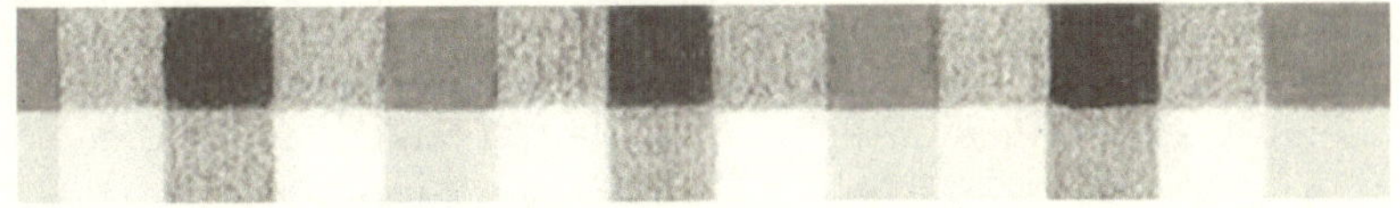

CRITICAL PERSPECTIVES FROM CANADA

EDITED BY
AMINA JAMAL,
JANE KU, AND
MARYAM KHAN

UNIVERSITY *of* **ALBERTA** PRESS

Published by

University of Alberta Press
1-16 Rutherford Library South
11204 89 Avenue NW
Edmonton, Alberta, Canada T6G 2J4
amiskwaciwâskahikan | Treaty 6 | Métis Territory
ualbertapress.ca | uapress@ualberta.ca

LIBRARY AND ARCHIVES CANADA CATALOGUING IN PUBLICATION

Title: South Asian feminisms in diaspora : critical perspectives from Canada / edited by Amina Jamal, Jane Ku, and Maryam Khan.
Names: Jamal, Amina, editor | Ku, Jane, editor. | Khan, Maryam (Lecturer in social work), editor.
Description: Includes bibliographical references.
Identifiers: Canadiana (print) 20250157373 | Canadiana (ebook) 20250157438 | ISBN 9781772128222 (softcover) | ISBN 9781772128451 (EPUB) | ISBN 9781772128468 (PDF)
Subjects: LCSH: South Asians—Canada—Social conditions. | LCSH: South Asians—Canada—Economic conditions. | LCSH: South Asians—Canada—Politics and government. | LCSH: South Asian diaspora. | LCSH: Feminism—Canada.
Classification: LCC FC106.S66 S73 2025 | DDC 305.8914/071—dc23

First edition, first printing, 2025.
First printed and bound in Canada by Houghton Boston Printers, Saskatoon, Saskatchewan.
Copyediting and proofreading by Angela Pietrobon.

GPSR: Easy Access System Europe | Mustamäe tee 50, 10621 Tallinn, Estonia | gpsr.requests@easproject.com

This book has been published with the help of a grant from the Federation for the Humanities and Social Sciences, through the Awards to Scholarly Publications Program, using funds provided by the Social Sciences and Humanities Research Council of Canada.

University of Alberta Press gratefully acknowledges the support received for its publishing program from the Government of Canada, the Canada Council for the Arts, and the Government of Alberta through the Alberta Media Fund.

Canadä

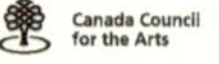

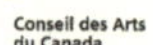

Amina dedicates this book to her beloved mother Kaniz Fatima Asar (d. 2009), whose caring and forceful presence is always near her heart.

Jane dedicates this book to Yu Chao Liu, who died on Father's Day during the pandemic, and whose loss became more keenly felt as she tried to reconnect with her childhood in India and when she needed help translating her memories to the present.

Maryam dedicates this volume to Kaushilya Weerapura, whose love has been healing.

Contents

Acknowledgements

WE ACKNOWLEDGE the graduate and undergraduate students whose questions, concerns, interactions, and practices within and outside the classroom inspired us to think seriously about their—and our—disparate connections to the South Asian experience in Canada. Thanks for motivating us to revive South Asian-ness as a site for renewing historical affinities, shared memories, and significant alliances that have been undermined by shifting economic, geopolitical, ideological transformations in the societies and states of the South Asian mainland. The project that eventually culminated in this edited volume also involved many of these students, some of whom need to be thanked individually. A special acknowledgement and thanks are due to Sonia Baweja, the project coordinator, website designer, copy editor, and symposium facilitator. We also thank all the research assistants and teaching assistants who worked with us in organizing and facilitating an online symposium in pandemic conditions. We especially acknowledge their interested participation in the discussions in addition to their notetaking and coordination responsibilities. Thank you to Anum Urooj-Sage, Belinda Ha, Enna Kim, Farah Virani-Murji, Isabella Eldeib, Katherine Graham, Samrit Brar, Sonia Baweja (again), and Oceana Nyala.

A very heartfelt thank you goes to Dr. Pramila Aggarwal, longtime Toronto activist, teacher, and friend, for being a collaborator and advisor through the entire project. We also want to thank Dr. Tania Das Gupta for her help in shaping our earlier thinking, and for her groundbreaking work on South Asian feminist activism. Finally, we thank all the dynamic South Asian feminists, activists, and community workers who participated in the symposium.

We are grateful for the financial and in-kind support that we received from many sources. The research symposium leading to this volume was partly funded by the Social Sciences and Humanities Research Council of Canada (SSHRC Participation grant number 611-2020-0191). We also acknowledge the support provided at Toronto Metropolitan University (TMU) by the Dean of Arts; Department of Sociology; Toronto Metropolitan Faculty Association; and Immigration and Settlement Studies program. We also appreciate the support of the Manulife Centre for Community Health Research (MCCHR) at Wilfrid Laurier University. In addition, Amina and Maryam would like to thank Dr. Jane Ku, Chair of Women's Studies, University of Windsor, for providing personal support in kind and cash for this project.

Introduction

AMINA JAMAL, JANE KU, AND MARYAM KHAN

THIS COLLECTION BRINGS TOGETHER diverse academic and activist performativities and interrogations by feminists who find themselves interpellated by the category of "South Asian" and "South Asian-ness," in spite of—or as a result of—their embeddedness in Canada, a settler colonial society located on the traditional ancestral lands of Indigenous Peoples. We recognize Canada's failures toward Indigenous populations and that South Asians, like other settlers and migrants, are entwined in the genocide and dispossession of Indigenous Peoples (Kennedy-Kish [Bell] and Carniol 2017; Tuck and Yang 2012). As anti-racist feminists, we acknowledge that the South Asian diaspora exists as an incommensurable category constructed for the exigencies of the colonial state that produces disjunctures for many feminist activists and academics included within the collectivity/community and identity represented by the "South Asian." Informed by these and other interstitial locations, this unique collection features feminists, especially emerging scholars, in Canada who intentionally came together to revive a diasporic and radical notion of a feminist community under the umbrella term "South Asian," to reclaim it from hegemonic and essentializing forces, and in response to a crisis of citizenship and nationalisms.

Some of the questions that motivate this book are the following:

- How do we move away from the hegemonic constructions of "South Asian" in contemporary global agendas of neoliberalism, populism, militarism, and state nationalisms, which also seep into our own research and activist projects?
- What kind of activist-academic subjects do we need to become in order to interrupt and intervene in the masculinist, heteronormative, and militaristic nationalisms that permeate self-representations of the South Asian diaspora in Canada?
- How do we reconfigure and resituate South Asian-ness as an identity informed by alliances with—rather than competition with—diverse equity and rights seeking groups, in particular Indigenous, Black, queer, and others?

This edited collection is a critical exploration of how a South Asian feminist politics may operate both as an affective positionality and as an activist basis for challenging identitarian and exclusionary discourses found in diasporic contexts in the Global North—mainly constituted of the Canadian, US, and European nations. From a transnational feminist perspective, these nation-states are unified in bolstering nationalisms and notions of nationhood that deploy exclusionary policies and tactics that adversely impact immigrants, refugees, and asylum seekers (Dua 2007; Grewal 2005; Walia 2014). Recent interventions by queer, postcolonial, and transnational as well as genealogically diverse, hybridized, and multi-faith feminist scholars and activists have drawn attention to the ways in which an unproblematized "South Asian" identity in diasporic situations can reproduce nationalism, patriarchy, and class, along with oppressive forms of religion, culture, and language, and bolster mythical histories of origin and return (Ku 2019a; Babar 2008; Narayan and Purkayastha 2011; Jamal 2015).

South Asian and South Asian-ness

In a provocative but indispensable boundary-setting plenary address, given at our symposium on critical South Asian diasporic feminisms, and included as an afterword to this book, anti-racist scholar and activist Sunera Thobani cautions us against "taking comfort in older identities and identifications [as this] no longer suffices to meet the challenges of our times." Thobani raises the questions that must necessarily guide any project that gestures toward community sharing through acts of community b(e)aring. Her concerns are worth engaging with for readers of this edited collection; indeed, many may prefer to read this book backwards, starting with Thobani's incisive reflections on the possibilities and limitations that we encounter in critical interrogations of identity/ies and "community." Thobani compiles important questions regarding the contestations of theory, knowledge production, and activism that inhere in discussions of histories of diaspora, colonialism, and postcolonialism, and that complicate our responses to the calamities of late capitalism and the disintegrating liberal-democratic order. Most pertinent to this volume is her enquiry: "What is it that is 'critical' about 'critical South Asian feminisms'? Where is this 'critical' approach directed?"

We read this not as an "ask" for definitions but as a rhetorical call for deeper interrogation of colonial homogenizing tendencies by mobilizing around the term "South Asian" and the South Asian feminist subject. We acknowledge the possibility of our project being mis/recognized as another liberal attempt to construct an "ethno-feminism" that might be positioned among a range of minority feminisms, ranked by their relationship to "white feminism" and demanding nationalist representation in the name of the autonomous Enlightenment subject. We look to the quintessential postcolonial critic Gayatri Spivak and her "deconstructionist variety of Marxism and feminism" (Chakrabarty 2012, 4). Following Dipesh Chakrabarty, we recall Spivak's epochal insight that the dilemmas of representation are always already entangled with the imperative to represent. To clarify, we do not plead "strategic essentialism," nor do we entertain charges of "epistemic violence," but rather argue that even a problematic strategy can sometimes lead to a satisfactory or at least useful outcome. As such, we use the identity South Asian feminisms "under erasure," that is, as a signifying practice employed by

Heidegger and later Derrida, and explained by Spivak (1997) thusly: "to write a word [concept], cross it out, and include both [the original word and the delete marker]" (xiv). The construct South Asian feminisms moves within and against essentialisms and epistemic violence, as at once a presence and an erasure, in a way that ensures the contradictory-ness of its meaning for our discussion. Returning to Dipesh Chakrabarty (2012), we attempt to write together "two different configurations" of South Asian-ness—as diasporics challenging both settler colonial and South Asian states, and at the same time as humans engaged in decolonization as a global project—first "through a collapsing of the person and the subject as in liberal or Marxist thought, and now through a separation of the two" (4-5). This duality is evident in the myriad discursive and embodied ways in which individual authors engage both South Asian (identity) and South Asian-ness (belonging) as a mode of identification, that is, as a "subject" interrogated through critique, and sometimes as a tension between these. Thus, the radical critique brought forward by South Asian feminism destabilizes the very historical, religious, cultural, and national forces that have ontologized South Asian-ness as a diasporic reality that we confront today, even if we refuse the (mis) category. We acknowledge that South Asian affiliation, as a desire, longing, and disavowal, is also suspect and requires ongoing vigilance by employing an "under erasure" practice.

As will become evident, the authors in this collection have varying understandings and practices of "criticality," and demonstrate a myriad of affinities/disaffinities, connectivities/disconnectivities, and varying relationships with South Asian-ness and feminisms. In her recollections about the feminist movement in Montreal in Chapter 1, for Dolores Chew—who traces her early critical awareness to Naxalbari communism in Bengal and the theories of subaltern studies scholars—"'South Asian'...eventually seemed to resonate best as a form of self-identification" in which to root her activism and scholarship. For Ameera Khan, a Bengali American transgender woman born and raised in the United States (US), it is the project of building an Islamic liberation theology (Chapter 15) that looms over her South Asian sociocultural affinity. Across and within the chapters, perceptive readers will easily discern the effort to challenge the status quo of South Asian-ness and South Asian feminisms, as contributors attempt to wrestle with ongoing colonialities, legacies of imperialism, climate and land justice, and settler colonial relations in Canada and elsewhere.

This diverse Canadian collection features seventeen scholars at different career levels and representing a range of geopolitical and cultural affiliations, including Parsi, Indo-Caribbean, North Indian, Bengali, Pakistani, South Indian, Bangladeshi, and Hakka Chinese. These scholars describe their struggles with gendered aspects of religious and cultural identities, issues of racism and white supremacy, postcolonial and diasporic identities and struggles, South Asian queerness, violence against women, and labour and organizing. They direct us away from culturalist recognitions and representations that tend to mythologize—and thus authorize—identity, culture, and religion. Instead, the scholars point to an interweaving of interests and hegemonies across national boundaries that enables the emergence of new modes of cultural and moral regulation and the continuation of older ones. These contributions collectively and individually interrogate the social, cultural, and political challenges relevant to notions of South Asia in Canada, and point to the possibility of developing a unique critical praxis.

Cultural Political Hegemonies and Transnational Feminism

Rising religio-militaristic nationalisms, patriarchal and heteronormative ideas about gender and culture, and intensifying discourses of cultural/ethnic purity in South Asia and elsewhere are social and political threats that raise the question of why and how a diasporic South Asian feminist space should be mobilized to counter such tendencies. Diverse scholars from queer criticism, anti-racism, transnational feminism, work and capitalism, migration and diaspora, anti-Black racism, and Indigenous literatures have brought forward insights into how South Asian feminism can be rethought and revitalized. There have been critiques of discourses of "community" and "nation" that are configured through heteronormative patriarchal and middle-class narratives that serve the interests of capitalism and male bourgeoisies (Gopinath 2005; Abu-Laban and Gabriel 2002; Joseph 2002; Khan 2018; Reddy 2017). In agreement with Miranda Joseph (2002) about the limitations of "community," we are dismayed that the South Asian "community" has become a neoliberal project and site of capitalist expansion rather than a cultural and social respite from the logics of the market. Such community discourses can be challenged by a queer analytical lens that encourages us to explore other "histories" of transnational linkages and "other" types of affinities (Gopinath 2005). They can also be challenged by building alliances among migrant women and other racialized cultural and ethnic groups to challenge the neoliberal global work regime (Joseph 2002; Mohanty 2013). Against the bordering tendencies of community and identity, critical anti-racist feminists (as well as the graduate students we supervise) compel us to theorize how the stabilizing of diasporic communities is related to anti-Blackness and the settler colonial expropriation of Indigenous lands (Day 2015; Ku 2019b; Lawrence and Dua 2005; Saranillio 2013; Tuck and Yang 2012).[1] South Asians are often cited as white-proximate model minorities in neoliberal nation-states like Canada and the US, and are used to measure Black and Indigenous communities' and individuals' participation in civic and economic structures (Prashad 2001). Other scholars such as Jamillah Karim (Islamic Monthly 2013); and Maria Khwaja Bazi (2016) have noted the persistence of what Bazi (2016) calls "aspirational whiteness" among South Asian and Middle Eastern Muslim immigrants—and we add, other immigrants—who try to integrate into the white community and be accepted by white people.

We advance a South Asian feminist scholarship from an intersectional, feminist, and critical approach (Ahmed-Ghosh 2015). Canadian scholars focusing on South Asian diasporas have taken an intersectional feminist perspective on specific issues impacting South Asians, such as gender, aging, employment, and migration (Aggarwal and Das Gupta 2013; Das Gupta 1994; Brown 2006; Soni-Sinha 2013). Our understanding of "intersectionality" (as developed by Black feminist scholars Kimberlé Crenshaw, Patricia Hill Collins, and others) is the opposite of the descriptive, additive ways in which this concept tends to be utilized to enumerate identifications; we view it as a radical concept that enjoins us to understand the ways in which practices of power create new and unnamed oppressions, which need to be highlighted and resisted. Furthermore, intersectionality is a powerful tool for developing a reflexive lens to understand the hierarchical and discriminatory practices through which a hegemonic South Asian-ness promotes some of its constituent identifications as desirable and demotes or erases other identities as less worthy. This focus is important in order to theorize the relationship of South Asian-ness to settler colonialism through questioning South Asian complicatedness in the ongoing practices of settler colonialism, anti-Black racism, and other local/global forms of violence. South Asians, like all settlers and migrants, must embrace the covenants made between the Indigenous Peoples and Europeans (Kennedy-Kish [Bell] and Carniol 2017). Examining the inherent hegemonies of South Asian-ness is a necessary space-clearing if we are to develop true solidarity with Indigenous and Black feminist struggles in Canada—in our classrooms, in our institutions, and at the larger societal level. With this collection, we also assert the political necessity of reclaiming the diasporic South Asian feminist space to challenge the emerging conservatisms, neoliberalisms, and nationalisms that are speaking in our name, from both the mainland and Canada.

The chapters in this volume indicate that diasporic activist involvement in South Asian politics seems to be accelerating in contradictory ways. For example, in Chapter 9, Sailaja V. Krishnamurti deepens concerns that Hindu groups in North America aggressively participate in attempts to undermine struggles against caste-based discrimination in academia (Feminist Critical Hindu Studies Collective 2022). At the same time, diasporic locations—for example, the Sri Lankan, Pakistani, and Myanmar diasporas—continue to be significant sites of political struggle for influencing homeland politics. Most recently, Pakistanis based in Europe and North America have become more vocal and activistic as both supporters and opponents of the government during Pakistan's deepening economic and political crisis (Husain 2022; News Desk 2022; Al Jazeera 2022).

Our analytical approach draws on and resonates with "transnational feminist practices," conceptualized by Grewal and Kaplan (1994) as attending to the spatial and temporal marking of diasporic experience in ways that "move beyond constructed oppositions without ignoring the histories that have informed these conflicts or the valid concerns about power relations that have represented or structured the conflicts up to this point" (17). Eschewing the relativistic tendencies of global feminism to construct a unitary category of gender (and, we would add, of oppression), the authors ask us to "articulate the relationship of gender to scattered hegemonies such as global economic structures, patriarchal nationalisms, 'authentic' forms of tradition, local structures of domination, and legal-juridical oppression on multiple levels" (17). Indeed, we use the notion "diasporic" intentionally to signal the affective connections between what Vijay Mishra (2007) calls the "classical diaspora" and the transnationalism of contemporary migrants of South Asian affiliation to Canada. The aim is to direct and focus attention on the "now" of the classical diaspora and the "here/there" aspects of transnationality. Diaspora is thus reconceptualized as diverse modes of living through—and countering—"scattered hegemonies," which may enable an "ethnic feminism" to cultivate "Otherwise-ness" and recognize opportunities for fostering transnational feminist practices within the scholarly and academic spaces we inhabit.

We have an obligation as feminist academics and activists in diasporic situations to challenge social and political threats that are common not only in the Global North but also across South Asia, including reassertions of religio-militaristic nationalisms, the rise of patriarchal and heteronormative ideas about gender and culture, and intensifying discourses of cultural/ethnic purity. There is also a need for a collectively shared effort and collaboration to align South Asian feminisms with other ongoing struggles by scholars and activists focussed on feminist, labour, and queer studies, whether or not they are affiliated with South Asian identities, in order to disrupt notions of diaspora/homeland as modern/traditional or good/bad or utopic/dystopic, as well as other hegemonic practices.

Scholarly Context

This collection is the culmination of three years of dialogue and connections among a group of feminist scholars and activists in Canada, which began as sporadic conversations around concerns that our graduate students raised about conflicting and diverse affiliations and investments in South Asian identity and politics. Methodologically, our first step was an informal discussion in the summer of 2018 with graduate students and colleagues, including visiting South Asian scholars and diasporic Canadian South Asians, at which we discussed the changing social and political realities of the post-9/11 era, both on the South Asian mainland and in Canada.

Although there has been productive South Asian and anti-racist feminist scholarship on the changes and shifts in the South Asian community, far less attention has been paid to feminist and queer concerns, intra-South Asian tensions related to heightened awareness of religious identities, the transnational rise of populist leadership and exclusionary nationalisms. Other issues that deserve urgent attention and feminist intersectional analysis are the identifications and dis/identifications of groups, such as Shia and Ahmadi Muslims, Tamils, and Hindu and Muslim Dalits, the intensification of anti-Muslim surveillance, and the association of Islam and Muslims with homophobia and transphobia (Das Gupta 2021; Kamran 2019; Varma and Seshan 2003). Amidst these social and political developments, there has been renewed questioning among South Asian scholars in diasporic and mainland locations about the possibilities and limitations of "South Asian" as an umbrella for community and regional organizing and as a diasporic identity (e.g., Kurien 2003; Ghosh 2013; Mohammad-Arif 2015).

While engaging with all of these aspects, our central concern was that the cultural-political domain and emotional force of "South Asian" as a diasporic identity were being actively appropriated by consumerist, capitalist, and neoliberal interests (e.g., Gopinath 2005; Grewal 2005). This led us to organize a roundtable as part of feminist sociology at the Canadian Sociological Association's annual conference, which sought to bring together scholars interested in the study of "South Asian-ness" in Canada. Encouraged by the level of participation and tenor of discussions, we developed a Social Sciences and Humanities Research Council of Canada Partnership Grant to expand our roundtable discussions into a two-day symposium, featuring about thirty participants as well as a strong team of graduate research assistants. This edited collection is a tangible outcome of the conversations that took place at the symposium, which was held online due to the COVID-19 pandemic. The choice to gather in a small group was deliberate as it offered a safe space for debating complex and possibly contentious issues around identity, faith, nation, sexuality, class, caste, and gender.

In informal and formal discussions, we mulled over "desi" queerness; divisive religion-, race-, and class-based diasporic politics; and feminism and the "community." We scrutinized national and populist discourses in Canada that link diasporic communities with post-9/11 security concerns. And we discussed how to respond to the racism directed against Chinese and other Asian groups amidst the COVID-19 pandemic. To enhance the degree of trust and confidentiality, the discussions were not recorded, but our team of research assistants took meticulous notes that generated key themes for this volume. We collectively affirmed the need to underline a fluid and inclusive South Asian identity in Canada that recognizes heterogeneous embodiments and histories that transcend South Asia as a geographic region—for example, Canadian-born generations, as well as those from East Asia, the Caribbean, East Africa, and the Middle East, and others with complex and convoluted ties to the idea of "South Asia."

Situating This Book in the Literature

This volume builds on the existing scholarship on South Asians in Canada, but also diverges from it in a significant way. We seek to centre the experiences and voices of marginalized and unclaimed identities within the larger category and to challenge both colonial/state and unexamined ideas about "community," with the explicit aim of deconstructing and reconstructing radical notions of South Asian-ness. This book reflexively constructs feminist anti-racist and critical knowledges and praxis that will help to counter the hegemonic representations of "South Asian" that can seep into our research, teaching, and activist projects in the Canadian context. For example, in Chapter 11, Maryam Khan dismantles a notion of South Asian community that is situated within the heteronormative ideals and compulsory heterosexuality found in discourses of "South Asian Muslim woman" configurations. The challenging of assumptions of normalcy and deviance embedded within unquestioned notions of community can erase queerness from Muslim women's lives, and from collective imaginings of a historical past solely involving heterosexual Islam.

Recent volumes on South Asian feminisms published in diasporic locations (important examples include Loomba and Lukose 2012; Roy 2012; Jha and Kurian 2018) have ably enhanced our understanding of feminist activism and organizing, mostly within the South Asian mainland. As such, they cleared an important scholarly space for this volume. While learning and benefiting from these collections, we felt the need for a different mode of conceptualizing and analyzing identity, one that begins with a focus on the diaspora community and examines feminist projects as transnationally circulating narratives that may sometimes align, sometimes misalign, and sometimes throw diasporic feminist practices out of sync with "homeland" feminisms. Colonial and postcolonial memories, economic imperatives, and affective ties connect diaspora with the mainland, but diasporas also have their own memories, struggles, and engagements that are specific to their present and future home space. To critically understand diasporic space, we eschew conventional histories of origin of the term "South Asian," both in its iteration as a disciplinary project of the multicultural Canadian state and in its identitarian embrace by self-anointed guardians, leaders, and "community spokespersons" (elite and educated men and women), who serve as nodal points for the expansion of exclusionary and purist cultural, political, and religious projects from the homeland. This book forges critical alternatives to masculinist, heteronormative, and militaristic nationalisms and diasporas through critical dialogues between graduate students, academics, community groups, and activist constituents while concurrently analyzing differences, sources of tensions, commonalities, and overlaps. We thus highlight the concerns and hopes of a newer generation of South Asian feminists, especially graduate students and emergent scholars. In doing this, we seek to invite younger generations to consider the appeal and utility of South Asian organizing. Indeed, this volume is a small step toward showcasing the richness and diversity of South Asian feminist scholarship, which tends to be obscured in dominant invocations of "identity" and "community" within South Asian studies as well as South Asian feminisms.

This collection reflects feminist disillusionment with nations and nationalisms, resulting from seventy-five years of violence between and within major South Asian states—whose victims have been heterogeneous in terms of gender, class, caste, religion, and so on. For example, in Chapter 6, Safiyya Hosein uses an auto-ethnographic approach to detail the parallels between the migration of indentured labour from the mainland to the Caribbean, belonging and identity within her family's life and journey, and the Marvel Muslim superhero character Kamala Khan.

This collection also revitalizes South Asian feminist politics by mobilizing around social justice, relationalities, and mutualities within the diaspora and in alliances with other political and rights-seeking groups (for example, Indigenous, Black, and queer). This broadens the context of South Asian-ness in Canada by signalling toward the intersectionalities of Sinophobia, Islamophobia, and rising Hindutva nationalisms, emphasizing the diasporic affects and effects of mainland violence, culture, and politics. This helps us develop a political framework that allows us to re-interpret our histories, and to build on relationships at multiple levels—from the personal to the macro-sociological—that challenge nationalist and global hegemonic forces. For example, in Chapter 14, Jane Ku interrogates nationalism as a site of affective belonging that is both cynical about and desiring of a different kind of politics, which can only be signalled by recuperating and building different relationships and connections.

We recognize the impossibility of an all-encompassing volume, and readers will no doubt note the absence of many key pieces of what should at least constitute a truly representative, even if illusionary, "South Asian feminism." Some particularly regretful limitations of this collection are the missing voices of Dalit feminists, disabled persons, and communities that would add accounts from Kashmiri, Afghan, and Rohingya women. We also acknowledge that there needs to be a more expansive and deeper engagement with urgent issues of transness and trans struggles that would augment the contribution of Ameera Khan. As well, chapters on class and social relations, migrant struggles, worker mobilizations, and more could be included. These erasures were not through oversight or lack of awareness, but rather were due to time and access constraints—and above all, our intention to avoid risking tokenism in the pursuit of "inclusion." As academics in Canada, we are especially aware of the urgent need to support Dalit struggles for inclusion and equity in North American institutions, and we recognize this volume is incomplete without the intervention of Dalit feminist voices. We also understand that it is not simply the presence/absence but the very terms of engagement of and with Dalit feminist voices in projects that demand a painstaking reflexivity and criticality. We agree that the persistence of Dalitness and similar caste-class "difference" within the "South Asian community," as well as the nature of such representation/engagement—as discussed by Dalit feminists such as Kazim (2022), Rege (1998), Guru (2020) and Patel (2016)—are likely to become touchstones for the claims of critical South Asian feminisms in Canada (see also Patel and Da Costa 2022). In this volume, Sailaja V. Krishnamurti's critique of the normalizing of Brahmannical Hinduism among diasporic scholars is a step toward such an examination of caste erasure.

Some of the erasures in this volume also stem from this project's informal and affective origins. Many of the authors were somewhat "self-selected," as these activists and academics had responded to our call at Congress 2019 and thus constituted a loosely formed "community of interest" around the critical feminist examination of South Asian-ess. These formed the core participants of a more formally constituted two-day workshop. In addition, the workshop acquired other participants through an unintentional "snowball" method, as individuals who heard about the project through interpersonal connections indicated their interest in joining us. Cognizant of the exclusivist character of South Asian academia, we later undertook a more intentional, directed, and wider recruitment process, which achieved some, albeit limited, results. We call to the wider activist and scholarly communities to engage with the aforementioned topics and identities in a meaningful way.

It is our hope that this collection will be of use to graduate students and academics researching and writing at the nexus of diasporic South Asian studies and intersectional, transnational, and Third World feminisms. We envisage this whole text, or a handful of chapters, featuring as readings in undergraduate and graduate syllabi in diasporic and settlement studies; social work and sociology courses on identity and lived experiences; Asian studies; and gender, women, and religious studies courses. The critical lens deployed throughout the volume will help elucidate for readers the geopolitical and transnational connections that follow bodies and identities across boundaries. We hope that this text will draw the attention of activists and community members who are organizing in South Asian diasporic contexts in Canada, in other settler colonial societies, and in the West more generally. It will also be informative for those in South Asia and elsewhere who are seeking to build solidarity and critical knowledge to challenge global hegemonies that require critique and reframing.

Organization of the Book

Continuing engagements among diverse South Asian feminists enabled us to translate our objectives into the four sections that follow this introductory chapter. Section One is titled "Identifications and Disidentifications." This section maps the history and processes by which "South Asian" emerged as a resistant mode of cultural and political self-identification to challenge discrimination and racism in Canada. It speaks to diasporic experiences and feminist memories of South Asian women in Canada by problematizing a long history of engagement with political, social, and epistemic structures that have enabled, but also limited, the scope of South Asian women's feminist identity and political organizing. The contributors revisit the diasporic trajectory of "South Asian-ness" in Canada and feminist memories of community organizing in the face of Eurocentric systems and structures. Some of these structures exist outside the diasporic community, as well as in colonized patriarchal traces within such communities. For example, the contributors reflect on their own experiences as racialized women through an implicit sense of "community"—even when the term "South Asian" was not yet in existence, as Dolores Chew notes in Chapter 1—and their experiences acquire intensity and urgency when juxtaposed with a more recent context. Chew, a professor of history and humanities at Marianopolis College, explores and theorizes a history of diasporic South Asian feminist activism over four decades. This chapter conveys the constant dialogic of praxis, which requires one to remain critical, question, dialogue, discuss, share, stay bold, remain unafraid, and retain and nurture communities of kindred spirits. In Chapter 2, Marshia Akbar draws attention to the erasure of Bangladeshi women among the categories of both "South Asian" and "Muslim." Based on an empirical study of Bangladeshi Muslim immigrant women who operate businesses in "Bangla Town" in Toronto, Akbar's chapter explicates how women's lived experiences are diverse and complex, as are their religious and spatial practices. The women in her study have constructed an ethnicity-based Bangladeshi Muslim group identity that not only challenges the notion of a single global Muslim identity but also participates in active place-making that interrelates their diverse identities with their workplaces. In Chapter 3, Mandeep Kaur Mucina constructs a genealogy of *izzat* as it appears throughout narratives, language, and the history of northern India, exposing izzat's movement from a system of morality to a tool for gender-based violence. Violence and the word for "honour" are both often intimately connected to immigrant South Asian cultures and religions in Canada, with very little discussion or research examining the significance of "honour" and its association with honour-based violence. Mucina examines the construct of izzat as the word for "honour" by engaging with narratives of second-generation Punjabi women who have survived "honour-based violence" within their family and/or community. This chapter aims at shifting dominant discourses that use honour-based violence as a tool to justify Orientalism and cultural racism toward South Asian bodies in the West, and focuses on exploring a deeper more nuanced understanding of izzat from northern India.

Section Two is titled "Unpacking the Problematics." This section maps the feminist diasporic imaginary of South Asian-ness through the reflections and experiences of women scholars and activists inhabiting different generational spaces. A rethinking of "South Asian" as identity and politics takes into account the discourses that colonize us as raced, gendered, and sexual subjects simultaneously. This section examines intersecting hegemonic nationalisms that challenge the possibilities for South Asian feminisms in Canada. South Asian-ness needs to be understood through the intersectionality of postcolonial racism, increasing white nationalism, and neoliberal capitalism, along with the globally circulating Hindutva ideology, post-9/11 Islamophobia, and post-pandemic Sinophobia, as well as re-emergent sexist, racist, and homophobic backlash. The contributors unsettle the myriad discursive representations of South Asian-ness with a shared assumption that representations in films, media, social media, literature, and political discourse have become more important than ever as a means of constructing the self and the other in modern nation-states. Resistance to oppressive and unjust modes of representing identity and otherness lies at the heart of feminist, anti-racist, queer, and Indigenous struggles in the contemporary era.

The chapters examine the challenges and possibilities presented to South Asian feminisms in Canada by the discursive representations of South Asian-ness that continue to regulate us in colonizing ways. We consider this an important attempt toward decolonizing our own understanding, by opening a path to a wider understanding of South Asian-ness and rejecting hegemonic identities imposed by neoliberal monopolistic versions of community and society. Each of the chapters in this section reflects a different engagement with the intersecting discourses that circulate within and across the diasporic community and transnationally. For example, in Chapter 4, Nayyar S. Javed draws on her struggle as a racialized practitioner of psychology and her encounter with racialized recipients of services to critically examine the discourses and practices in her field. Revisiting the theories of Edward Said (1979) and Frantz Fanon (1967; 2004), Javed frames her experiences and her work in mental health services in Saskatchewan to problematize "imposter syndrome" among racialized women, interpreting it as a "protective strategy individuals facing the challenges of discrimination use to survive" in a settler colonial context. In Chapter 5, Sarah Shah broadens "Muslim" identity by examining two trends noted in an empirical study in Toronto. A non-binary Pakistani Muslim with roots in the US and Canada, Shah asks us to understand Muslim reflexivity not as a monolithic phenomenon but as involving two divergent trends: exclusivity, which frames only one approach to Islam as correct, and inclusivity, which frames multiple approaches as correct. These novel findings have implications for better understanding the role of religiosity/Islam in diasporic identity formation and practices. The author locates their study as an important contribution to South Asian feminisms, and as a reminder to include religion (Islam) in analyses of identity formation and existence in the diaspora. Instead of solely concentrating on the ethnic facet, religious identity can be a meaningful tool for activism and analysis to examine Pakistani post-immigration identity construction.

In Chapter 6, Safiyya Hosein underlines the erasure of Indo-Caribbean Muslim representation in scholarship on South Asia through an autoethnographic examination of her own response to the experiences of Kamala Khan, a Ms. Marvel hero. Hosein traces parallels with Kamala Khan's inherited stories of migration beginning with the Partition of India in 1947 and her eventual arrival in the US, and her own family's traumatic migrations out of India to Trinidad and then Canada. As an Indo-Caribbean woman, Hosein locates her scholarship in the tumultuous chasms of historic geographic displacement and multiple migrations rooted in coloniality (indentured slavery), which have defined her claims to the notion of South Asian-ness. By critically reflecting on her own sense of relatability with Marvel's heroine and comparing these to her ambivalent relationship with persons of "mainland" South Asian descent, Hosein draws attention to the general undermining of Indo-Caribbean people within the larger South Asian community in North America.

For many South Asians, the legacies of 9/11 and the War on Terror are lived in ways that sometimes escape the notice of contemporary theorizing around Islamophobia and anti-Muslim racism in Western contexts. Extremist violence from militant groups such as the Tehrik-e Taleban Pakistan and Islamic Jihad continues to be a major issue for many Pakistanis and Afghans, and is experienced virtually almost daily through local, "ethnic," and conventional news reports about the bombings of mosques, shrines, bazaars, and schools, along with military and police outposts. In Chapter 7, Kanwal Khokhar analyzes Canadian media and popular representations of Rehab Dughmosh, a Canadian woman charged with terrorism offences, and notes disconnects between the realities of gendered radicalization and deradicalization processes in the Western world. Khokhar calls for further research on female terrorism that is attentive to gendered experiences of diaspora that are negotiated through multiple femininities. We accept the use of "terrorism" very hesitantly, being aware of its wider deployment by powerful states and entities to delegitimize popular resistance movements, especially by racialized people and those under occupation, such as the Palestinians. In this case, we see Khokhar's use of the term "terrorism" as related to the experiences of many in Pakistan and Afghanistan, where a particular ideological and repressive version of Islam became weaponized—and was later discredited—for exigencies of geopolitical enmities. We also see her contribution as an attempt to widen the motivations and desires attributed to "terrorist" subjectivities. In another examination of the theme of violence, in Chapter 8, Peruvemba S. Jaya brings the issue of gender identity to the forefront of community construction by problematizing the silencing of women and girls in response to violence within the family. Peruvemba undertakes a critical analysis of *Because We Are Girls*, a 2019 Canadian documentary film directed by Baljit Sangra and funded by the National Film Board of Canada. The film is about Jeeti, Kira, and Salakshana Pooni, three Punjabi Canadian sisters from Williams Lake, British Columbia who went public in adulthood about allegations of childhood sexual abuse by a relative. Bringing together ethnic identity and postcolonial feminist theories, Peruvemba questions diasporic claims of "community" when the latter fails to be a safe place for women and girls. The chapter also speaks to the challenges of resistance against an oppressive diasporic community that has been constituted through migration and experiences of racism and other hegemonies.

Section Three is titled "Not All Together: Gender, Sexuality, Class, and Diverse Patriarchies." Examples of diasporic South Asian women's projects interrupt normative expressions and understandings of gender, sexuality, class, caste, and diverse cis-heteropatriarchies. As an instinctive space of sisterhood for women scholars and activists, feminism can easily obscure the practices of power that are implicated within identitarian labels such as South Asian feminisms or women of colour and racialized women. Important interventions by queer and Dalit scholars, as well as others marginalized in the area of South Asian studies, have broadened and nuanced feminism's engagement with gender, class, caste, and diverse expressions of faith in ways that require a radical restructuring of diasporic feminism and its projects and make possible new imaginings of community (Puar 2007; Gopinath 2005). In Chapter 9, Sailaja V. Krishnamurti draws attention to the normalizing of Brahmanical Hinduism and the erasure of caste even within South Asian feminist groups. Krishnamurti invites South Asian feminists of *savarna* (dominant and upper caste) Hindu descent to examine their relationship with Hindu community formations, and to identify the ethical responsibilities that come with this self-reflection. Chapter 10, by Ayesha Mian Akram, calls into question the notion of a homogenous South Asian Muslim identity by providing an account of the ongoing violence against the Ahmadiyya Muslim community, especially the unjust exclusionary designation of this community as "non-Muslim" by the Pakistani state in 1974. This resulted in institutional persecution, the concealment of Ahmadi identities, and the mass migration of Ahmadis out of Pakistan into diasporic contexts. Mian Akram highlights the burden of identity for second-generation Pakistani Canadian Ahmadi Muslims in different situational contexts. The chapter reveals how the oppressive power of heteropatriarchies and nationalism continues to shape the lives of diasporic subjects who have never even visited the mainland and marginalize women and religious minorities, re-orienting feminists of South Asian Muslim descent to their responsibility for challenging these hegemonies. In Chapter 11, Maryam Khan engages in a critical discourse analysis of queerness and how it is taken up in scholarly literature (empirical studies) on South Asian Muslim women in Global North diasporas. Due to imperial and colonial legacies, queerness in its many expressions and forms is often invisibilized and eradicated from South Asian Muslim women's lives and identities. Substantial research on gay male South Asian identities and experiences dominates contemporary scholarship, leaving a gap on queer South Asian Muslim women. For Khan, the landscape of South Asian feminisms has not been easy to navigate, due to the competing chasms between Islamic feminism, queer politics and life, and South Asian-ness. The author locates herself and this chapter in the liminal spaces that exist between the regulated and patrolled borders of South Asian and Islamic feminisms and queerness. This chapter adds to the critical literature on how queer South Asian Muslim women are constructed through mutually exclusive and static understandings of Muslim, South Asian, and women. For instance, common tropes constructing Muslim women involve static, Orientalist, exotic, and fundamentalist perspectives. It is important to examine and tease out how these tropes are thriving in contemporary empirical research on queer South Asian Muslim women from critical feminist, transnational, and intersectional perspectives.

Section Four, the final section of the collection, is titled "Anti-Racist Feminism and Settler Colonialisms: Solidarities, Activism, and Futures." The chapters featured in this section entreat us to be critically reflexive about our modes of self-identification and our collective objectives, so that our self-constructed South Asian-ness does not become an alibi for academic illiteracy and scholarly complacency toward feminist resistances and complicities in changing local, national, and global conditions. The contributors pose incisive questions and proffer critical insights about the futures of South Asian feminisms, organizing, and activism. Feminist organizing in Canada and other diasporic locations, inspired by critical race theory and postcolonial theories, must be nuanced and multilayered so as to go beyond the conventional constructions of state and dominant society versus community, West and the rest, white/non-white, and so on. As part of the necessary space clearing, we need to engage with situated accounts of women's organizing and agency that are overshadowed in colonial and anti-colonial projects of nation-building, with their hegemonic constructions of gender and erasures of race, class, and cultures. Organizing counter-hegemonic feminist collective strategies demands nuanced ways of building alliances across the many "isms" that generate positionality and communities. As part of this effort, Farah Mahrukh Coomi Shroff, in Chapter 12, provides a much-needed account of South Asian Parsi women's experiences of support, empowerment, and independence, along with their struggles for women's rights. Drawing on an oral herstory project conducted by and for Parsi women, Shroff shares life stories of participants and their struggles, triumphs, and life-sustaining bonds. The voices of Parsi and Zoroastrian women are often overlooked in South Asian discourses and under-represented in South Asian feminisms. Due to such reasons, the author vociferously takes up space in South Asian feminisms to highlight her own voice and those of other Parsi and Zoroastrian women in Canada and the US. Shroff makes it clear that South Asian feminisms need to acknowledge and celebrate the gains made by Parsi women. In Chapter 13, Aaliya Khan looks at real and imagined spaces as sites of agency and power for Muslim women in Canada who attempt to reclaim physical space for themselves and their communities in Western liberal contexts. Her chapter seeks to account for the spatial implications of racializing and gendering practices, in addition to outlining how these practices are present in the politics of space. Khan locates her chapter and self as "complicated" within South Asian feminisms. A Kenyan-born Muslim of South Asian heritage, the author identifies religion (Islam) as her main connecting and entry point into the larger South Asian community in the Greater Toronto Area, to forge alliances and community-building toward social justice and against Islamophobia.

In a critical intervention for South Asian feminist organizing, in Chapter 14, Jane Ku both asserts and challenges South Asian feminism as an entry point to politics and solidarity. She explores the historicity of Chinese Indian nationalism as a performance in order to better intervene in and analyze the contemporary politics of Euro-American imperialism, racism, gender, and bordering practices, and to develop transnational feminist collaboration and analysis. Explicating these performances as a production of lived embodied experiences through identifying and reconstructing memories and biographies, the chapter attempts to enact a translation practice that transcends colonizing and reductive representations by highlighting hyper-visibilities as well as absences and erasures. Through such practices, Ku argues, cultural translation can produce new cultural meanings to unsettle borders, histories, and identities, and to challenge the reductive task of the translator as one who works across distinct and discrete communities and cultures, between insiders and outsiders, and across intersectionalities. Similarly, in Chapter 15, Ameera Khan explores principles for the formation of an inclusive and non-judgmental faith-based community of diasporic Muslims. Speaking as a trans Muslim woman, Khan decries neoconservative narratives in Islamic culture for their frequent invocation of Islamic concepts to justify heteronormativity and cisnormativity. In response, she points to some traditional and historical theologies, such as the work of Ibn Hazm and the *fatwā* of the grand mufti of Al-Azhar, to suggest that these neoconservative efforts are incongruent with Islam itself, in both spirit and law. Khan makes a persuasive case for adopting Islamic liberation theology as a lens through which to cultivate social and theological acceptance of queerness. Drawing from personal experience, as well as the contemporary Islamic theories of Amina Wadud (1999) and Scott Kugle (2010), she draws the line between the past and present to invest in "our future as Muslims." By refuting some aspects of modern neoconservative theologies and cultural stigmas that narrowly define Islam and Shari'ah, specifically with regard to the inclusion of transgender, gender non-conforming, and "homosexual" Muslims, Khan points to the dangers of adopting ahistorical and amoral approaches and indicates the deeply powerful, transformative, and communally liberatory concepts that Islam can be and has been. She invokes an Islam that is inclusive, progressive, and better equipped to take the Muslim *Ummah* into the future.

Conclusion

The volume concludes with an afterword by South Asian feminist scholar and long-time anti-imperialist activist Sunera Thobani that may be read as a philosophical manifesto for future critical engagements with South Asian diasporic critical studies. Thobani argues that South Asian feminists can no longer rely solely on feminist ideals that do not disturb class, neoliberal, and settler colonial injustices. Even when filed under feminist transnationalism, South Asian feminisms can be seeped in and further colonial and imperial discourses. Thobani's critiques fundamentally challenge and question the very construction of a critical diasporic South Asian feminism as a home or tool for intervening in these political times. Thobani's warning about the pitfalls of projects like this is well-received. One of the lessons learned is that even critical feminist gatherings can become over-infused with intimacy and sharing, thereby lessening the space and time available for much needed reflexivity and self-critique. Spaces that might provide relief for racialized women from the performative demands of Eurocentred academia can simultaneously erase and authorize exclusion and marginalization. We continue to be reflexive about our own project and ask readers to be reflexive as they engage with this volume, since it speaks to the networks and connectivities that represent

South Asian feminism as well as the absence of linkages that underlie our own diasporic imaginary. These are important flags for us and, we hope, for emerging scholars, as spaces that will require feminist attention and engagement in the future.

The work for South Asian feminism lies in building real solidarities and learning from social movements of Indigenous and Black communities in Canada and elsewhere. Further, it requires us to question how South Asian feminisms collide with, and inadvertently collude with, geopolitical imperialism in naming violence, participating in ideological wars, and furthering capitalist interests. As we prepare this volume, right-wing populism and backlash against hard-won feminist, 2SLGBTQ+, and minority group rights are trammelling those rights with impunity everywhere, including in self-proclaimed bastions of freedom and democracy such as the US and India. Global expressions of outrage at human rights violations by states such as Saudi Arabia and Israel are addressed through merely bureaucratic exercises. The most urgent crisis facing the international community at the time of writing—if one indeed exists—is Israel's siege of Gaza, which has been described by UN experts as "collective punishment" and "ethnic cleansing" (OHCHR 2023). Israel's right-wing government has threatened to wipe out the entire city of Gaza in retaliation for a Hamas attack, and has placed 2.1 million Palestinian inhabitants under, in the words of Israeli defence minister Yoav Gallant, "a complete siege...no electricity, no water, no food, no fuel" (Fabian 2023). The large-scale dehumanization of Palestinians and Muslims in the war rhetoric has in turn instigated attacks on Palestinians in Western societies. The Western hemisphere is already grappling with the Russian invasion of Ukraine and the militaristic response of the US and its European allies, with increased fears of nuclear conflict or at least another Cold War as the US fights to maintain its global dominance against the emerging specter of "Eurasian" solidarity (Pindell 2022; Mampilly 2022; World Economic Forum 2022). The heartening news is that large numbers of individuals and groups across global, racial, and religious divides—including states such as South Africa—are pushing back for peace and justice (International Court of Justice

2024). Even so, the local, national, and global apprehensions that initiated this feminist project threaten to become more ominous and uglier as states in the Global South are pushed by the US to prove their loyalty to the prevailing Western global order.

Against this overwhelming scenario, it is intuitive for us to strengthen South Asian feminism as a movement, a project, and a transnational practice. In fact, Thobani's critique of current iterations of critical South Asian feminism warrants a pause for reflection and action. This challenge in many ways has been embraced by the diverse contributors of this collection. South Asian feminist politics have been and are carving out a path to unsettle hegemonic discourses surrounding South Asian-ness as it relates to identities, communities, histories, geographies, lived experiences, and related affinities. The scholarship featured in this collection engages with transnational, feminist, critical, and intersectional perspectives that seek to dismantle normative, cisheteropatriachal, and cisgendered practices and ideas. The construction and discourse of South Asian-ness in Canada are broadened through this collection, as it sheds light on the nuances and complexities of politics originating from the mainland and their implications for the diasporic populace.

The editors have attempted to centralize marginalized voices that collectively challenge the status quo in South Asian communities. Finally, we recognize that this collection, like every other of its kind, is by no means exhaustive or complete. Indeed, we own the gaps and silences that are part of this volume and hope that it will inspire others to broaden and deepen the conversation. Overall, this collection paves a path forward, toward fostering more critical dialogues that will point to a socially just praxis and pedagogy in critical diasporic South Asian studies in Canada.

Note

1. For a detailed account of whiteness and the model minority, see Dennis (2018), Islamic Monthly (2013), and Bazi (2016).

References

Abu-Laban, Yasmeen, and Christina Gabriel. 2002. *Selling Diversity: Immigration, Multiculturalism, Employment Equity, and Globalization*. Toronto: University of Toronto Press.

Aggarwal, Parmila, and Tania Das Gupta. 2013. "Grandmothering at Work: Conversations with Sikh Punjabi Women in Toronto." *South Asian Diaspora* 5 (1): 77–90.

Ahmed-Ghosh, Huma. 2015. *Asian Muslim Women: Globalization and Local Realities.* New York: SUNY Press.

Al Jazeera. 2022. "PM Khan Gone: Pakistan's Political Crisis Explained in 400 Words." April 10. https://www.aljazeera.com/news/2022/4/10/pakistans-political-crisis-all-you-need-to-know.

Babar, Aneela. 2008. "New 'Social Imaginaries': The Al-Huda Phenomenon." *Journal of South Asian Studies* 31 (2): 348–363.

Bazi, Maria Khwaja. 2016. "Black Muslim Americans: The Minority Within a Minority." *Fair Observer*, February 22. http://www.fairobserver.com/region/north_america/black-muslim-americans-the-minority-within-a-minority-34590/.

Brown, Judith M. 2006. *Global South Asians: Introducing the Modern Diaspora*. Cambridge: Cambridge University Press.

Chakrabarty, Dipesh. 2012. "Postcolonial Studies and the Challenge of Climate Change." *New Literary History* 43 (1): 1–18. https://doi.org/10.1353/nlh.2012.0007.

Das Gupta, Tania. 1994. "Political Economy of Gender, Race and Class: South Asian Immigrant Women in Canada." *Canadian Ethnic Studies* 26 (1): 59–73.

Das Gupta, Tania. 2021. *Twice Migrated, Twice Displaced: Indian and Pakistani Transnational Households in Canada*. Vancouver: UBC Press.

Day, Iyko. 2015. "Being or Nothingness: Indigeneity, Antiblackness and Settler Colonial Critique." *Journal of Critical Ethnic Studies Association* 1 (2): 102–121.

Dennis, Elisabeth. 2018. "Exploring the Model Minority: Deconstructing Whiteness Through the Asian American Example." In *Cartographies of Race and Social Difference*, edited by George J. Sefa Dei and Shukri Hilowle, 33–48. Berlin: Springer.

Dua, Enakshi. 2007. "Exclusion Through Inclusion: Female Asian Migration in the Making of Canada as a White Settler Nation." *Gender, Place and Culture: A Journal of Feminist Geography* 14 (4): 445–466.

Fabian, Emmanuel. 2023. "Defense Minister Announces 'Complete Siege' of Gaza: No Power, Food or Fuel." *The Times of Israel*, October 9. https://www.timesofisrael.com/liveblog_entry/defense-minister-announces-complete-siege-of-gaza-no-power-food-or-fuel/.

Fanon, Frantz. 1967. *Black Skin, White Masks*. Translated by Charles Lam Markmann. New York: Grove Press.

Fanon, Frantz. 2004. *The Wretched of the Earth*. Translated by Richard Philcox. New York: Grove Press.

Feminist Critical Hindu Studies Collective. 2022. "Hindu Fragility and the Politics of Mimicry in North America." *The Immanent Frame*, November 2. https://tif.ssrc.org/2022/11/02/hindu-fragility-and-the-politics-of-mimicry-in-north-america/.

Ghosh, Sutama. 2013. "'Am I a South Asian, Really?' Constructing 'South Asians' in Canada and Being South Asian in Toronto." *South Asian Diaspora* 5 (1): 35–55. http://dx.doi.org/10.1080/19438192.2013.724913.

Gopinath, Gayatri. 2005. *Impossible Desires: Queer Diasporas and South Asian Public Cultures*. Durham: Duke University Press.

Grewal, Inderpal. 2005. *Transnational America: Feminisms, Diasporas, Neoliberalisms*. Durham: Duke University Press.

Grewal, Inderpal, and Caren Kaplan. 1994. "Introduction: Transnational Feminist Practices and Questions of Postmodernity." In *Scattered Hegemonies: Postmodernity and Transnational Feminist Practices*, edited by Inderpal Grewal and Caren Kaplan, 1–33. Minneapolis: Minnesota University Press.

Guru, Gopal. 1995. "Dalit Women Talk Differently." *Economic and Political Weekly* 30 (41/42): 2548–2550. http://www.jstor.com/stable/4403327.

Guru, Gopal. 2020. "Dalit Women Talk Differently." In *Dalit Feminist Theory: A Reader*, edited by Sunaina Arya and Aakash S. Rathore, 150–153. London: Routledge.

Husain, Khurram. 2022. "Where Does Pakistan's Economy Go from Here?" *Dawn News*, October 16. https://www.dawn.com/news/1715309.

International Court of Justice. 2024. Application of the Convention on the Prevention and Punishment of the Crime of Genocide in the Gaza Strip (South Africa v. Israel). Press release no. 2024/3. January 12. https://www.icj-cij.org/index.php/case/192.

Islamic Monthly, The. 2013. "Black, Muslim, American: Interview with Dr. Jamillah." February 27. http://theislamicmonthly.com/black-muslim-american-interview-with-dr-jamillah-karim/.

Jamal, Amina. 2015. "Piety, Transgression and the Feminist Debate on Muslim Women: Transnationalizing the Victim-Subject of Honor-Related Violence." *Signs: Journal of Women in Culture and Society* 41 (1): 55–79.

Jha, Sonora, and Alka Kurian. 2018. *New Feminisms in South Asia: Disrupting the Discourse Through Social Media, Film, and Literature*. New York: Routledge.

Joseph, Miranda. 2002. *Against The Romance of Community*. Minneapolis: University of Minnesota Press.

Kamran, Tahir. 2019. "The Making of a Minority: Ahmadi Exclusion Through Constitutional Amendments, 1974." *Pakistan Journal of Historical Studies* 4 (1–2). https://muse.jhu.edu/article/811903.

Kazim, Rafia. 2021. "Who Will Speak for the Pasmandaa Women?—Dalits, Women, Muslims, and the Politics of Representation." *Journal of International Women's Studies* 22 (10), Article 8. https://vc.bridgew.edu/jiws/vol22/iss10/8.

Kennedy-Kish (Bell), Babkonda, and Ben Carniol. 2017. "A Two-Road Approach to Ethical Practice." In *Social Work Ethics: Progressive, Practical, and Relational Approaches*, edited by Elaine Spencer, Duane Massing, and Jim Gough, 270–281. Don Mills: Oxford Press.

Khan, Maryam. 2018. "Intersectional Identities and Resistance Strategies of LBTQ Muslim Women." PhD Diss., York University.

Ku, Jane. 2019a. "Journeys to a Diasporic Self." *Canadian Ethnic Studies* 51 (3): 137–154.

Ku, Jane. 2019b. "Intentional Solidarity as a Decolonizing Practice." *Intermédialités / Intermediality*, no. 34 (Fall). https://doi.org/10.7202/1070870ar.

Kugle, Scott Siraj al-Haqq. 2010. *Homosexuality in Islam: Critical Reflection on Gay, Lesbian, and Transgender Muslims*. London: Oneworld Publications.

Kurien, Prema A. 2003. "To Be or Not to Be South Asian: Contemporary Indian American Politics." *Journal of Asian American Studies* 6 (3): 261–288. https://doi.org/10.1353/jaas.2004.0020.

Lawrence, Bonita, and Enakshi Dua. 2005. "Decolonizing Antiracism." *Social Justice* 32 (4): 120–143.

Loomba, Ania, and Ritty A. Lukose. 2012. *South Asian Feminisms: Contemporary Interventions*. Durham: Duke University Press.

Mampilly, Zachariah. 2022. "The Du Bois Doctrine: Race and the American Century." *Foreign Affairs*, September 6. https://www.foreignaffairs.com/united-states/web-du-bois-doctrine-race-america-century.

Mishra, Vijay. 2007. *The Literature of the Indian Diaspora: Theorizing the Diasporic Imaginary*. Milton Park: Taylor & Francis.

Mohammad-Arif, Aminah. 2015. "Introduction: Imaginations and Constructions of South Asia: An Enchanting Abstraction?" *South Asia Multidisciplinary Academic Journal* 10 (10). https://doi.org/10.4000/samaj.3800.

Mohanty, Chandra T. 2013. "Transnational Feminist Crossings: On Neoliberalism and Radical Critique." *Signs: Journal of Women in Culture and Society* 38 (4): 967–991. https://doi.org/10.1086/669576.

Narayan, Anjana and Bandana Purkayasthab. 2011. "Talking 'Gender Superiority' in Virtual Spaces: Web-Based Discourses of Hindu Student Groups in the US and UK." *South Asian Diaspora* 3 (1): 53–69. https://doi.org/10.1080/19438192.2010.539035.

News Desk. 2022. "Overseas Pakistanis Protest Against 'Regime Change.'" *Global Village Space*, April 16. https://www.globalvillagespace.com/overseas-pakistanis-protest-against-regime-change/.

OHCHR (Office of the High Commissioner for Human Rights). 2023. "UN Expert Warns of New Instance of Mass Ethnic Cleansing of Palestinians, Calls for Immediate Ceasefire." Press release. October 14. https://www.ohchr.org/en/press-releases/2023/10/un-expert-warns-new-instance-mass-ethnic-cleansing-palestinians-calls.

Patel, Shaista. 2016. "Complicating the Tale of 'Two Indians': Mapping 'South Asian' Complicity in White Settler Colonialism Along the Axis of Caste and Anti-Blackness." *Theory & Event* 19 (4). muse.jhu.edu/article/633278.

Patel, Shaista, and Dia Da Costa. 2022. "'We Cannot Write About Complicity Together': Limits of Cross-Caste Collaborations in Western Academy." *Engaged Scholar Journal: Community-Engaged Research, Teaching, and Learning* 8 (2): 1–27. https://doi.org/10.15402/esj.v8i2.70780.

Pindell, James. 2022. "No, It's Not the World Against Russia. In Fact, It's Far from It. Why a Lot of Nations Aren't on Board With Economic Sanctions." *Boston Globe*, March 16. https://www.bostonglobe.com/2022/03/16/nation/no-its-not-world-against-russia-fact-its-far-it-why-lot-nations-arent-board-with-economic-sanctions/.

Prashad, Vijay. 2001. *The Karma of Brown Folk*. Minneapolis: University of Minnesota Press.

Puar, Jasbir. 2007. *Terrorist Assemblages: Homonationalism in Queer Times*. Durham: Duke University Press.

Reddy, Vanita. 2017. "Affect, Aesthetics, and Afro-Asian Studies." *Journal of Asian American Studies* 20 (2): 289–294.

Rege, Sharmila. 1998. "Dalit Women Talk Differently: A Critique of 'Difference' and Towards a Dalit Feminist Standpoint Position." *Economic and Political Weekly* 33 (44): WS39–WS46.

Roy, Srila. 2012. *New South Asian Feminisms: Paradoxes and Possibilities.* London: Zed Books.

Said, Edward W. 1979. *Orientalism*. New York: Vintage Press.

Sangra, Baljit, dir. 2019. *Because We Are Girls*. Montreal: National Film Board of Canada. https://www.nfb.ca/film/because-we-are-girls/.

Saranillio, Dean Itsuji. 2013. "Why Asian Settler Colonialism Matters." *Settler Colonial Studies* 3 (3/4): 280–294.

Soni-Sinha, Urvashi. 2013. "Intersectionality, Subjectivity, Collectivity and the Union: Perceptions of the 'Locked-Out' Hotel Workers in Toronto, Canada." *Organization: The Journal of Organization Theory and Society* 20 (6): 775–793. https://doi.org/10.1177/1350508412453364.

Spivak, Gayatri Chakravorty. 1997. "Translator's Preface." In *Of Grammatology*, by Jacques Derrida, ix–lxxxvii. Baltimore: Johns Hopkins University Press.

Tuck, Eve, and K. Wayne Yang. 2012. "Decolonization Is Not a Metaphor." *Decolonization: Indigeneity Education & Society* 1 (1): 1–40.

Varma, S. J., and Radhika Seshan. 2003. *Fractured Identity: The Indian Diaspora in Canada.* Jaipur and New Delhi: Rawat Publications.

Wadud, Amina. 1999. *Qur'an and Woman: Rereading the Sacred Text from a Woman's Perspective*. Oxford: Oxford University Press.

Walia, Harsha. 2014. *Undoing Border Imperialism*. Chico: AK Press.

World Economic Forum. 2022. "President Xi Jinping's Message to the Davos Agenda in Full." January 17. https://www.weforum.org/agenda/2022/01/address-chinese-president-xi-jinping-2022-world-economic-forum-virtual-session/.

I

Identifications and Disidentifications

1

The Dialogic of Praxis

DOLORES CHEW

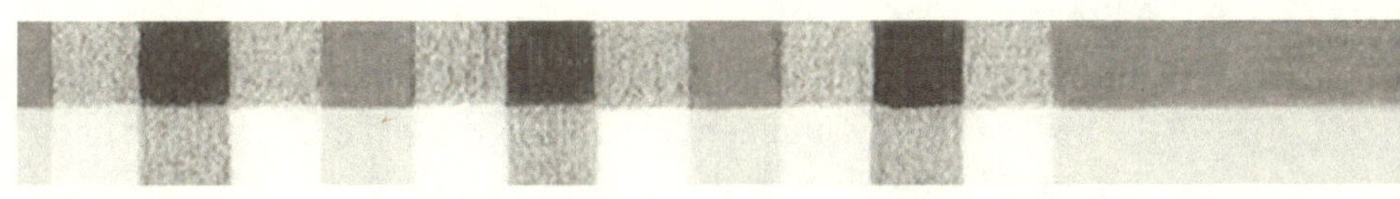

THIS CHAPTER EVOLVED from the keynote I gave at the Critical South Asian Feminisms symposium, in July 2021, in what is now called Canada, northern Turtle Island.[1] I am grateful and honoured to have been part of this rich and exciting gathering of intergenerational scholars and activists, a diverse and dynamic group whose contributions enrich ongoing South Asian feminist intellectual work and activism that go back decades. The symposium, and subsequently this volume, demonstrate that networks of a committed sisterhood have been forged.

For me, academic work and activism have always gone hand in hand, spanned multiple areas, and been grounded in my South Asian identity. And so, using my personal trajectory, in this chapter I will explore a history of diasporic South Asian feminist activism over four decades, beginning when "South Asian" was a rarely used moniker. The location of the work and activism is mostly Montreal and Quebec, while the issues are transnational as well as local. I have learned over the years and will try to convey in this chapter the constant dialogic of praxis, which invites one to remain critical, question, dialogue, discuss, share, stay bold, remain unafraid, and retain and nurture communities of kindred spirits.

My engagements to a large extent reflect that I was born and raised in postcolonial India, in Calcutta (now Kolkata). After migrating to Canada and given the shifting forms of identification, however, "South Asian" eventually seemed to resonate best as a form of self-identification. Friendships and collaborations with other South Asians deepened my knowledge and understanding. And so, over the course of this chapter, while my grounding in India will be apparent, "South Asian" becomes more apt as a descriptor.[2]

A Starting Point

Putting together my keynote for the symposium made me focus on the lineage, legacy, and heritage that converged in the four elements identified in the symposium title: critical/diasporic/South Asian/feminisms. I began by locating us historically, which makes for a good place to start this chapter.

In Canada, the Komagata Maru incident of 1914 has become a watershed moment for those of us who are of South Asian origin.[3] While the South Asian presence in Canada predates 1914, that event marked us as staking a claim, even as it clearly identified and racialized us—and in the colonial framing, slotted us into the category of "hewers of wood and drawers of water." As multi-generational scholars dig deeper into the Komagata Maru incident and South Asian history in Canada, we will develop more contextualized and detailed accounts of our presence; build alliances with others who were also excluded by racist legislation and policies; and develop collaborative relationships with Indigenous Peoples to challenge our racialization. The Komagata Maru incident tangibly demonstrates the links between South Asia and the diaspora that were strong then, and that remain so today. For example, in 1914, anti-colonial Ghadar links existed, as what was happening in *watan* was reflected here,[4] and vice versa.[5]

During the 1970s and 1980s, South Asian feminists in Canada were inspired by developments in different parts of South Asia. In India, an intersectional understanding of violence against women and a new feminism emerged after the Mathura rape case (Shanti 2021; Omvedt 1990).[6] In Pakistan, the military dictator General Zia ul

Haq imposed his own interpretation of Islam to promulgate repressive measures such as the Hudood ordinances, which were strongly challenged by the Women's Action Forum (WAF). This gave women and feminism a profile and legitimacy in that country as they became the only organized political opposition (Mumtaz and Shaheed 1987). In other parts of South Asia, the limitations and problematic aspects of the "nationalism" that had inspired many in the anti-colonial movements became more evident. Bangladesh emerged from Pakistan in 1971 after a bloody struggle, evidence that religion alone could not sustain a national identity; there was growing resistance in Kashmir against unfulfilled promises made in 1948 (United Nations 1948), demonstrating that self-determination was a strong force; and the legislative marginalization of Tamils in Sri Lanka illustrated how nationalism can degenerate into ethnic exclusivity. In other regions of South Asia, the discontent of those forcibly included in postcolonial nation-states also led to self-determination movements and government use of military force to stamp them out. And these struggles continue. All of this fed our understanding and work here in the diaspora. While we were inspired by the feminist engagements in South Asia, a new kind of diasporic and anti-racist feminist activism was growing in Canada as well (Canadian Encyclopedia 2016), evinced in the emergence of diasporic South Asian and immigrant women's centres and new groups.[7] For me, this was reflected in my involvement in the founding of South Asian Women's Community Centre (SAWCC) in Montreal in 1981 and its subsequent development and hurdles—including our being labelled as "home breakers," and racism and marginalization within the broader feminist and women's movement.

My South Asian feminist consciousness and praxis was informed by my activist involvement, the theoretical insights of feminists and postcolonial scholars, and movements from below like Naxalbari, which among other things generated greater interest in and writing about subaltern movements more generally (Banerjee 1980). The work of one of the theoreticians of the subaltern studies school, Gayatri Spivak (2010), has become ubiquitous in critical analytic engagement.[8] Developments in emerging feminist movements in

South Asia gave rise to an outpouring of writing and publishing that foregrounded women's experiences. This was happening outside India as well.[9] My own academic work deepened my feminist understanding and knowledge of patriarchy. I was developing my gender analysis toolbox. The urgency of bringing women's experiences to the fore was palpable.

Along with this was a growing awareness of how the process of Othering essentialized women. I remember early in my graduate work reading Mary Daly (1978) and her calling out of "suttee." It disturbed me, not because I condoned the horrific act, but because I felt deep discomfort with the sweepingly generalized way that Daly dealt with it. At this time, I was also arriving at conclusions in my own historical research on women in colonial Bengal. I concluded that upper-caste male reformers in colonial Bengal who were concentrating on ameliorating the situation of women were reactive, more concerned with the colonial critique of the status of "their" women than with the situation of women per se. These patriarchal, Hindu, upper-caste social reform movements negatively impacted degrees of autonomy that had been normative for women of so-called marginalized castes. This, for me, was also a lonely time. Working in isolation as a young woman and mother, at a time when there was little written on this topic, I experienced a degree of self-doubt about the conclusions I was arriving at.

Doing Intersectionality Before It Became a Noun

A while back I was approached to contribute to a collection on intersectionality. "What's that?" I asked. And when I got the explanation, I responded, "Oh that! It's what we've been doing all this time." I make this point as an example of how analytic concepts and categories often emanate from lived experiences and realities. This is an excellent example of the dialogic of praxis. A good friend of many of us, the late Aziz Choudry, who left us too soon, and who recognized the importance of the dialogic of praxis in social movements, encouraged us to document what we were doing so that our theory could be grounded in action and movements.

One of the reasons for the genesis of SAWCC was the absence of spaces and resources that spoke to our linguistic and cultural needs as migrant women from South Asia. Over the years in SAWCC we have asserted our right to be where we are and who we are. We work with networks of other women's centres in Quebec, with a work style and functioning that serve our community best. For example, we have been questioned about why we admit men into our spaces. Our response is that we privilege women and women's needs, but at times need to include men. As an organization that works with newcomers and refugee claimants, we also provide services to men. Living as we do in Quebec, where the issue of language is very fraught, we have asserted our right to provide services in languages that are understood by the centre's users, even as we provide free French and English language classes so we can assist women to become autonomous and economically independent in this province.

In the 1990s, the late Madeleine Parent, a good friend and ally, worked hard to open up the Fédération des femmes du Québec (Quebec Women's Federation; FFQ) to migrant women's organizations, and to build ties with Femmes autochtones du Québec/ Quebec Native Women (FAQ/QNW). SAWCC members have worked with FAQ and have sat on the FFQ board. In the FFQ, SAWCC has brought greater awareness of the challenges facing migrant women. While it had at times been a struggle for SAWCC to work with the FFQ, this has changed. There is greater understanding and awareness in the federation of intersectionality, and of how accommodations are needed to ensure equality rights in a province with strong (French) linguistic nationalism. SAWCC has contributed to these developments.[10] At SAWCC, the ability to communicate and work in French has been difficult to grapple with, given that English is already a colonial language that many of our members have been forced to adopt. Beyond language, as racialized migrant women, we contend with systemic and structural inequalities.

During the Harper years,[11] when the terms "barbaric cultural practices," "honour" crimes, and "forced marriage" came to be used very often in certain circles, SAWCC (2014) put out a statement to reiterate the need for public education for government bodies and women's organizations. We emphasized the racist and colonial underpinnings of discussions in Canada on "honour killings" and "forced marriage,"[12] and the manner in which such discourses tend to essentialize crimes that are ultimately about violence against women and children. We argued: "Focusing on cultural specificities is often politically motivated, erroneous, dangerous, racist and totally misplaced. We strongly believe all efforts and funds should focus on eliminating *violence against women and children* without cultural essentialism. Anything else is a disservice to all the many and continuing victims of patriarchal violence" (SAWCC 2014, 1; emphasis original).

The SAWCC statement did not minimize the issue of violence against women, but pointed out the fallacy of essentializing communities, and women and children in those communities. Moreover, it did not adopt a defensive position but drew attention to the racism inherent in such labelling. Our ability to frame and present our position was based on our political understanding of the way race and gender work to marginalize communities. It was also informed by our work in our communities, where we have to confront the patriarchal policing of women and violence against women—as with the protest against the murder of Rajinder Prabhneed Kaur in July 2021 (CBC News 2021), or when the murder of Milia Abrar in 1998 (Gazette 2008) was used by some in the community to exercise control by warning young women not to live life on their own terms. We continue to speak out against conservative, patriarchal attitudes, and so we struggle within and without.

Problematizing "South Asian": Personal "Plus"

The Critical South Asian Feminisms symposium was enriched with the multiple identities reflected in the topics and the participants, including those less often heard about—Hakka Chinese, Kashmiri, Indo-Caribbean Muslim—making the concept of diaspora tangible and tactile! This resonated with me, as I trace my origins to Melaka Chinese (Malaysia), Malayali (Kerala), Sikh (Punjab), Irish and Dutch

(Burgher).[13] To simplify things and reflect my cultural subjectivities, I describe myself as Anglo-Indian, a community recognized by that name in India's constitution.

My identities have been alternatingly liberating, joyful, and burdensome, but they allow me to empathize with many who embody fractured, colonized, and racialized identities. It has also meant that never seeming to quite "belong" equipped me for experiences in Canada. In 1964, as my mother, sister, and I were at the airport in Calcutta, my stomach tightened in knots as an official looked down, glowering and saying loudly, "Chinese!" This was at a time when India had gone from "Hindi-Chini bhai-bhai"[14] to the tensions of the Sino-Indian war, when it became pragmatic to permit some confusion—"they are from Burma" was safer. On one hand, the possibility that this official might put the kibosh on a trip that I was so excited about, because our passports were Indian but our name Chinese, seemed so unfair that I burst out crying. On the other hand, as I grew up, I had to also contend with the gendered identity "Anglo-Indian woman," which in some circles was a euphemism for an "easy lay" (Chew 2002; 2021)!

While I was growing up, nationalism was in the air after the partition of the independent subcontinent into secular India and Pakistan. At the Catholic girls' school I attended, we were educated with an ethos of secularism, liberal democracy, inclusion, and service to the nation. During those decades, wars—the Sino-India war in 1962, and Indo-Pak wars in 1965 and 1971—had an impact on me. There was a horror of being identified as Chinese during the Sino-India war, and the partisanship of the Indo-Pak wars, when Pakistan was the enemy. When I came to Montreal and met students from Pakistan at university, I quickly realized that there was more we shared than there were dissimilarities. And later, when I visited Pakistan, but for my inability to read the Urdu script I felt completely at home. However, when a South Asian student group I was part of at my university in Montreal prepared an exhibition on South Asia, I noticed a difference in narratives—a consequence of the history textbooks we had studied. For my Pakistani colleagues, Aurangzeb was the best Mughal ruler and Akbar was an apostate. In Indian textbooks, Akbar was lauded as a tolerant ruler and Aurangzeb was condemned as an oppressive religious bigot! This was one of my first lessons in the nationalist renderings of history. Today history has become even more of a battleground, and WhatsApp university a primary source!

After living in Canada for many decades, I found "Indian" origin seemed less relevant as I worked and struggled together with others with shared culture and origins from the Indian subcontinent. Years ago, we would discuss what nomenclature would be most appropriate—sub-conty?[15] South Asian? In parts of Canada, especially west of Quebec, for many years, "East Indian" was generically used, but this has given way to the more widely accepted "South Asian." But, of course, among South Asians, there are multiple other identities reflective of ethnicity, religion, caste, class, and region—e.g., Bengali from East or West Bengal, Tamil from Tamil Nadu or Jaffna, and so on. And so, the term "South Asian" itself remains very broad (as does "feminisms").

Nationalism/s

More than ever, today nationalism is exploited for populist ends. Hegemonizing discourse facilitates militarization and the use of violence by power brokers. When I teach nationalism to my students, I often begin by quoting lines from Tagore's "Mind Without Fear" from his poetry collection *Gitanjali*, where he celebrates the liberatory aspects of nationalism even as he warns of its dark side:

> *Where the mind is without fear and the head is held high*
> *Where knowledge is free*
> *Where the world has not been broken up into fragments*
> *By narrow domestic walls*
> Where words come out from the depth of truth
> Where tireless striving stretches its arms towards perfection
> Where the clear stream of reason has not lost its way
> Into the dreary desert sand of dead habit
> Where the mind is led forward by thee
> Into ever-widening thought and action

> Into that heaven of freedom, my Father, let my country awake.
> (1913; emphasis mine)

In Quebec, we live in a laboratory of nationalism. Before the 1950s, undeniably, French Quebecers were an oppressed group in an English-dominated world. This was exacerbated by the control exercised by the Catholic Church. But in the 1950s, change began with the Quiet Revolution. With the election of the Parti Québecois (PQ) in 1977, nationalism was more coherently articulated in the legislature. At the time, there were also many who identified with the overall social democratic platform of the PQ.[16] But gradually the ethos of solidarity dissipated, as the party moved to the right and the politics of neoliberalism, reaction, and exclusion.

In 2013, a PQ government tabled legislation to advance secularism, with a "Charter of Values" directed against "ostentatious" religious symbols, particularly impacting individuals who wear head coverings for religious reasons (Chew 2015; SAWCC 2013).[17] "Secularism" has a specific meaning within the context of Quebec, as it is translated from the concept of *laïcite*, which emerged from post-revolutionary republican France with its strong anti-clerical outlook, coupled with the reaction to the Catholic Church's strong hold on Quebec society for centuries. This reactionary understanding of secularism generates a highly dichotomized separation of church/religion and state/politics, something I have identified as "secular fundamentalism" (Chew 2007). The unproblematized normativity of Euro-Christian culture in public and government spaces and holiday observances in Quebec is very present.[18] In 2019, the Coalition Avenir Quebec (CAQ) succeeded in passing Loi 21, which bans the wearing of religious symbols by anyone in public service or a position of authority. This includes public school teachers, prosecutors, and judges. In summer 2022, the CAQ passed Loi 96 (extending the language law, Bill 101, passed by the PQ in 1977), which drastically narrows the space and opportunities for anglophones (English speakers) and allophones (those whose mother tongue is neither English nor French, but who are often accused of favouring English over French).[19] This has very detrimental impacts for newcomers to Quebec, who are expected to communicate in French for services—government, social services, and so on—within six months of arrival.

Along with different understandings of secularism, the issue of Quebec nationalism also creates fissures among feminists. Nevertheless, those who identify as intersectional feminists, whether sovereigntist or not, have put forward a more nuanced meaning of solidarity through their shared struggles and histories. For example, the alliances formed in recent struggles for justice and equality for racialized and migrant women reflect a rich understanding and class awareness.[20] SAWCC's active presence on the FFQ's board has helped direct the struggle. The passage of Loi 21 disproportionately targets Muslim women, but also Sikhs and Jewish men, to the point of forcing them to leave the province to find employment (Gilmour 2019). Legal challenges are making their way through the court system, and in the legal appeal in Quebec, the FFQ together with LEAF (Women's Legal Education and Action Fund) obtained intervenor status (FFQ 2022b). I write this to demonstrate that years of work to build alliances, share lived experiences, and challenge exclusionary hegemonic feminist thinking and discourse have borne fruit (FFQ 2019).[21]

What should nationalism mean for us as critical diasporic South Asian feminists in terms of subcontinental identities, as well as those of settler-migrants in Canada? Our geographical location in the diaspora informs our lives and affords incredible opportunities to meet and exchange, without the divisions and conflicts fueled in South Asia. We share experiences as women whose bodies get conflated with patriarchal or national honour, even as they are subjected to interpersonal violence and the violence of war and militarism. Our intersectional feminist analysis will help guide our work, especially now as Hindutva ethno-nationalism is shaping diasporic relations around caste, gender, and religion (The Breach 2024).

Allyship in Colonized Spaces

I remained unaware of the impact of colonialism on Indigenous Peoples for a very long time. Growing up in postcolonial India, harbouring patriotic (and at times nationalist) sentiments, and believing that an India free from colonial rule was a better India, there was a huge gap in my knowledge and awareness. For example, when I was growing up, it was normal for children to use pistols, holsters, hats, and boleros to play "Cowboys and Indians." When I came to Canada, in my ignorance and naïveté I assumed I was coming to a white country. And even as I became more politicized in terms of racism and gender, in general I remained ignorant of Indigenous realities. Even when in 1987, the High Commissioner for South Africa to Canada, Glen Babb, visited an Indigenous reserve in Manitoba to demonstrate Canada's hypocrisy in its criticism of South Africa's apartheid system, I still didn't comprehend how widespread systemic racism was toward Indigenous people. I saw Babb's visit as a political ploy and the situation on the Manitoba reserve as an exception, not the norm.

The Oka Crisis in the summer of 1990 finally compelled me to embark on a steep learning curve to learn as much as I could about Indigenous realities in Canada. I participated in many solidarity demonstrations and pow wows at Kanehsatake. I heard Katsi'tsakwas Ellen Gabriel speak at an International Women's Day event that I helped organize as part of Femmes de diverses origins/Women of Diverse Origins.[22] Later, I also became involved with the movement to raise awareness about Missing and Murdered Indigenous Women and Girls, making the connections between racism and gendered and sexual violence. I learned about "settler colonialism."[23] I read and watched documentary films as part of my self-education about colonial dispossession and the genocide against Indigenous Peoples. But it took the Truth and Reconciliation Commission of Canada's work on the history of residential schools and its 94 Calls to Action (TRC 2015), including in the sphere of education, which implicates me directly as an educator, to bring home to me the magnitude of the impact of the centuries of settler colonialism and racism. This transformed me from a somewhat passive student of the history of colonialism who engaged in some activism, to someone who was now compelled to very actively contribute in whichever way I could to end the ongoing colonization. And that process is ongoing. I educate myself to grasp the principles of decolonizing methodology and to use them in my teaching, and work to bring de-colonizing into all the spaces I am part of, always keeping in mind what Mi'kmaq scholar Marie Battiste says: "Nothing about us, without us" (as quoted in Cote-Meek 2017).

As critical South Asian diasporic feminists, we have work we need to do in our communities in this regard. One of the developments for example, from the perspective of SAWCC, is the need to move beyond solidarity to critical allyship, as we learn and inform ourselves of the meaning of decolonization in the realities of the settler-colonial state that we live in. We are often indirectly (or perhaps more directly) complicit in colonialism here, even as we are so very cognizant of the histories of colonialism in our countries of origin, and of the colonial gaze and racist essentializing that we as folks with origins in South Asia have been and continue to be subjected to. At our Annual General Meeting in June 2015, SAWCC adopted a territorial acknowledgement that included a commitment to acting in solidarity with Indigenous Peoples in tangible ways, in order to consciously move beyond solidarity to critical allyship as authentically as possible (SAWCC 2015).

I have come to understand how traces of colonialism remain even after its formal end, and how they seep into everything. My own educational, research, and teaching trajectory has been a process of unlearning and appreciating how hierarchies of inequality proliferate ideologically, even when one is consciously trying to avoid them. It took me a long time to become comfortable and assured enough to study Anglo-Indian women. Despite my non-Western perspectives, it was not easy for me to disrupt the liberal arts canon and adopt alternative methodological approaches to knowledge acquisition and production. Critical diasporic South Asian feminism must be involved in issues that are not always "South Asian," precisely because "South Asian" is a form of discourse of power that produces hierarchies (Haque and Patrick 2015; Haque 2009). Thus, as South Asian feminists, we also attend to the marginalization of Dalit-Bahujans and Indigenous/Adivasis that is spilling out into diasporic spaces (The Breach 2024). To challenge different hegemonies, our allyship building work can also lead to teaching people in Canada about European colonialism in India. For example, I shared with Indigenous leader Katsi'tsakwas Ellen Gabriel a piece written by Sudha Bharadwaj (2022), a prisoner of conscience in India who has spent many years working with and legally representing Indigenous/Adivasi people. Katsi'tsakwas had just signed a public letter calling for the release of political prisoners in India. While not identical, there were many parallels that I thought Katsi'tsakwas would recognize. This campaign to get political prisoners in India released also demonstrates the links, interventions, and actions that we as critical diasporic South Asian feminists can make in these fraught times, in support of efforts toward democracy and equality in South Asia.[24]

Conclusion

The dialogic of praxis, where I bring my experience of activism and scholarship, makes me tease out personal subjectivities and identify lessons garnered through collaborative work with kindred spirits. I have tried to pose conundrums and dilemmas that exist or that may rear up in our path, together with possible ways to identify and counter them. As with critical alternatives to what may be destructive and divisive nationalisms, the strength of consistent grassroots organizing and coalition building to counter powerful hierarchies has produced knowledge about struggle, but also knowledge that is counter-hegemonic, which can be comforting in the face of seemingly relentless behemoths. These are indeed exciting times, and the work we are doing affords tremendous opportunities for future knowledge production, for affirmation about the paths less trodden that we walk on, and for meaningful and vibrant South Asian diasporic feminisms.

Notes

1. "For some Indigenous peoples, Turtle Island refers to the continent of North America. The name comes from various Indigenous oral histories that tell stories of a turtle that holds the world on its back. For some Indigenous peoples, the turtle is therefore considered an icon of life, and the story of Turtle Island consequently speaks to various spiritual and cultural beliefs" (Robinson 2018).

2. India is a hegemon in South Asia, and there is a need in our work in Canada to remain conscious of how this can influence our work here.
3. For general notes about this incident, see Johnston (2006) and CBC News (2016).
4. *Watan* in Punjabi and Urdu means homeland.
5. For more, see the special issue of *Socialist Studies* dedicated to the Ghadar Movement (D'Souza and Tirmizey 2018).
6. 1947 was the year that India achieved independence from British colonialism and the Indian subcontinent was partitioned into India and Pakistan. Despite the violence and tragedy of that time, when at least 1 million people died and approximately 14 million people fled their homes and crossed borders, there was still hope for an improved life now that colonialism had ended. For example, with independence, universal adult suffrage was introduced. There was no need to agitate for voting rights for women. However, within a couple of decades after independence and its promises of equality, the realities of gender inequality (along with other inequalities) became more apparent. The rape of 16-year-old Mathura by a police constable rocked the entire nation (see Shanti 2021).
7. My reflections here utilize my subjective experience as a founding member of the South Asian Women's Community Centre (SAWCC). It's important to note that SAWCC continues to straddle political activism and service provision, a difficult position for many community organizations that attempt to maintain their grassroots, feminist, and radical vision. In many respects, a diasporic organization with which SAWCC shares a lot is London, UK's Southall Black Sisters (Gupta 2003).
8. Gayatri Spivak's essay "Can the Subaltern Speak?" is *de rigueur* in many academic courses that utilize a critical theoretical approach. For me, the foundational text of the subaltern studies group, Ranajit Guha's *Elementary Aspects of Peasant Insurgency in Colonial India* (1983) and Edward Said's *Orientalism* (1978), were very influential in making colonial and subaltern realities visible for me, and informed my analysis and understanding.
9. Texts that dealt with women's participation in larger movements and struggles in India and elsewhere made visible the fact that female sexuality, so central to women's experience and also key to the essentializing of women, needed to be a significant aspect of our understanding, researching, and writing. Today this may seem so normative that it doesn't bear mentioning, but in the 1970s and 1980s it was definitely not so. Works that influenced me a lot included Stree Sakti Sanghatana's *We Were Making History* (1989), Domitila Barrios de Chungara's *Let Me Speak!* (1978), Margaret Randall's *Sandino's Daughters* (1981), and Kumkum Sangari and Sudesh Vaid's *Recasting Women* (1989).
10. For example, with the passage in 2022 of an amendment to the language law in Quebec, the pressure on organizations and institutions like ours has increased. In this instance, however, as a result of our work and the work of other intersectional feminists in Quebec, including those belonging to the majority community, strong solidarity pronouncements and interventions were made.
11. Stephen Harper of the Conservative Party was prime minister of Canada from 2006 to 2015.

12. Traditions of "arranged marriage" are long-standing and continue in many communities around the world. However, equating all "arranged marriages" with "forced marriage" is totally erroneous. This in no way denies that violence and coercion may come into play, as with many things in the context of patriarchal violence. However, equating "forced marriage" with "arranged marriage" does a disservice to individual young women and men who continue to choose this way of selecting their marriage partner. Moreover, there is an implicit assumption that self-choice marriage is free of violence, something we know is absolutely untrue.

    Horrifyingly, the booklet with information to prepare for the Canadian Citizenship Test contains a section under the sub-heading "The Equality of Women and Men in Canada" that states: "men and women are equal under the law. Canada's openness and generosity do not extend to *barbaric cultural practices* that tolerate spousal abuse, "*honour killings*," female genital mutilation, *forced marriage* or other gender-based violence. Those guilty of these crimes are severely punished under Canada's criminal laws" (Immigration, Refugees and Citizenship Canada 2021; emphasis added). The citizenship test also contains questions about "honour" killings. It is high time this document was revised and this outrageous, inflammatory and racist language edited out.

13. "Burgher" is a term used to identify people of mixed European and Asian ancestry.
14. This slogan of "India-China solidarity" came from the postcolonial non-aligned stance of the early Cold War period at the Bandung conference of 1955, when literally and figuratively Zhou-en-Lai (China's head of government and foreign minister) and Jawaharlal Nehru (India's prime minister) embraced. Things soured in 1962 with the Sino-India war, and people of Chinese origin in India were regarded with suspicion. Many were taken away and placed in internment camps far from their homes, businesses, and livelihoods. Many lost everything they had. Overnight, people of Chinese origin became pariahs. As a young child, I absorbed these tensions, and sought protection by eliding this part of my identity with the Burmese connections we had through my mother—who like many Indians had lived all her life in Burma, which until 1937 was part of the British empire of India and Burma, until she became a refugee in India after Japan invaded (Frayer 2021).
15. Sub-conty, as in being from the Indian sub-continent.
16. For my more detailed elaboration of this, see Chew (2015).
17. Prior to this, the previous government, led by the Liberal Party of Quebec, opened the floodgates with the Bouchard-Taylor Commission, demonstrating that various governments in Quebec, overly nationalist or not, engage with and deploy issues of "identity" based on language and cultural exclusivity. SAWCC has been involved in public deliberations regarding this issue, making suggestions concerning the various iterations of these proposals, asserting that inclusion and accommodations are essential to assure equality rights for all.
18. This proposed legislation was met with opposition from community and civil society organizations, some political parties, and even a former PQ premier. In 2014, the PQ lost in elections to the Liberals, who in turn lost to the Coalition Avenir Quebec (CAQ) in 2018.

19. For more context, until 1998, Quebec had confessional school boards—Catholic and Protestant. In addition, these boards' schools could be English or French. Some elders today, recounting their arrival in Montreal as children whose mother tongues were neither English nor French, remember being directed to Protestant schools. The Protestant School Board of Greater Montreal (PSBGM) was in a predominantly English-speaking district and offered French immersion and English language programs. The PSBGM has become the English Montreal School Board (EMSB) and offers French immersion, English monolingual, and bilingual programs in its schools.
20. See, for example, the statement issued by the Regroupement des centres des femmes du Québec (2021) voicing concerns about how Bill 96 would further inequality for migrant communities in Quebec. Also see the statement published in *Pivot* initiated by the FFQ and signed in support by several groups in Quebec, including the Women of Diverse Origins (Femmes de diverses origins) and SAWCC (FFQ 2022a).
21. At the time of writing, this was the status of the legal process. Then on February 29, 2024, the Quebec Court of Appeal upheld the constitutionality of Loi 21, and on January 23, 2025, the Supreme Court of Canada granted leave to hear a court challenge against the law.
22. Organizing for International Women's Day was resurrected by the group that formed: Femmes de diverses origines/Women of Diverse Origins (FDO-WDO).
23. In India, our experience was of "colonialism." True, some Europeans "stayed on" after independence, but most returned "home" upon retirement. India was never a settler-colonial state.
24. Critical diasporic South Asian feminists have been taking up this challenge with respect to Afghanistan, India, and Pakistan. What is in place augurs positively for future continued work in this regard.

References

Banerjee, Sumanta. 1980. *In the Wake of Naxalbari.* Calcutta: Subarnarekha.

Barrios de Chungara, Domitila. 1978. *Let Me Speak!* New York: Monthly Review Press.

Breach, The. 2024. "Hindu Far Right Pressured a Canadian University into Cancelling a Critical Lecture." September 19. https://breachmedia.ca/hindu-far-right-pressured-a-canadian-university-into-cancelling-a-critical-lecture/.

Bharadwaj, Sudha. 2022. "India's President Droupadi Murmu and 'An Unbroken History of Broken Promises.'" *The Quint.* July 23. https://www.thequint.com/voices/opinion/india-has-droupadi-murmu-as-president-and-unbroken-history-of-broken-promises-chhattisgarh-tribals-maoist-violence.

Canadian Encyclopedia. 2016. "Women's Movements in Canada: 1960–85." September 12. https://www.thecanadianencyclopedia.ca/en/article/womens-movements-in-canada-196085.

Canadian Encyclopedia. 2018. "Turtle Island." November 6. https://www.thecanadianencyclopedia.ca/en/article/turtle-island.

CBC News. 2016. "Justin Trudeau Apologizes in House for 1914 Komagata Maru Incident." May 18. https://www.cbc.ca/news/politics/komagata-maru-live-apology-1.3587827.

CBC News. 2021. "Parc-Extension Rally Against Domestic Violence Calls for Legislative Changes." July 30. https://www.cbc.ca/news/canada/montreal/parc-extension-rally-domestic-violence-south-asian-women-community-centre-1.6125089.

Chew, Dolores. 2002. "The Search for Kathleen McNally and Other Chimerical Women." In *Translating Desire*, edited by Brinda Bose, 2–29. New Delhi: Katha.

Chew, Dolores. 2007. "Secular Feminism Today: Lessons from Canada and India." *Pakistan Journal of Women's Studies: Alam-e-Niswan* 14 (1): 87–96.

Chew, Dolores. 2015. "Feminism and Multiculturalism in Quebec: An/Other Perspective." In *Canadian Woman Studies: An Introductory Reader*, 3rd ed., edited by Brenda Cranney and Sheila Molloy, 12–25. Toronto: Inanna.

Chew, Dolores. 2021. "The Personal Can Be Political: Deconstructing Representations of Anglo-Indians." In *Anglo-Indian Identity Past and Present in India and the Diaspora*, edited by Robyn Andrews and Merin Simi Raj, 253–277. Cham, Switzerland: Palgrave Macmillan.

Cote-Meek, Sheila. 2017. "Supporting the TRC's Calls to Action." *University Affairs*. https://universityaffairs.ca/opinion/supporting-trcs-calls-action/.

Daly, Mary. 1978. *Gyn/Ecology: The Metaethics of Radical Feminism*. Boston: Beacon Press.

D'Souza, Radha, and Kasim Tirmizey, eds. 2018. "The Ghadar Movement." Special issue, *Socialist Studies* 13 (2). https://socialiststudies.com/index.php/sss/issue/view/1859.

Fédération des femmes du Québec (FFQ). 2019. "Le projet de loi ne vise pas la laïcité mais les femmes musulmanes." Press release, May 29.

Fédération des femmes du Québec (FFQ). 2022b. "La Loi 21: Une atteinte au droit fondamental d'égalité des genres." April 20. https://ffq.qc.ca/portfolio-items/la-loi-21-une-atteinte-au-droit-fondamental-degalite-des-genres/.

Fédération des femmes du Québec (FFQ). 2022a. "Réforme de la loi 101: quells impacts sur les femmes?" *Pivot*, June 11. https://pivot.quebec/2022/06/11/reforme-de-la-loi-101-quels-impacts-sur-les-femmes/.

Frayer, Lauren. 2021. "Tensions with China Revive Old Fears for Indians of Chinese Descent." *NPR.org*. December 12. https://www.npr.org/2021/12/12/1059976638/india-china-conflict-chinatown-chinese-indians.

Gilmour, Matt. 2019. "Young Sikh Teacher Leaves Quebec for B.C. Over Bill 21 Religious Symbols Exclusion." *CTV Montreal*. August 14. https://www.ctvnews.ca/montreal/article/young-sikh-teacher-leaves-quebec-for-bc-over-bill-21-religious-symbols-exclusion/.

Guha, Ranajit. 1983. *Elementary Aspects of Peasant Insurgency in Colonial India*. Delhi: Oxford University Press.

Gupta, Rahila. 2003. *From Homebreakers to Jailbreakers: Southall Black Sisters*. London: Zed Books.

Haque, Eve. 2009. "Homegrown, Muslim and Other: Tolerance, Secularism and the Limits of Multiculturalism." *Social Identities* 16 (1): 79–101.

Haque, Eve, and Donna Patrick. 2015. "Indigenous Languages and the Racial Hierarchisation of Language Policy in Canada." *Journal of Multilingual and Multicultural Development* 36 (1): 27–41.

Immigration, Refugees and Citizenship Canada. 2021. *Discover Canada: The Rights and Responsibilities of Citizenship*. https://www.canada.ca/content/dam/ircc/migration/ircc/english/pdf/pub/discover.pdf.

Johnston, Hugh. 2006. "Komagatu Maru." *The Canadian Encyclopedia*. February 7. Last modified October 12, 2021. https://www.thecanadianencyclopedia.ca/en/article/komagata-maru.

Mumtaz, Khawar, and Farida Shaheed. 1987. *Two Steps Forward, One Step Back?* London: Zed Books.

Omvedt, Gail. 1990. *Violence Against Women: New Movements and New Theories in India.* New Delhi: Kali for Women.

Randall, Margaret. 1981. *Sandino's Daughters.* Vancouver: New Star Books.

Regroupement des centres de femmes du Québec. 2021. "Message from l'R des centres de femmes du Quebec on Bill 96." December 9. https://www.sawcc-ccfsa.ca/EN/message-from-lr-des-centres-de-femmes-du-quebec-on-bill-96/.

Said, Edward. 1978. *Orientalism.* New York: Pantheon Books.

Sangari, Kumkum, and Sudesh Vaid. 1989. *Recasting Women.* New Delhi: Kali for Women.

Sanghatana, Stree Shakti. 1989. *We Were Making History.* New Delhi: Kali for Women.

Shanti, Nishtha. 2021. "The Mathura Rape Case of 1972: A Watershed Moment in India's Rape Law." *feminisminindia.com*. September 2. https://feminisminindia.com/2021/09/02/mathura-rape-case-1972-watershed-moment-india-rape-laws/.

South Asian Women's Community Centre (SAWCC). 2013. "Mémoire pour la consultation concernant loi no 60, Charte affirmant les valeurs de laïcité et de neutralité religieuse de l'État ainsi que d'égalité entre les femmes et les hommes et encadrant les demandes d'accommodement." https://www.sawcc-ccfsa.ca/EN/wp-content/uploads/2022/01/Charterenglish.pdf.

South Asian Women's Community Centre (SAWCC). 2014. "Crimes d'honneur et mariages forcés: violence envers les femmes et les enfants." *Bulletin* (Mai): 1. https://www.sawcc-ccfsa.ca/EN/wp-content/uploads/2017/06/05_May_2014.pdf.

South Asian Women's Community Centre (SAWCC). 2015. "Moving & Powerful Historic Moment—SAWCC and Indigenous Solidarity." *Bulletin* (August): 2.

Spivak, Gayatri Chakravorty. 2010. "'Can the Subaltern Speak?': Revised Edition, from the 'History' Chapter of Critique of Postcolonial Reason." In *Can the Subaltern Speak?: Reflections on the History of an Idea*, edited by Rosalind C. Morris, 21–78. New York: Columbia University Press.

Tagore, Rabrindranath. 1913. "Mind Without Fear." In *Gitanjali: Selected Poems*. Translated by Rabrindranath Tagore. London: MacMillan & co. https://web.archive.org/web/20120721220852/http://www.schoolofwisdom.com/history/teachers/rabindranath-tagore/gitanjali/.

Truth and Reconciliation Commission of Canada. 2015. *Truth and Reconciliation Commission of Canada: Calls to Action*. https://ehprnh2mwo3.exactdn.com/wp-content/uploads/2021/01/Calls_to_Action_English2.pdf.

United Nations Security Council. 1948. Resolution 47 (1948) / [adopted by the Security Council at its 286th meeting], of 21 April 1948. https://digitallibrary.un.org/record/111955/.

2

Placing Muslim Identity

Experiences of Bangladeshi Immigrant Women Operating Businesses in Toronto

MARSHIA AKBAR

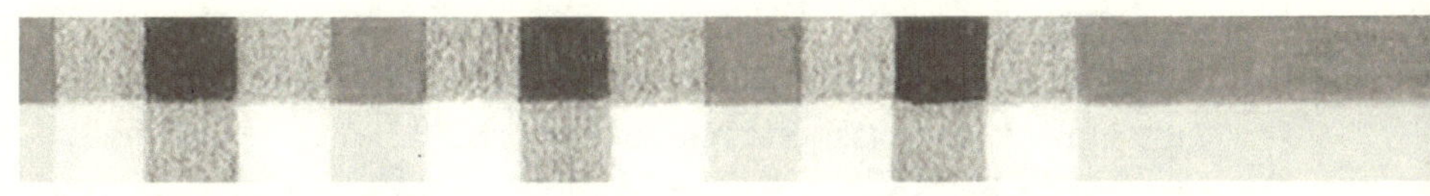

Introduction

In the aftermath of the 9/11 attacks, Orientalist views of Islam and Muslims as primitive and violent gained a new momentum in the West (Said 1979; Zine 2006). While all Muslims face increased scrutiny and surveillance, Muslim women, particularly those who wear the *hijab*, have become the main target of Islamophobic discourses. Muslim women are frequently represented as docile, static, and homogenous in Western media, and the hijab is constructed simultaneously as a symbol of oppression and terrorism (Aziz 2012). Within this context, the debates regarding Muslim immigrant women's engagement in paid work and their presence in the public sphere have also intensified. Some have suggested a direct link between Muslim immigrant women's religious practices and their lower labour market participation compared to non-Muslim women in the UK, the US, and Canada (Ram et al. 2000; Dale et al. 2002; Kibria 2008; Halder 2012; Mohammad 2013). This view suggests that conservative Islamic principles regarding gender segregation and women's dress codes often restrict Muslim women's physical mobility and their engagement in paid work. Others insist instead that religious practices and Islamic dress codes often allow Muslim women to negotiate masculine "public" places (Ruby 2006; Mirza 2013; Nagra 2011; Zimmerman 2014). This binary view of restricted/liberated Muslim women often overlooks the ethno-cultural diversity among Muslim immigrant women, as well as their agency, diverse religious beliefs, and practices. There is a call for recognizing the complexity, plurality, and fluidity in Muslim women's identity construction, to understand and recognize their diverse religious and spatial practices (Moghissi, Rahnema, and Goodman 2009; Abu-Lughod 2002).

Recognizing South Asian diversity is crucial, as it significantly shapes processes of identity construction, as well as settlement, integration, and diasporic relations in Canada. With the externally imposed label "South Asian," the complexity of community is reduced to a single homogeneous category. It encompasses a multitude of gender, class, ethnic, religious, national, and linguistic subsets. Initially grounded in geography and colonial history, this category has since evolved into a racial marker within the context of Canada. Consequently, "South Asian" has acquired connotations of an ethnicized and geographically bounded "race," entailing unfavourable implications within Canadian society (Ashutosh 2014; Rajiva 2013; Ghosh 2014a; Chilvers and Walton-Roberts 2014).

This chapter makes a meaningful contribution toward dismantling the monolithic portrayal of Muslim South Asian women. It achieves this by investigating the impact of religious identities, encompassing religious practices and beliefs, on the participation of Bangladeshi Muslim immigrant women in entrepreneurial ventures outside their home. Additionally, it explores how these women attribute significance to their workplaces within Toronto's Bangla Town neighbourhood.

The study employs an intersectionality framework to examine the multifaceted dimensions of Bangladeshi Muslim women's identities and spatial practices, with a particular focus on three key aspects: group making, body making, and place making. Intersectionality, initially introduced by Kimberlé Crenshaw (1988; 1991), elucidates how "race becomes gendered" and "gender becomes racialized" in the distinct experiences of domestic violence among Black women. Critiquing the limitations of considering gender and race in isolation, Crenshaw argues that social categories such as gender, race, class, and ethnicity co-constitute, mutually reinforce, and normalize each other. While intersectionality has gained widespread acceptance as a theoretical approach (McCall 2005), the exploration of the intersecting identities of Muslim women is relatively recent. Only a handful of studies have delved into how Muslim women residing in the West navigate their identities at the crossroads of race, ethnicity, gender, and religion (Zimmerman 2014; Latif et al. 2018; Mirza 2013; Essers and Benschop 2009). Furthermore, their intersectional identities in the context of paid employment and the workplace have not been extensively examined in the literature (see Latif et al. 2018). Use of the intersectionality framework to comprehend the identities and employment integration of South Asian immigrant women is also limited (Bannerji 1995; George and Ramkissoon 1998; Zaidi et al. 2014; Aurora 2015; Srivastava and Ames 1993). By concentrating on group making, body making, and place making through an intersectional lens, this study highlights the intricate relationships between identities, religious practices, and the workplace. Additionally, by incorporating a geographical perspective into intersectionality, the study illustrates that a workplace is not a static container with fixed meanings. Instead, it takes on diverse meanings for Bangladeshi Muslim women, shaped by their varied religious values and practices.

Identity, Paid Work, and Muslim Immigrant Women

The literature indicates contrasting opinions about the ways in which Islamic practices influence Muslim immigrant women's paid work outside the home (Dwyer 2008; Berns-McGown 1999; Moghissi 2007; Mohammad 2005a, 2005b; Ruby 2006). In the context of migration, as Moghissi (2006) suggests, transformation of identities often drives Muslims toward more conservative practices. Racism and the loss of previous social positions along with minority status in countries of settlement encourage South Asian Muslims, who in their homeland are diverse in their religious practices, to develop strong associations with conservative Islam and emphasize practices that allow them to identify with a larger Muslim Ummah (community) in post-migration contexts in Canada, Britain, and the US (Dale et al. 2002; Halder 2012; Islam 1997; Kibria 2008, 2011; Moghissi 2006; Mohammad 2013; Siraj 2011). Several studies illustrate how the consolidation of conservative Islamic symbols and practices in South Asian Muslim communities constrains women's engagement in paid work outside the home. Mohammad (1999, 2005a, 2005b) illustrates how British Pakistani immigrant women's "gender" roles are often policed and monitored in particular locations, especially outside the home, by imposing Islamic dress codes such as the hijab. Community surveillance and parental regulations seek to control and limit women's access to particular spaces (such as educational centres or the labour market) that are perceived as a threat to Islamic ideology. Similarly, Halder (2012) describes how the inclination toward preserving a global Muslim identity among Bangladeshi Muslims in Toronto influences women's physical appearance and their attitude toward paid work. Peer pressure and social expectations affect their involvement in paid work outside the home. Studies conducted in the UK claim that South Asian Muslim women are not involved in ethnic businesses located outside the home due to religious restrictions (Ram et al. 2000). Along with facing patriarchal oppression within their own communities, Muslim women also experience oppression, racism, and Islamophobia in society at large, as they are constructed as backward, uneducated, and oppressed by others (Mohammad 1999; Zine 2006). Khattab and Hussein (2018) found that most Muslim women in the UK face significant discrimination in the labour market, regardless of their multiple ascriptive identities, generation, and levels of qualifications compared to their white British Christian counterparts.

While these studies highlight Muslim women's marginalization within and outside their own communities, other studies highlight the complex meanings of the veil in terms of how they negotiate their religious identities to engage in paid work (Bartkowski and Read 2003; Hoodfar 2001). Hoodfar (2001) argues that wearing the veil often allows Muslim women to negotiate masculine spaces. Similarly, Ruby (2006) draws on a study of Pakistani Muslim women in Canada to illustrate the ways in which women negotiate places within and outside Muslim communities by embracing the hijab. She argues that women protect themselves from the male gaze in a sexist society by covering their beauty and sexuality. Similarly, Tiilikainen (2003) argues that Somali women in Finland embrace the veil as a marker of their religious identity. Muslim women usually do not perceive the veil as a boundary between themselves and public spheres; they wear the veil to enter into gender-biased "public" space, gain respect in the community, and practice modesty (Abu-Lughod 2001; Berns-McGown 1999).

Some scholars emphasize an intersectionality approach to understand and recognize Muslim immigrant women's diverse religious and spatial practices (Latif et al. 2018; Mirza 2013; Zimmerman 2014; Essers and Benschop 2009). Zimmerman (2014) examines how young American Muslim women negotiate their identity at the intersection of race, gender, and religion, and within their own personal context, and develop strategies to resist stigmatization as they claim a Muslim American identity. While they adopt American values of individual liberty, they also resist assimilative influence by wearing the hijab. Similarly, Latif et al. (2018) discuss how Muslim professional women express or suppress different aspects of their identities at work in Canada while confronting stereotypes and navigating organizational interactions. In another study, Mirza (2013) applied the notion of the "embodied intersectionality" of race, gender, and religion to demonstrate how professional Muslim women's internal experiences are shaped by external Islamophobic discourses, and to show how they resist those discourses in their daily lives in Britain. Essers and Benschop (2009) examine how the entrepreneurial activities of Moroccan and Turkish women intersect with their gender, ethnicity, and religion. Through the notion of "boundary work"—the strategies people adopt to maintain (dis)alignment with different social positions "to react to processes of inclusion and exclusion tied to various identity categories" (406)—their study describes how women utilize religious norms to justify their individual decisions to become entrepreneurs. Women highlight verses from the Qur'an that support women's involvement in paid work and gender equality. They challenge patriarchal interpretations of religious norms that restrict women's presence in "public" domains, including entrepreneurship.

In addition to these intersectional studies, research indicates how the post-9/11 "War on Terror" climate in Canada has notably affected the encounters of South Asian Muslims in comparison to their non-Muslim counterparts (Jamil and Rousseau 2012). The pervasive atmosphere of fear and suspicion associated with escalated security and anti-terrorism apprehensions has cast a shadow over the lives of Muslims in Canada (Akram-Pall and Moodley 2016; Hirji 2010). Agrawal's (2013) findings suggest that among various South Asian sub-groups, Bangladeshis and Pakistanis experience the least post-migration gains in their human capital, which is a possible indication of religion-based bias. These studies imply that the intersection of religious identity with other social dimensions can affect South Asian women's employment opportunities.

Building on this literature and using an intersectionality approach, this study illustrates how Bangladeshi Muslim immigrant women construct diverse religious identities to engage in business activities outside the home in Toronto, and how their religious beliefs and practices shape the meanings of their workplace. The findings reveal how a small group of Bangladeshi women construct their religious identities through the lens of their ethnic identity and cultural practices, and how they link their religious views and practices to their business activities in varied ways. The study describes how the construction of identities and places are often interrelated. Some Bangladeshi women redefine the meanings of "public" workplaces by adopting business strategies that reflect their religious practices. Their experiences underscore the diversity among South Asian communities in Canada concerning paid work and workplace dynamics, and the significance to feminist politics.

Methods and Research Participants

Qualitative methods were implemented to gather data for the study. Field work was conducted around the intersection of two major Toronto streets, Danforth and Victoria Park avenues, a neighbourhood known as Bangla Town, which has the largest residential and business concentrations of Bangladeshi immigrants in Toronto (Ghosh 2014b; Akbar and Preston 2023). In 2016, about 30 percent of Bangladeshi immigrants resided in this neighbourhood (Akbar 2016). Qualitative methods allowed for a detailed examination of business operators. I engaged in participant observation at the South Asian Women's Rights Organization (SAWRO),[1] a Bangladeshi community-based organization that provides employment and social services to Bangladeshi women. Volunteering there helped me gain the trust of community members, gain insights through discussions with community leaders, and recruit participants, including two key informants who worked in different community-based organizations involved with the Bangladeshi community.

In-depth semi-structured interviews were conducted with twelve Bangladeshi Muslim immigrant women operating businesses in the neighbourhood. They described their migration experiences, labour market barriers, religious practices, employment decisions, and experiences at their workplace in detail. All participants had migrated to Canada as dependents of their husbands or relatives. At the time of the interviews, they operated formal retail and service businesses. Like the Korean self-employed women studied by Kwak (2002), most Bangladeshi immigrant women I interviewed did not have paid work before migrating to Canada. Only three out of twelve had participated in the paid labour market in Bangladesh. Despite their lack of work experience in Bangladesh, all but one of the women who participated in the interviews were of working age, ranging from 24 to 60 years old. The majority were mothers, and six had preschool-aged children. Like most recent immigrants in Canada, the participants possessed a high level of educational qualifications. Of the participants, four had a college diploma, five had a university degree, and three had graduated from high school.

According to the 2016 census, nearly half of Bangladeshi immigrants (48.3 percent) arrived in Canada after 2000 (Akbar 2016). But most business operators in this study belonged to the pre-2000 cohort of Bangladeshi immigrants. Only one-third of the participants had arrived after 2000, and among the women who had arrived before

2000, two had lived in Canada for close to twenty-five years and six for more than fifteen years. As Green and colleagues (2016) and Li (2001) have suggested, the longer period of stay may have helped these women acquire the financial capital needed to invest in formal businesses. Unlike most Bangladeshi immigrants (52 percent) who reside in rental apartments, the participants in this study were homeowners, which is evidence of their financial success (Akbar 2016).

Group Making: Not Just Muslim but Bangladeshi Muslim

The Bangladeshi women who participated in the study provided a distinct view of their religious identity to justify their engagement in businesses outside the home. Instead of relating themselves to a global Muslim identity, as suggested by several studies (Dale et al. 2002; Halder 2012; Kibria 2008, 2011; Moghissi 2006; Mohammad 2013), they constructed an ethnically Muslim identity. Differentiating themselves from "other" Muslims was a crucial component of their identity construction. Some examples of the frequent comments from women who claimed a distinct Bangladeshi Muslim identity to justify their involvement in business activities were: "We are not like other Muslims" (Nupur); "Bangladeshi Muslims are different from Middle Eastern Muslims" (Rebeka); and "Bangladeshi Muslims are not like Afghani Muslims" (Nishat). Their comments reflect their perceptions of the differences between themselves and other Muslims. Their narratives also reveal their concerns about Islamophobia and Orientalist stereotypes of Muslim women, which have been exacerbated in the post-9/11 era. To avoid further racialization, social exclusion, and the risk of hate crimes, these women distanced themselves from Middle Eastern Muslims, who are often portrayed as terrorists in Canadian and other Western media.

Using cultural practices to mark her difference, Nupur stressed that Bangladeshi Muslim women are more progressive than Afghani and Arab Muslim women, because "Bengali" culture is less restrictive about women's clothing and their involvement in "public" affairs. She also noted a lack of shared cultural values with Muslim women from other countries. An emphasis on ethno-religious identity was also articulated by Mariyam: "We Bangladeshis are different. We are not extremist, we don't follow conservative religion, like Afghans and Pakistanis. Bangladeshi culture is a liberal culture; Bangladeshi women are educated and smart. Women in Bangladesh don't stay in a 'Khacha'/cage [women are not confined to the home] like Arab women. They [Arabs] follow conservative Islam, they made it up to silence women...we follow progressive Islam."

Mariyam emphasized her ethnic identity to construct Bangladeshi immigrants as progressive and liberal Muslims, as opposed to conservative Muslims from other countries. Drawing a binary division between conservative and liberal Muslims, she confirmed her disassociation with extreme Islamic norms. "We are not extremists" is another common statement in Bangladeshi women's narratives, possibly in response to the depiction of Muslims as violent extremists in Western media. Bangladeshi women who follow religious rituals daily and identify themselves as devout Muslims also differentiate themselves from Muslims who endorse radical Islam. Rebeka, a hijab wearer, expressed her worries about how Bangladeshi Muslims are perceived in Toronto due to the extremist activities of Muslims from other countries: "The problem is people don't know very well that Muslims are different. They [non-Muslims] think all Muslims are alike, and there is no difference. If a Middle Eastern man commits a violent act like [a] suicide bombing, the next day people will hate us, but Bangladeshi Muslims never committed any violent crime. A few [radical] people are ruining Bangladeshi Muslims' reputation."

Most Bangladeshi women interviewed resisted the concept of a single, global Muslim identity. Instead, they underscored the attributes that distinguished them from other Muslims. By highlighting their ethnic identity and distinct cultural practices, the Bangladeshi women challenged the inclination to stereotype Muslim immigrant women. This approach served as a means of protecting themselves from Islamophobia and enabled their active engagement in entrepreneurial endeavours. Concurrently, they drew a distinction between themselves and other groups of Muslim women, often utilizing a binary framework of liberal/conservative that was frequently influenced by Western media narratives. Additionally, their emphasis on their ethno-religious identity set them apart from other South Asian Muslim and non-Muslim subgroups. Engaging in what can be termed as "boundary work" within their identity construction, the Bangladeshi women, similar to Moroccan and Turkish women in the Netherlands (Essers and Benschop 2009), justified their involvement in entrepreneurship outside the home.

Body Making: Hijab vs. Modesty in the Workplace

For the hijab-wearing Bangladeshi women in the study, veiling was an embodied religious symbol through which they made their religious identity visible (Mirza 2013; Gökarıksel 2009). They challenged the notion that veiling is inherently associated with women's seclusion from "public" places. They perceived it as a religious and cultural symbol, not an instrument of women's seclusion. Their opinions reflected one of the underlying notions of the Canadian multiculturalism policy, which promotes inclusivity of ethnic, religious, and cultural diversity (Halder 2012; Nagra 2011). Rebeka, who ran a restaurant, viewed her hijab as a symbol of the religious and cultural practices that she had every right to follow, exactly the way other religious groups follow their customs and beliefs: "Here when one sees a woman with hijab, they think that [she] is very backward, but maybe that's not the case...All communities have their own beliefs and practices; they don't give up their culture. Jewish people follow their own religion, Hindus follow their own religion, but what is wrong if a Muslim woman follows her religion?" Rebeka's opinion concurs with the argument that women often construct the hijab as a mechanism to assert their religious identity in their workplace (Al Wazni 2015; Mirza 2013; Predelli 2004; Ruby 2006; Tiilikainen 2003).

Only a few studies outline the experiences and perceptions of non-veiled Muslim women. Non-veiled Muslim women are often considered to be integrated into the dominant society in North America and Europe, unlike their veiled counterparts (Fadil 2011; Kepel 1994). Fadil (2011) argues that Muslim women's decisions to not veil stem from their (own) cultivation of a specific religious agency, one that is primarily structured along liberal ethical lines. Affirming this notion, a few of the Bangladeshi women interviewed for this study stressed their liberal views about Islamic dress codes. Shahin, a beautician, believed that Muslim women should not associate modesty with clothing: "I don't think your clothing can protect you. I don't know why women here are so much into dress code. Even in Islam it says only to be decent in dressing up. Modesty is not about clothing; it is about how you think and behave. I [have] felt really worried and upset about conservative behaviours."

Most of the non-hijab wearers agreed that wearing the hijab is not necessary for Muslim women, even though they also believed that being modest in one's dress and behaviour is important. Most of the women interviewed stated that they were not conservative, but said that they made sure to be seen as modest women, especially since they worked in "public" places where they interacted with different people. Highlighting her multiple identities as a wife, mother, Muslim, and Bangladeshi woman, Dipika, who ran a clothing store, pointed out how these intersecting identities required her to be a modest woman in the neighbourhood: "I am not conservative, but I don't think we should be that indecent, because we are Bangladeshi and Muslim. And I am married as well, [and] have kids, so I don't think I should be indecent. I work and meet people every day, so I do everything within the limit of decency. I try to create a good impression among the customers... I wear everything, *salwar kamij*, shirt-pant, suit, [as] those do not expose the body." Dipika strived to maintain modesty as a Muslim woman by dressing in certain types of clothing to interact with customers at her workplace.

Another group of business operators took a flexible approach to their clothing. According to Nupur, Bangladeshi women should be flexible in selecting clothes to adapt to the places in which they live and work. She described how she changed her style when she quit her job at a daycare centre and started a restaurant. She used to wear "Western" clothes (e.g., shirt and pants) at the daycare centre to reduce the distance between herself and her non-Bangladeshi coworkers. After starting the restaurant, she began wearing traditional Bangladeshi clothing (salwar kamij) to represent herself as an insider to Bangladeshi customers and employees: "I tell this to everyone, that you should present yourself based on the norms of the place [where] you are. I used to wear shirt-pant [shirts and pants] when I worked at the daycare centre. I presented myself the way they are...Here, I work in [a] Bengali area, [and] Bengali customers come here mainly, so I wear our traditional dress. Look at other Bengali girls, they are also following the same idea. When they work at Tim Hortons, they wear [a] shirt and pant[s]." Since Nupur worked in a Bangladeshi neighbourhood and sold meals to Bangladeshi customers, wearing traditional attire at her workplace seemed reasonable and modest to her. Her explanation sheds light on how Bangladeshi women practice diverse ways of dressing to fit in with various workplace environments. Bangladeshi women's choice of clothing styles reflects their multiple views about religious practices, despite their agreement that women's modest outfits and behaviour are important at workplaces where they interact with other people.

Place Making: Ethnic vs. Religious Setting

Women play active roles in shaping the meanings of their work locations and people's experiences in them (Rodó-de-Zárate 2014; Valentine 2007). Bangladeshi women maintain the ambience of their workplace through diverse cultural and religious practices and business decisions.

Nupur emphasized her Bengali ethnic identity and cultural aspects in applying business strategies. Her ideologies were reflected in the food menu and ambience within her restaurant. On the walls of the restaurant, there were several posters for Bengali cultural festivals that generally unite different religious groups (e.g., Bengali New Year, Independence Day, and International Language Day). Bengali newspapers were kept on the side tables, and Bengali movies and drama serials were played every day on the television. She took extra care in making sure that the food reminded customers of authentic homemade Bengali food. She provided an outlet for Bangladeshis to socialize and retain cultural practices.

Nupur described the cultural significance of Bangladeshis gathering over snacks and tea in her restaurant: "We Bengalis like *adda* [social gathering], we are *addabaj* [fond of socialization] and we love food. There is no source of entertainment for Bangladeshis here. So eventually, people come to the restaurants and spend time with family and friends. They have tea, snacks, and discussions, like *deshi* style... you feel good, and you feel connected to the culture because all the time you study or work and do not get opportunity to enjoy your own food and culture, speak in your own language. So that's why my restaurant is a good place to socialize."

While her restaurant nurtured "Bangaliness," it also exhibited the coexistence of different religions. She served both halal and non-halal food to attract both Muslim and non-Muslim Bangladeshis and maximize her business opportunities. In recruiting a Bengali Hindu chef for her restaurant, Nupur also showed an example of inclusivity. Her strategies to create a symbolic Bangali space in her restaurant appealed to many Bangladeshis, but some conservative Muslim Bangladeshis criticized her for recruiting a non-Muslim chef. She explained: "I decided to recruit him [the chef] because he has very good knowledge of Bengali traditional food. He does not have [an] ego like many chefs. So, that is the point, we can work together. His religious background is not important to me. In my restaurant, all religions are equal. I know many Bangladeshis who are *'gora'* [conservative] Muslims [who] avoid my restaurant because the chef is Hindu. They think he does not know how to handle halal food. But, he knows, and I supervise him." Despite facing criticism, Nupur had adopted business strategies that complied with her ethnicity-based religious identity to construct a Bengali space in her restaurant.

Shahin had created an inclusive space in her beauty parlour by challenging conservative Islamic principles regarding gender segregation. To increase her income, she provided haircuts and hair colouring services to men and women, and she attracted a fair number of male customers on a daily basis. Operating a unisex beauty parlour in her neighbourhood was quite challenging, since Islamic social practices emphasize gender separation in workplaces

(Dhaliwal 1998; Ram et al. 2000). Bangladeshi Muslim women usually do not provide aesthetic services to men. However, the majority of Shahin's customers were Bangladeshi and non-Bangladeshi men from different ethnic and religious backgrounds. She emphasized her hybrid Bangladeshi Canadian identity to justify her business decisions: "We are now Canadians; we live here, and we need to adopt Canadian systems. Here men and women from all backgrounds work together without any restrictions, [and] they study together. This is completely [about] working relation[s, which] is different than other social relations...I do not see any difference between men and women customers. The most important thing for me is to be successful in my business." By including male customers, Shahin ensured her business success. Her economic interests and Bangladeshi Canadian identity encouraged her to transcend conservative Islamic gender roles regarding the separation of men and women in "public" business locations.

In contrast, Soniya—a hijab wearer—had adopted a different set of strategies to attract customers to her restaurant. She exclusively targeted Muslim customers from different ethnic and cultural backgrounds. She stressed the power of religion in uniting people from different parts of the world, and incorporated this notion in her business strategy. Her restaurant was decorated with images of Islamic architecture, *hajj*, and the *kaaba*. She played spiritual and religious songs in her restaurant and served only halal food. Her food menu mainly included a wide range of kabob and tandoori meats and breads, signature food items of Muslims in South Asia and the Middle East. Soniya described her rationale for creating a Muslim space: "Businesses are very competitive in this area. I need a large customer base to survive, so I think targeting Muslims is an effective strategy...and they can relate to me. When they see that I wear the hijab, they respect me. We have commonalities, like we eat halal food, [and] this is very important for Muslims. This is a very good restaurant for Muslims in this area. Once people come here, they inform their friends and relatives. They order food for different events, and that's how I get customers...I do not want to limit myself by serving only Bengalis." Utilizing Islamic symbols was a key strategy behind Soniya's business success. Her emphasis on Muslim identity had shaped the ways in which she made business decisions and created a space for Muslims in her restaurant.

The narratives of Nupur, Shahin, and Soniya indicate how their identities and workplaces were co-constructed (Valentine 2007), although they had redefined their "public" workplaces, by adopting business strategies that reflected their intersecting ethnic, gender, and religious identities. In defining their workplaces, they had also created a boundary between who was included and/or excluded from their business.

Conclusion

This study employed an intersectionality approach to examine the agency and active roles of Bangladeshi Muslim immigrant women in asserting their religious identities and spatial practices in Toronto. Despite their growing presence in Canada, Bangladeshis are often grouped under broader categories like South Asian or the Muslim diaspora, overshadowing their unique identity and diversity (Islam 1997). These generalizations fail to capture the historical and cultural uniqueness of the Bangladeshi community and its internal variations. Furthermore, Western discourse frequently portrays Muslim women through an Orientalist lens, viewing them as passive and backward, while South Asian women are often homogenized into a single ethnicized and racialized group. This study has addressed these distortions by centring on the intricate tapestry of cultural and religious practices among Bangladeshi immigrant women entrepreneurs. Furthermore, it makes a valuable contribution to the ongoing discourse surrounding the diverse identities within South Asian diasporic feminism.

The Bangladeshi women in this study held a range of contrasting views regarding their relationship with their religious, cultural, and business practices, and had constructed boundaries to assert their religious identities and to challenge specific racialized and gendered discourses around modesty and Islamic radicalism. Their emphasis on an ethnicity-based religious identity had also set them apart from other Muslim South Asians (such as Pakistanis), as well as non-Muslim South Asian subgroups. The diverse religious practices of these women had influenced their business strategies and the ways they defined their workplaces and identities. Their active roles in shaping their workplaces through different ethno-cultural and religious symbols, food menus, and customer targets demonstrate how their multifaceted identities influenced the meanings they attributed to their workspaces. This illustrates how these Bangladeshi Muslim immigrant women's distinct gender, ethnic, and religious identities influenced them to challenge Islamophobic narratives perpetuated by Canadian media. They actively defined their embodied identities and the significance of their workplaces in diverse ways.

This case study involving Bangladeshi Muslim immigrant women highlights the intricate and multifaceted nature of South Asian identities, and the necessity of using feminist intersectionality to explore the oversimplification of the label "South Asian" and transcend gender, national, and religious boundaries to acknowledge nuances within and among South Asian subgroups (Ashutosh 2008). However, the study is limited, as it is based on a unique group in one Toronto neighbourhood, where one-third of Toronto's Bangladeshis reside. Women in mixed neighbourhoods may offer different insights into how they navigate their religious practices and paid work.

Note

1. The South Asian Women's Rights Organization (SAWRO) was established in 2005 in order to assist Bangladeshi women residing in Toronto to overcome their poverty, unemployment, and other sociocultural issues (Akbar 2016).

References

Abu-Lughod, Lila. 2001. "Women on Women: Television Feminism and Village Lives." In *Women and Power in the Middle East,* edited by Suad Joseph and Susan Slyomovics, 103-114. Philadelphia: University of Pennsylvania Press.

Abu-Lughod, Lila. 2002. "Do Muslim Women Really Need Saving? Anthropological Reflections on Cultural Relativism and Its Others." *American Anthropologist* 104 (3): 783-790.

Agrawal, Sandeep K. 2013. "Economic Disparities Among South Asian Immigrants in Canada." *South Asian Diaspora* 5 (1): 7-34.

Akbar, Marshia Tashmim. 2016. "Does Workplace Matter? Identities and Experiences of Bangladeshi Immigrant Women Operating Businesses in Toronto." PHD diss., York University.

Akbar, Marshia, and Valerie Preston. 2023. "Entrepreneurial Activities of Canadian Bangladeshi Women in Toronto: A Family Perspective." *Journal of Ethnic and Migration Studies* 49 (11): 2817-2836.

Akram-Pall, Saadia, and Roy Moodley. 2016. "'Loss and Fear': Acculturation Stresses Leading to Depression in South Asian Muslim Immigrants in Toronto." *Canadian Journal of Counselling and Psychotherapy* 50 (3-S): S137-S155.

Al Wazni, Anderson Beckmann. 2015. "Muslim Women in America and Hijab: A Study of Empowerment, Feminist Identity, and Body Image." *Social Work* 60 (4): 325-333.

Ashutosh, Ishan. 2008. "(Re-)Creating the Community: South Asian Transnationalism on Chicago's Devon Avenue." *Urban Geography* 29 (3): 224-245.

Ashutosh, Ishan. 2014. "From the Census to the City: Representing South Asians in Canada and Toronto." *Diaspora: A Journal of Transnational Studies* 17 (2): 130-148.

Aurora, Monisha. 2015. "The Experiences of Second-Generation South Asian Female Students Who Are Attending Universities in Canada." Master's thesis, University of Western Ontario.

Aziz, Sahar F. 2012. "The Muslim 'Veil' Post-9/11: Rethinking Women's Rights and Leadership." Policy brief. Institute for Social Policy and Understanding. https://doi.org/10.7282/T33200FJ.

Bannerji, Himani. 1995. *Thinking Through: Essays on Feminism, Marxism and Anti-Racism*. Toronto: Canadian Scholars' Press.

Bartkowski, John P., and Jen'nan Ghazal Read. 2003. "Veiled Submission: Gender, Power, and Identity Among Evangelical and Muslim Women in the United States." *Qualitative Sociology* 26 (March): 71-92.

Berns-McGown, Rima. 1999. *Muslims in the Diaspora: The Somali Communities of London and Toronto*. Toronto: University of Toronto Press.

Chilvers, Simon, and Margaret Walton-Roberts. 2014. "Introduction: Deconstructing the (Re) Construction of South Asian Identities in Canada." *Diaspora: A Journal of Transnational Studies* 17 (2): 121-129.

Crenshaw, Kimberlé Williams. 1988. "Foreword: Toward a Race-Conscious Pedagogy in Legal Education." *National Black Law Journal* 11 (1): 1-14.

Crenshaw, Kimberlé. 1991. "Mapping the Margins: Intersectionality, Identity Politics, and Violence Against Women of Color." *Stanford Law Review* 43 (6): 1241-1299.

Dale, Angela, Nusrat Shaheen, Virinder Kalra, and Edward Fieldhouse. 2002. "Routes into Education and Employment for Young Pakistani and Bangladeshi Women in the UK." *Ethnic and Racial Studies* 25 (6): 942-968.

Dhaliwal, Spinder. 1998. "Silent Contributors: Asian Female Entrepreneurs and Women in Business." *Women's Studies International Forum* 21 (5): 463-474.

Dwyer, Claire. 2008. "The Geographies of Veiling: Muslim Women in Britain." *Geography* 93 (3): 140-147.

Essers, Caroline, and Yvonne Benschop. 2009. "Muslim Businesswomen Doing Boundary Work: The Negotiation of Islam, Gender and Ethnicity Within Entrepreneurial Contexts." *Human Relations* 62 (3): 403–423.

Fadil, Nadia. 2011. "Not-/Unveiling as an Ethical Practice." *Feminist Review* 98 (1): 83–109.

George, Usha, and Sarah Ramkissoon. 1998. "Race, Gender, and Class: Interlocking Oppressions in the Lives of South Asian Women in Canada." *Affilia* 13 (1): 102–119.

Ghosh, Sutama. 2014a. "A Passage to Canada: The Differential Migrations of South Asian Skilled Workers to Toronto." *Journal of International Migration and Integration* 15 (August): 715–735.

Ghosh, Sutama. 2014b. "Everyday Lives in Vertical Neighbourhoods: Exploring Bangladeshi Residential Spaces in Toronto's Inner Suburbs." *International Journal of Urban and Regional Research* 38 (6): 2008–2024.

Gökarıksel, Banu. 2009. "Beyond the Officially Sacred: Religion, Secularism, and the Body in the Production of Subjectivity." *Social & Cultural Geography* 10 (6): 657–674.

Green, David Alan, Huju Liu, Yuri Ostrovski, and Garnett Picot. 2016. "Immigration, Business Ownership and Employment in Canada." Analytical Studies Branch Research Paper Series. Ottawa: Statistics Canada. https://www150.statcan.gc.ca/n1/pub/11f0019m/11f0019m2016375-eng.htm.

Halder, Rumel. 2012. "Immigration and Identity Negotiation Within the Bangladeshi Immigrant Community in Toronto, Canada." PHD diss., University of Manitoba.

Hirji, Faiza. 2010. *Dreaming in Canadian: South Asian Youth, Bollywood, and Belonging*. Vancouver: UBC Press.

Hoodfar, Homa. 2001. "The Veil in Their Minds and on Our Heads: Veiling Practices and Muslim Women." In *Women, Gender, Religion: A Reader*, edited by Elizabeth A. Castelli, 420–446. New York: Palgrave Macmillan.

Islam, M.S. 1997. "Bangladeshi Immigrants in Toronto: Towards an Alternative Way to Meet Cultural Needs." *The Journal of Social Studies*: 57–70.

Jamil, Uzma, and Cécile Rousseau. 2012. "Subject Positioning, Fear, and Insecurity in South Asian Muslim Communities in the War on Terror Context." *Canadian Review of Sociology/Revue canadienne de sociologie* 49 (4): 370–388.

Kepel, Gilles. 1994. *The Revenge of God: The Resurgence of Islam, Christianity, and Judaism in the Modern World*. University Park: Penn State Press.

Khattab, Nabil, and Shereen Hussein. 2018. "Can Religious Affiliation Explain the Disadvantage of Muslim Women in the British Labour Market?" *Work, Employment and Society* 32 (6): 1011–1028.

Kibria, Nazli. 2008. "The 'New Islam' and Bangladeshi Youth in Britain and the US." *Ethnic and Racial Studies* 31 (2): 243–266.

Kibria, Nazli. 2011. *Muslims in Motion: Islam and National Identity in the Bangladeshi Diaspora*. New Brunswick: Rutgers University Press.

Kwak, Min-Jung. 2002. "Work in Family Businesses and Gender Relations: A Case Study of Recent Korean Immigrant Women." Master's thesis, York University.

Latif, Ruby, Wendy Cukier, Suzanne Gagnon, and Radia Chraibi. 2018. "The Diversity of Professional Canadian Muslim Women: Faith, Agency, and 'Performing' Identity." *Journal of Management & Organization* 24 (5): 612–633.

Li, Peter S. 2001. "Immigrants' Propensity to Self-Employment: Evidence from Canada." *International Migration Review* 35 (4): 1106–1128.

McCall, Leslie. 2005. "The Complexity of Intersectionality." *Signs: Journal of Women in Culture and Society* 30 (3): 1771–1800.

Mirza, Heidi Safia. 2013. "'A Second Skin': Embodied Intersectionality, Transnationalism and Narratives of Identity and Belonging Among Muslim Women in Britain." *Women's Studies International Forum* 36 (Jan–Feb): 5–15.

Moghissi, Haideh, ed. 2006. *Muslim Diaspora: Gender, Culture and Identity*, vol. 2. London: Routledge.

Moghissi, Haideh, Saeed Rahnema, and Mark J. Goodman. 2009. *Diaspora by Design: Muslims in Canada and Beyond*. Toronto: University of Toronto Press.

Mohammad, Robina. 1999. "Marginalisation, Islamism and the Production of the 'Other's Other.'" *Gender, Place and Culture* 6 (3): 221–240.

Mohammad, Robina. 2005a. "Negotiating Spaces of the Home, the Education System and the Labour Market: The Case of Young, Working-Class, British-Pakistani Muslim Women." In *Geographies of Muslim Women: Gender, Religion, and Space*, edited by Caroline Nagel and Ghazi-Walid Falah, 178–200. New York: Guilford Press.

Mohammad, Robina. 2005b. "British Pakistani Muslim Women: Marking the Body, Marking the Nation." In *A Companion to Feminist Geography*, edited by Lise Nelson and Joni Seager, 379–397. Hoboken: Wiley.

Mohammad, Robina. 2013. "Making Gender Ma(r)king Place: Youthful British Pakistani Muslim Women's Narratives of Urban Space." *Environment and Planning A* 45 (8): 1802–1822.

Nagra, Baljit. 2011. "Unequal Citizenship: Being Muslim and Canadian in the Post 9/11 Era." PHD diss., University of Toronto.

Predelli, Line Nyhagen. 2004. "Interpreting Gender in Islam: A Case Study of Immigrant Muslim Women in Oslo, Norway." *Gender and Society* 18 (4): 473–493.

Rajiva, Mythili. 2013. "'Better Lives': The Transgenerational Positioning of Social Mobility in the South Asian Canadian Diaspora." *Women's Studies International Forum* 36 (Jan–Feb): 16–26.

Ram, Monder, Balihar Sanghera, Tahir Abbas, Gerald Barlow, and Trevor Jones. 2000. "Ethnic Minority Business in Comparative Perspective: The Case of the Independent Restaurant Sector." *Journal of Ethnic and Migration Studies* 26 (3): 495–510.

Rodó-de-Zárate, Maria. 2014. "Developing Geographies of Intersectionality with Relief Maps: Reflections from Youth Research in Manresa, Catalonia." *Gender, Place and Culture* 21 (8): 925–944.

Ruby, Tabassum F. 2006. "Listening to the Voices of Hijab." *Women's Studies International Forum* 29 (1): 54–66.

Said, Edward W. 1979. *Orientalism.* New York: Vintage.

Siraj, Asifa. 2011. "Meanings of Modesty and the Hijab Amongst Muslim Women in Glasgow, Scotland." *Gender, Place and Culture* 18 (6): 716–731.

Srivastava, R. P., and Michael Ames. 1993. "South Asian Women's Experience of Gender, Race, and Class in Canada." In *Ethnicity, Identity, Migration: The South Asian Context*, edited by Milton Israel and Narendra K. Wagle, 123–141. Toronto: University of Toronto.

Tiilikainen, Marja. 2003. "Somali Women and Daily Islam in the Diaspora." *Social Compass* 50 (1): 59–69.

Valentine, Gill. 2007. "Theorizing and Researching Intersectionality: A Challenge for Feminist Geography." *The Professional Geographer* 59 (1): 10–21.

Zaidi, Arshia U., Amanda Couture-Carron, Eleanor Maticka-Tyndale, and Mehek Arif. 2014. "Ethnic Identity, Religion, and Gender: An Exploration of Intersecting Identities Creating Diverse Perceptions and Experiences With Intimate Cross-Gender Relationships Amongst South Asian Youth in Canada." *Canadian Ethnic Studies* 46 (2): 27–54.

Zimmerman, Danielle Dunand. 2014. "Young Muslim Women in the United States: Identities at the Intersection of Group Membership and Multiple Individualities." *Social Identities* 20 (4–5): 299–313.

Zine, Jasmin. 2006. "Unveiled Sentiments: Gendered Islamophobia and Experiences of Veiling Among Muslim Girls in a Canadian Islamic School." *Equity and Excellence in Education* 39 (3): 239–252.

3

Transgressing Boundaries of *Izzat*

Resisting, Surviving, and Understanding Honour-Related Violence Through the Stories of South Asian Women

MANDEEP KAUR MUCINA

Introduction

My doctoral research examined how second-generation Punjabi Canadian women negotiate, resist, and ultimately reclaim their honour, or *izzat*, after being exiled from their family and/or community for engaging in perceived unacceptable sexual relationships. The women spoke about impossible choices they have navigated throughout their lives, from displacement to reclamation of their izzat. Their narratives of the violence they experienced through fear, shame, guilt, and anger—and their pleas for empathy—cannot be encapsulated in the contemporary discourse of honour-related violence (HRV) deployed in feminist attempts to protect women.

South Asian critical feminists have spent a great deal of time and energy deconstructing the racist and sexist discourses that underlie dominant mainstream perspectives about South Asian women and family violence. Scholars such as Sherene Razack, Yasmin Jiwani, Himani Bannerjee, Uma Narayan, Lila Abu-Lughod, Inderpal Grewal, Rupaleem Bhuyan, and Amina Jamal have been pivotal in giving me, a South Asian Sikh Punjabi woman, the language to challenge neoliberal, racist, and sexist discourses that are part of the everyday narratives of Western society. These critiques, analysis, and arguments are embedded in anti-racist, post-structural feminist, anti-colonial, and cultural theories that are pivotal to not only this research but also the conversations I have in my Punjabi community. I recognize and pay homage to their work, because without it I would not be able to take this conversation to the next level.

The next level or stage in the conversation involves going beyond a critique/analysis/dismantling of racist discourses that fog second-generation South Asian women's stories of violence. This research is aimed at raising consciousness for both individuals and communities. This involves acknowledging and confronting the patriarchal family violence distressing South Asian communities in Canada. It also involves maintaining a strong hold on how culturally racist discourses are waiting to take up our stories and use them to diametrically oppose the values of the West and the East, in order to portray a fabricated picture that the West is beyond patriarchy and violence against women.

I draw on in-depth interviews conducted with five women over two years, in addition to my own experience, to conceptualize a new understanding of HRV. You will hear from Lakshmi, Tara, Durga, Parvati, and Makavidya,[1] who shared their life histories and stories of resistance after being exiled from their family and/or community. Their stories speak to the complexities of HRV in the West, specifically how it unravels in Punjabi families and is reconstructed from a colonial lens that centres white supremacy and heteropatriarchy. Challenging the dominant discourses that frame family violence in South Asian communities, the women described resisting/reclaiming their izzat while surviving layers of patriarchy, violence, and racism throughout their lives (Mucina 2018, 2021).

Methodology and Analytical Framework

For this research, I use a discursive framework to guide the analysis and methodology, including critical intersectionality and narrative inquiry. I am an insider when it comes to the Punjabi diaspora, this research, and the issue of HRV, and I align myself with the women I interviewed. My ontology shapes how I understand women's stories and how I represent them in my writing. I am a cisheterosexual, able-bodied, brown woman with an evolving class status and a Sikh Punjabi understanding of izzat. I am also a survivor of displacement from my family because of izzat.

The stories of the five women are the backbone of this research and this chapter, as is my narrative. Through narrative inquiry methods, I was able to focus on how izzat took shape in their lives. Narrative therapy follows a similar trajectory of restructuring stories, so that the teller and listener engage in a therapeutic alliance (White 2004). The basic premise of narrative therapy is that we make sense of our lives through stories (Brown and Augusta-Scott 2007).

I begin this chapter by deconstructing Western discourses that perpetuate colonial logics of Orientalism on the backs of second-generation women and girls who have been killed in the name of honour. Then, I focus on the narratives of the women I interviewed, engaging briefly with an emergent theme: being exiled for transgressing boundaries. Finally, I offer a framework for understanding HRV as a continuum that can be part of women's stories throughout their lives, challenging current framings that focus on extreme acts of violence, in order to consider honour or izzat in thinking about interpersonal or family violence.

Honour Discourses in the West and Their Impact on Second-Generation South Asian Women

HRV has become oversimplified and been associated with marked bodies in the West for decades (Baker, Gregware, and Cassidy 1999; Meetoo and Mirza 2007; Papp and Kay 2012; Sanghera 2007). Significant capital is filtered into liberal feminist discourses that frame HRV as a problem in migrant communities that can be resolved by civilizing brown bodies (see Papp and Kay 2012). This currency in the construction and maintenance of honour discourses allows institutions like Immigration and Citizenship Canada to maintain a strong hold on who gets into Canada and how migrants assimilate.

These discourses fuel the ongoing surveillance of marked bodies, particularly Muslim bodies defined as a threat to Western imperialism (Razack 2008).

Sherene Razack (2004) has contextualized how forced marriages manifest power and control in migrant households: "There is little doubt that both arranged and forced marriages spring from an impulse to control women's sexuality, and that such controls are exercised more vigorously when communities feel themselves to be losing control...We need to see migrant communities in context. First, instead of seeing them as composed of foreign newcomers and uninvited guests, we might view them as populations displaced by colonialism and now under siege in late capitalism. As communities they struggle for survival in an increasingly racist context" (140). Migrant communities are confronted with capitalist, imperialist, hegemonic whiteness that casts them as "immigrants, aliens, [and] strangers" (Ahmed 2010, 5). The racism that migrant families encounter fuels heteropatriarchy inside and outside their homes, and women feel the effects of these intersecting institutions of power in how their bodies are constantly regulated (Espiritu 2001; Jiwani 2006).

Second-generation South Asian women are situated in a liminal space between the heteropatriarchy enacted in mainstream society that intersects with their experiences of racism and historical colonialism and the heteropatriarchy inside their family and community that uses their body as a space to enact power and control over their cultural identity (Ahmed 2000; Aujla 2000; Handa 2003; Puar 1994; Rajiva 2013). As Yasmin Jiwani (2006) states, "It is the convergence of these internal and external patriarchies that demands scrutiny" (23).

Furthermore, as second-generation immigrants, the women of this study shared their stories while situated on the unceded or treaty territories of many Indigenous communities in the settler colonial nation called Canada—communities that continue to fight acts of genocide and colonial violence to protect their land, culture, and identity. The presence of Punjabi immigrants on these territories is in large part due to the colonial global network that moves disposable bodies according to capitalist endeavours (Byrd

2011). The logic of colonialism relies on capitalism, heteropatriarchy, and pillars of white supremacy that define racialized bodies as expendable labourers useful for the project of resource extraction (Tuck and Yang 2012). White supremacy and colonialism rely on the enslavement of Black bodies, the genocide of Indigenous bodies, and Orientalism and war in the East to maintain a narrative of Western superiority (Bonds and Inwood 2016). As a diasporic community and generation, we live in and benefit from the settler colonial society that feeds and breeds violence toward Indigenous women, who have been targeted for violence since colonial occupation began on this land. I cannot speak about violence against women without recognizing Indigenous women's struggles and the thousands of murdered and missing Indigenous women (National Inquiry into MMIWG 2019).

Second-generation immigrants raised in the West from birth or childhood are defined as aliens (Ahmed 2000), serving the imagination of a colonial state such as Canada. The second-generation body is a site of hope for assimilation, as regulation is framed within that ideal. The second generation is expected to strive for the egalitarian Western ideals of "equality" by denouncing their family's culture, traditions, and practices. This regulation is framed as "choice" and as the "freedom" that Canada provides second-generation youth, particularly women, to choose between patriarchies, whether internal or external. The second-generation South Asian woman is expected to challenge the heteropatriarchy of her community and embrace the "liberal" values of the West as they are portrayed in the media. Yet, this embrace comes at a cost: she must renounce all ties to her family and community and continue to suffer the racism, oppression, and sexist values of the West. As second-generation women, our bodies become a place for our families to demonstrate their resistance to the racism in these new nations they have migrated to, while in the outside world, we are managing capitalist heteropatriarchy in spaces that we must constantly maneuver, as well as the racism, Orientalism, and colonialism evident in Western society.

Surviving HRV: Stories of Being Excommunicated/Displaced

Sara Ahmed (2010) articulates a metaphor—feminist killjoy—that encapsulates how the threat of a woman's transgressions creates distinct moments of panic, anger, and shame in a family and community when a woman breaks down or discloses her transgressions:

> To be the object of shared disapproval, those glances that can cut you up, cut you out. An experience of alienation can shatter a world. The family gathers around the table; these are supposed to be happy occasions. How hard we work to keep the occasion happy, to keep the surface of the table polished so that it can reflect back a good image of the family. So much you are not supposed to say, to do, to be, in order to preserve that image. If you say, or do, or be anything that does not reflect the image of the happy family back to itself, the world becomes distorted. You become the cause of a distortion. You are the distortion you cause. Another dinner, ruined. To become alienated from a picture can allow you to see what that picture does not and will not reflect. (1)

A "feminist killjoy" is a woman who disrupts the status quo, speaks out against hegemony, and essentially shifts something inside each person at that table. The six women in this study, including myself, knew our choices went against family codes and a moral order that our family was invested in preserving—underneath claims of happiness. Yet, to disclose our world to them was "to be willing to cause unhappiness, even if unhappiness [was] not [our] cause" (Ahmed 2010, 3).

For Lakshmi, being queer was part of this disclosure, and after she came out to her family, some of her siblings made a collective stand to excommunicate her, thus taking away their mother's choice to have a relationship with her daughter. Lakshmi described her anger at her siblings for taking away her opportunity to come out to her mother on her own terms, all to maintain their judgments on her sexuality: "If I go there [to tell her], and my mother says to me,

'I don't want to see your face again, I don't approve of this, get out of my sight.' Let her say that to me, and do not let you [the siblings] decide that she can't even manage the news. Don't take that agency away from her, She's going to be the one to say that to me, let her decide that." From her siblings' perspective, Lakshmi would bring their mother shame and unhappiness, and they saw it as their role to protect her from their sister's transgressions.

The removal from the family table is not a cordial affair but a violent experience. There is very little choice embedded in women's removal from the table. It is a misconception that women are "choosing" to become "feminist killjoys," not only in their families but also in society, and this misconception risks minimizing the pain of women's displacement/exile from their families and/or community. Women exercise agency, strength, and resiliency when they take control over their own lives and self-determine when the family table is no longer safe for them, or when they challenge the family status quo knowing they will lose family and community support. The concept of choice, the rejection associated with choice, and the capacity to exist beyond the family and/or community are themes that emerged from this research, yet these are rarely discussed in honour discourses.

The Continuum of HRV

Within the general discourses of violence against women and girls, scholars such as Aysan Sev'er (2002) emphasize the climate of misogyny that surrounds extreme cases of not only intimate partner violence but also gender-based violence that targets women and girls. Sev'er uses the concept of a continuum of violence to consider the "culture of machoism, widespread misogyny, and the troubling nature of work and intimate relations all over North America" (75), and demonstrates the triangulation of power, control, and sexuality in this continuum, which sets men/boys against women/girls at various personal and structural levels.

Taking Sev'er's lead, as well as the direction of other feminist scholars who insist on a broader discussion of gender-based violence, particularly concerning the family unit (see Eichler 1997;

Korteweg 2012), I have theorized a continuum of HRV. This continuum emerges from the women's stories, from my own comprehensive literature review, and from my frontline experience as a social worker focussed on violence against women. Furthermore, I consulted with frontline social workers in Toronto working with women fleeing situations of HRV and forced marriage. In Table 4.1, I have strategically placed the forms of violence in a specific order to demonstrate the prevalence of each in women's lives. This model is a tool for engaging in conversations about HRV, and thus makes it possible to piece together all the individual, collective, and institutional elements that are involved in a complex HRV narrative. As the women in this study articulated, most of their experiences did not go past forms of displacement/exile (5) and forced marriage (6). This research is about expanding our consciousness and practice to think beyond the extreme cases of honour killings to consider women's everyday encounters with the regulating of their bodies, encounters that sit on a continuum.

The women's stories reveal that guilt and shame bind women to izzat. The fear of going beyond the boundaries set by her parents stopped Tara from pushing her family too much at a young age: "We didn't have any boyfriends in high school...I never did. I just didn't. Also, I didn't even know people went out to parties. My first dance was the spring fling and that was in Grade 12, and then at that point, I would ask, 'Can I go to a dance?' and my mom would say, 'Ask your dad.' And then that was stopped. I'm like, 'I'm not going to ask Dad.'"

As Tara reflected on these moments in her life, she expressed a lot of pain associated with the constrictions in her life and the nonverbal cues that surrounded these moments. The phrase *"hor na ne khe khanna?"* (What will other people think?) was used frequently by Tara, Parvati, and Lakshmi in their stories. Within this phrase is the construction of shame surrounding women's behaviour and the guilt of putting parents through a confrontation with their community when they start gossiping about their daughter. Lakshmi articulated this construction in her story and described her siblings' preoccupation with shame and izzat: "Yeah, I think that shame is tied really closely to this idea of honour, because I don't think if you

TABLE 4.1. Continuum of Honour-Related Violence: Transgressions and Consequences

<table>
<tr><th>Honour-related violence within the home</th><th>Examples</th><th>Navigating heteropatriarchy, racism, Islamophobia, sexism, homophobia, transphobia, colonialism, and classism</th></tr>
<tr><td>Emotional violence to control behaviour and transgressions</td><td>Experiencing guilt and shame associated with your body.

Receiving verbal and nonverbal cues for what are acceptable and unacceptable boundaries.

Being told that your actions will lead to the death of parents and elders as a way of deterring you from behaviours that transgress izzat or honour.</td><td rowspan="3">Feeling pressure from friends to participate in activities that could lead to transgressing boundaries of izzat or honour.

Being told your family is "cruel," "unusual," or "barbaric" for placing controls on your life.

Encountering silence or gaslighting from counselling professionals when speaking about your story or experience.

Fearing child protection getting involved and defining your family as barbaric.

Feeling pressure from friends, acquaintances, and professionals who suggest that any choice between family and so-called "freedom" should always be freedom.

Being triggered by media depictions of honour violence that define South Asian/Muslim communities as barbaric.

Having to justify needing support or help when describing your story to service providers; having to prove the impact of emotional abuse to get support/services.

Encountering difficulties in shelter systems that are usually full of young people who are fleeing very different situations (e.g., parental neglect, sexual abuse, drug addiction).</td></tr>
<tr><td>Economic violence to control behaviour and transgressions</td><td>Having no financial control and limits placed on your access to education.

Having limits placed on who you can engage with outside of the family.

Having limits placed on what activities you can engage in outside the family home.</td></tr>
<tr><td>Confinement and threats</td><td>Experiencing interventions by extended family that involve various forms of coercion.

Experiencing confinement, control over social mobility, phone calls being tracked, being watched and followed by family members.

Being threatened with being taken to another country.

Being threatened that your parents will die by suicide.

Being threatened with murder.</td></tr>
</table>

TABLE 4.1. Continuum of Honour-Related Violence: Transgressions and Consequences (cont.)

Honour-related violence within the home	Examples	Navigating heteropatriarchy, racism, Islamophobia, sexism, homophobia, transphobia, colonialism, and classism
Physical violence	Witnessing physical violence against your mother, siblings, or care providers because of transgressions. Experiencing physical violence because of transgressions.	Experiencing financial constraints after being excommunicated that lead to a precarious lifestyle.
Displacement or excommunication and violence	Being forced into an arranged marriage. Being excommunicated if you continue transgressing. Being displaced from your family and community. Being excommunicated from your family and community.	
Forced marriage/non-consensual marriage	Being coerced to marry a chosen suitor against your will, under duress, and/or without full, free, and informed consent from both parties (forced marriage can occur abroad or in Canada).	
Honour-related killing	Experiencing physical violence that leads to murder instigated by shame or potential shame due to a perceived transgression of the boundaries of izzat or honour.	

ask them what honour is, they could explain that, you know. Maybe in my family, they would explain it as being a good Sikh."

Reflecting on the continuum, the regular encounters of emotional violence for women are largely controlled through a process of implementing guilt and shame for transgressing family codes of conduct. Guilt and shame are useful tools of control, particularly for women, because of how intimately they are internalized. Brené Brown (2006) has conducted extensive research on shame and its impact on women. She defines shame as "an intensely painful feeling or experience of believing we are flawed and therefore unworthy of acceptance and belonging" (45). Brown notes that a common response to shame is to flee from those who view you as flawed or bad. Brown's research is very applicable to the construction of izzat and/or honour and the regulation of women's bodies. For Brown, the shame resiliency theory is a "web of layered, conflicting, and competing expectations that are, at the core, products of rigid sociocultural expectations" (46).

Themes of guilt run through Parvati's story. She shared a common family narrative, where her father described encountering shame in his community because of the transgressions the women in his family had made against the social order. Parvati witnessed each of her sisters being exiled from the family because of this, as well as her mother leaving her father. The impact this had on her father led to Parvati's own guilt and conviction to not bring shame to her father's honour. This became a significant contributing factor leading to Parvati's commitment to her father, confined her to pleasing her father to protect his izzat. Parvati was trapped in an abusive marriage, and after finding a way out was forced into another marriage that suited her sister and father more than herself and her dreams for her future. When she was hospitalized due to post-traumatic stress, she became unwilling to protect her father's izzat and let it control her life: "When I was hospitalized, and it gave me an opportunity to think, okay, every time I've tried to do things my father's way, [and] he said anything, I've done it. Boom. When is enough enough? So I decided enough was enough. That's why I was willing to be disowned, but it was kind of mutual. If you're willing to disown me, I'll disown you back. You can't disown me twice in one lifetime. So that's how I fought."

Fear associated with shame and guilt for going against the social order is also evident in Tara's story. She described never saying no to her family, and the responsibility she continued to take on: "Family responsibility is a huge thing, so you don't really think about that. You're just like, 'Okay, I have to do this.'" The first time Tara said no to her parents, the events led her to marry a man she did not love and was not ready to live with forever. She described tremendous long-lasting guilt for that part of her life: "Even my mom said, 'You always were a good girl.' And it's true, I did everything that they asked me to, it's just this one thing that I was like, 'No'...Even to this day, my mom says, because she regrets, she says, 'I wish I had just let you date him.' Because I was like, 'Mom, he was not the man I was going to marry, you know what I mean. But I wish you would have let me date him because I would have found that out on my own, right?'" Tara felt guilty about going against the social order, and her mother regretted making decisions about her daughter's future based on her fear of being shamed by the community.

As much as shame becomes a tool to control women in private homes, I would also suggest it is useful on a systemic and social level for effectively controlling and maintaining or perpetuating racist stereotypes of marginalized communities, such as Muslim and/or South Asian communities in Canada, particularly in a post-9/11 world. After the deaths of Jassi Sidhu (Dawson 2017), Amandeep Atwal (Bains 2005), and Aqsa Parvez (Mitchell 2008), the South Asian community found itself in a similar web of shame, where many people felt cornered or powerless in their choice of how to speak about the deaths of these three women, who were framed as victims of their culture and religion. The community felt isolated, and the most common response was to either deny these acts or defend the culture and religion. As a social worker in both British Columbia and Ontario at the time of these three tragic murders, I witnessed these narratives within the South Asian circles in which I was living and working. Collective shaming has devastating impacts on every individual in the community, because it leads not only to denial but to silencing survivors currently struggling with violence. Most family or community responses deflect discussions of "honour" by agreeing that such deaths are due to femicide, or family violence. This, in my opinion, is a response to the shame associated with the sociocultural expectations placed on the "good" immigrant who has strayed from the boundaries of how they should behave in Canadian society. Media perpetuates this shame, and as a result, we have a community of women who are silenced, remain trapped, and feel powerless to voice their stories of izzat or honour.

Since empathy is the opposite or counter-emotion to shame, I agree with Brown's (2006) work on empathy as a way to increase resiliency to shame responses. An empathic response involves "mutual support, shared experience, and the freedom and ability to explore and create options" (47). Empathy requires a great deal of engagement between individuals and communities, yet it can be the most powerful tool for critical consciousness-raising for both. When I asked the women in my study what they would say if they could speak to their family, our community, and the world about their experience, their responses varied. However, each thread came back to an element that was missing in their personal stories: having an open dialogue; being able to share with their family what choice they were making and why; being able to tell our community the impact their expectations were having on their lives; and being able to tell the media to back off so that their family and our community could figure this out on their own.

Lakshmi wanted to ask her family: "Who are you hurting when you are do[ing] this? Are you examining how you are being hurt when you also do this?" She was speaking to the impact her exile would have on her siblings, their children, and future generations who would not have an opportunity to know her. Tara reflected on what she would do differently in hindsight, and offered insights for other young women who might be going through something similar:

> If your parents feel this way, you're not going to change them. You're just not going to change them. So, I mean, try to do it in as

> loving [a] way as possible...But...your happiness is your happiness, go for that. You are not responsible for their happiness, but...try to do it in a way that is loving...The one thing that I [w]ould change [is] to be able to collaborate with them. Let's come together with a solution. Do you know what I mean? "I love you, you love me, this is what I want, but let's do it together. Let me understand where you're coming from, [and] I want you to understand where I'm coming from, and let's do it together."

Ultimately, empathy was the response each of the women expected from the world. Instead, they received more shame and guilt for how they chose to challenge the boundaries placed around their bodies and their behaviour.

Conclusion

Our community needs to hear the voices of second-generation women and their struggles with izzat, and about the shame and guilt that come from community judgment when a young woman is defined as ruining her family's izzat. Conversations that need to occur inside our communities are essential to the change we seek as second-generation South Asian women. The voices of second-generation women are seldom a part of these community conversations. Finally, there is a need for us to confront the discourses of "honour" that shape racist stereotypes of South Asian women, families, and communities. National and international discourses must engage with survivor stories and voices, and these voices must be present when any change in policy or practice is contemplated and implemented. As I have spoken about throughout this chapter, institutions play a big role in shifting heteropatriarchy and gender-based violence and, as a result, the lives of women on a national and international level. We must be part of the conversation for this change to happen, and it must begin now.

Note

1. The names in this chapter are pseudonyms chosen by the author.

References

Ahmed, Sara. 2000. *Strange Encounters: Embodied Others in Post Coloniality*. London: Routledge.

Ahmed, Sara. 2010. "Feminist Killjoys (and Other Willful Subjects)." *The Scholar and Feminist Online* 8 (3). http://sfonline.barnard.edu/polyphonic/print_ahmed.htm.

Aujla, Angela. 2000. "Others in Their Own Land: Second-Generation South Asian Canadian Women, Racism, and the Persistence of Colonial Discourse." *Canadian Women Studies* 20 (2): 41-47.

Baker, Nancy V., Peter R. Gregware, and Margery A. Cassidy. 1999. "Family Killing Fields: Honour Rationales in the Murder of Women." *Violence Against Women* 5 (2): 164-184.

Bains, Camille. 2005. "Amandeep Atwal Was a Starry-Eyed Teen With Big Dreams and a Secret Love Affair That She Thought Would Get Her Killed If It Was Ever Discovered by Her Parents." Canadian Press NewsWire, Canadian Press Enterprises.

Bonds, Anne, and Joshua Inwood. 2016. "Beyond White Privilege: Geographies of White Supremacy and Settler Colonialism." *Progress in Human Geography* 40 (6): 715-733. https://doi.org/10.1177/0309132515613166.

Brown, Brené. 2006. "Shame Resilience Theory: A Grounded Theory Study on Women and Shame." *Families in Society* 87 (1): 43-52.

Brown, Catrina, and Tod Augusta-Scott. 2007. "Introduction: Postmodernism, Reflexivity, and Narrative Therapy." In *Narrative Therapy: Making Meaning, Making Lives*, edited by Catrina Brown and Tod Augusta-Scott, ix-xliii. Thousand Oaks: Sage.

Byrd, Jodi. 2011. *The Transit of Empire: Indigenous Critiques of Colonialism*. Minneapolis: University of Minnesota Press.

Dawson, Fabion. 2017. "Jassi Sidhu: The Tragedy of a Forbidden Love." *Vancouver Sun*, September 10. https://vancouversun.com/news/local-news/jassi-sidhu-the-tragedy-of-a-forbidden-love.

Eichler, Margrit. 1997. *Family Shifts: Families, Policies and Gender Equity*. Oxford: Oxford University Press.

Espiritu, Yen Le. 2001. "We Don't Sleep Around Like White Girls Do: Family Culture, and Gender in Filipina American Lives." *Signs* 26 (2): 415-440.

Handa, Amita. 2003. *Of Silk Saris and Mini-Skirts: South Asian Girls Walk the Tightrope of Culture*. Toronto: Women's Press.

Jiwani, Yasmin. 2006. *Discourses of Denial: Mediations of Race, Gender, and Violence*. Vancouver: UBC Press.

Korteweg, Anna. 2012. "Understanding Honour Killing and Honour Related Violence in the Immigration Context: Implications for the Legal Profession and Beyond." *Canadian Criminal Law Review* 16 (2): 33-58.

Meetoo, Veena, and Heidi Mirza. 2007. "There Is Nothing Honourable About Honour Killings: Gender Violence and the Limits of Multiculturalism." *Women's Studies International Forum* 30 (3): 187-200.

Mitchell, Bob. 2008. "Charge Upgraded in Daughter's Death: Dad of Aqsa Parvez, 16, Faces First-Degree Count." *Toronto Star*, June 18.

Mucina, Mandeep Kaur. 2018. "Exploring the Role of Honour in Son Preference and Daughter Deficit Within the Punjabi Diaspora in Canada" *Canadian Journal of Development Studies* 39 (3): 426-442. https://doi.org/10.1080/02255189.2018.1450736.

Mucina, Mandeep Kaur. 2021. "Witnessing, Grieving and Remembering: Letters of Resistance, Love and Reclamation From Daughters of Izzat." *International Journal of Child, Youth, & Family Studies* 12 (1): 13-30. https://doi.org/10.18357/ijcyfs121202120081.

National Inquiry into Missing and Murdered Indigenous Women and Girls (MMIWG). 2019. *Reclaiming Power and Place: The Final Report of the National Inquiry into Missing and Murdered Indigenous Women and Girls.* https://www.mmiwg-ffada.ca/final-report/.

Papp, Aruna, and Barbara Kay. 2012. *Unworthy Creature: A Punjabi Daughter's Memoir of Honour, Shame and Love.* Toronto: Freedom Press Canada.

Puar, Jasbir. 1994. "Resituating Discourses of 'Whiteness' and 'Asianness' in Northern England: Second Generation Sikh Women and Constructions of Identity." *Socialist Review* 24 (1): 21-54.

Rajiva, Mythili. 2013. "'Better Lives': The Transgenerational Positioning of Social Mobility in the South Asian Canadian Diaspora." *Women's Studies International Forum* 26 (Jan-Feb): 16-26.

Razack, Sherene. 2004. "Imperiled Muslim Women, Dangerous Muslim Men, and Civilized Europeans: Legal and Social Responses to Forced Marriages." *Feminist Legal Studies* 12 (October): 129-174.

Razack, Sherene. 2008. *Casting Out: The Eviction of Muslims from Western Law and Politics*. Toronto: University of Toronto Press.

Sanghera, Jasvinder. 2007. *Shame: True Story of a Girl's Struggle to Survive.* London: Hodder & Stoughton.

Sev'er, Aysan. 1999. "Exploring the Continuum: Sexualized Violence by Men and Male Youth Against Women and Girls." *Atlantis: Critical Studies in Gender, Culture and Social Justice* 24 (1): 95-104.

Tuck, Eve, and K. Wayne Yang. 2012. "Decolonization Is Not a Metaphor." *Decolonization: Indigeneity Education & Society* 1 (1): 1-40.

White, Michael. 2004. *Narrative Practice and Exotic Lives: Resurrecting Diversity in Everyday Life.* Adelaide: Dulwich Centre.

II

Unpacking the Problematics

4

Is Feeling Like an Imposter a "Syndrome" or a "Protective Response" to the Colonial Gaze?

NAYYAR S. JAVED

WRITING AS a practising psychologist and a social activist of South Asian descent in Saskatchewan, here I will reflect on the journey of racialized foreign-trained professionals to a prohibited territory that I refer to as "elite white institutions." Their journey, in my opinion, takes a toll on their well-being, which Euro-American psychological discourses attribute to their psychological deficit, but which conceals the traumatic colonial relations pervasive in those institutions. My education at the University of Saskatchewan did not train me to note the psychological impact of colonialism, racism, and sexism, or the possibilities of "other" psychologies developed in non-European contexts. It was only through working with racialized clients that I began to see these oppressive forces in their mental health, and thus the need to embark on a journey to explore the relationship between psychology and colonialism.

My reflections are based on the stories shared with me by racialized foreign-trained professionals during my practice as a psychologist, and as a social activist engaged in anti-racism work with other immigrant women within the Saskatchewan Intercultural Association and the City of Saskatoon's Race Relations Committee. Their stories also resonate with my own journey as a foreign-trained professional South Asian woman. Like with many racialized immigrant women, my credentials were not accepted in Canada, even though I had studied in the US and taught at the university level in Pakistan. On each step of the journey to eventually acquiring my practitioner's licence, I was treated as an imposter who really did not have what it took to be working in a place reserved for white people only. Despite this humiliating treatment, like many other racialized foreign-trained professionals whose stories have inspired me, I do not recall having any symptoms of "imposter syndrome." I have been acutely aware of the need to have survival strategies in what Bannerji (1995) describes as "the theatre of cruelty."

Imposter syndrome emerged in the discourses of Euro-American psychology in 1978. This syndrome is characterized by a fear-based mindset dominated by a deep sense of self-doubt. It is attributed to women and minorities engaged in intellectual work in what Andrews (2021) describes as elite white institutions. In this chapter, I intend to unpack its attribution to racialized immigrant professionals. I will refer to the stories of my clients who belong to this group in order to explore the validity of this diagnosis. I synthesize the themes of their stories to build a framework for understanding the specificity of their reality, and to propose the importance of including a contextual analysis and understanding of whiteness in the diagnosis of imposter syndrome. I argue that the neglect of a broader social context enhances the mental health profession's use of its authoritative status to legitimize gender, race, and class oppression to protect the privilege of the dominant groups.

The South Asian community is culturally, regionally, linguistically, and religiously heterogeneous, and lives in different parts of Canada. As I trace the historical roots of the contemporary legal, economic, and social apartheid for immigrants, I refer to the history of South Asians in Canada with the acknowledgement of my limitations in capturing their realities. South Asian Canadians are the second-largest group among visible minorities, and have a long history of experiencing different layers of discrimination since their arrival in British Columbia in 1903 (University of the Fraser Valley 2022; Basran and Bolaria 2004). The literature on South Asian migration to Canada is replete with evidence of legal, economic, and social measures taken by the state and society that may be deemed as legal, economic, and social apartheid. Despite the South Asian community's resilience in confronting these disasters, the community continues to face challenges in the contemporary era. The persistence of colonial thinking manifested in the neoliberal economic system (Bolaria and Li 1988), the rise of the extreme right—including the support it gets from right wing politicians who shamelessly promote hate (CRIAW 2022)—and unexpected crises such as 9/11 and the COVID-19 pandemic create a breeding ground for racial hostility in the public, and in public policies. How this context affects immigration policies, recent immigrants, racialized foreign-trained professionals, and the deterioration of immigrants' health and the mental health risk this poses are the questions explored in this chapter.

Unpacking Imposter Syndrome

Postcolonial scholars (Duran 2019; Fanon 2004; Said 1979) help us understand the impact of colonial representation expressed through the assumption of being unfit to belong and perform in elite white institutions. Duran and Fanon provide insight into the complicity of mental health discourses and practices in the perpetuation of colonial relations in the broader context in general, and in elite white institutions in particular, as they are organized to safeguard white privilege. The role Euro-American psychology has played in protecting white privilege is manifested in the diagnoses and theories of personality development. The diagnosing of racialized immigrant professionals as afflicted with imposter syndrome while they seek psychological services due to the impact of being treated as imposters reveals the colonial embeddedness of mental health discrepancies.

Imposter syndrome is conceptualized by Clance and Imes (1978) as a mental state dominated by a deep sense of self-doubt about one's intellectual abilities and fear of being fraudulent, and a fear of exposing one's self-perceived intellectual deficit. Individuals afflicted with this syndrome are viewed as more prone to developing mental health disorders such as depression and anxiety. This syndrome has not yet been included in the American Psychological Association's *Diagnostic and Statistical Manual of Mental Disorders* (DSM 2022), which is used for diagnosing "disorders," but it has gained enormous salience in mental health practices, despite challenges to its validity put forth by feminist psychologists who view it as an attempt to partially shift the responsibility for the impact of gender-based discrimination from the oppressive patriarchal context onto women. I have tried to make a similar argument to that of feminist psychologists to raise questions about this attribution of gender-based discrimination to racialized immigrant professionals. They get depressed and anxious not because they view themselves as imposters, but because they have been treated as imposters, fraudulent and inferior to their privileged white coworkers. They are fearful because of the surveillance under which they work.

My clients' experiences reflect a coercive pressure to either accept their inferiority and carry on or go somewhere else. The reason that drove them to seek help was a painful struggle to resist the pressure to internalize an inferior professional identity. Duran (2019) describes the intensity of the emotional pain caused by this pressure as wounding to the soul. He sees this pressure as a force that tears apart the very core of the human psyche. The experiences my clients have described point out racial discrimination in the constrictions of a professional identity that racialized immigrant professionals are supposed to accept, the implications of which they are supposed to tolerate. In understanding how their experience has been misconstrued, I propose that it is external forces, rather than any psychological deficit within individuals belonging to a racialized group, that have been misdiagnosed as imposter syndrome. Such a misdiagnosis of identity further creates obstacles for this group in surviving within elite white institutions.

The struggles my clients reported undergoing are best described as a border crossing through a barbed-wire territory, guarded to protect white privilege. Their credentials were devalued, their work experiences in their countries of origin were dismissed and considered irrelevant, and their accents, languages, and cultural backgrounds were viewed as deficiencies. Those who needed opportunities for internships and residency in order to receive their license to practice had faced consistent rejections. Even those who had studied in Canada and finished their coursework had often been denied these opportunities for fulfilment of their license requirements. One of my female clients of South Asian background had completed her coursework in counselling psychology, but was unable to find an internship, having experienced several rejections. She was often told rejection was "good for her." The professor responsible for finding her an internship told her that he had tried his best by informing potential employers that she "was not like other Indians and Pakistanis."

The difficulties my clients had faced in getting residencies and internships can be explained by a comment made by an employment counsellor who worked at a settlement agency in Saskatchewan. At a forum on the difficulties faced by foreign-trained immigrant professionals, she legitimized the discrimination reflected in the policies of regulatory bodies by saying that "caution [is] necessary for the protection of public security." The assumptions underlying such comments come from institutional policies embedded in colonial representations that portray the colonized as a threat. Thus, strategies to annihilate the threat are implemented through the subjugation and obstacles that racialized immigrant professionals face in entering elite white institutions. Many of these professionals do not succeed. Those who do continue to experience subjugation and coercion to accept an inferior professional identity.

Experiences of Racialized Professionals

Most of my clients have experienced differential treatment in their jobs. They have recounted working harder than their white colleagues who held positions classified as professional, with a huge difference in salaries. The impact of being forced to live with an inferior professional identity can be illustrated with the case of two racialized Egyptian immigrant professional women (El Bialy and Youssef) employed by a Canadian university (Khan 2021). El Bialy joined the

Canadian university in 2011, and prior to this, she had worked in Egypt as a professor. Youssef joined the university in 2006 as a doctoral student, then was hired in 2017 for a full-time teaching position. Youssef was, prior to that, employed as a lecturer at Ain Shams University. Both women were highly qualified academics who had taught in universities in their country of origin (Egypt). They were hired at the level of support staff by the Canadian university, but assigned the responsibilities usually performed by an associate professor. When they finally raised the issue of pay equity with the administration, they were told that other foreign-trained graduates would envy their positions. In addition, the administration decided to reclassify the job and downgrade their responsibilities. The union found no recourse, while acknowledging the racism in their case. Their efforts to seek justice were met with persistent harassment, which took a toll on their mental health. However, both women refused to give up and approached the human rights tribunal. The article recounting their story ends with the grim news that both women went on subsequent stress leaves, are facing changes to their positions (from academic to administrative), and are awaiting news from the human rights tribunal.

This is not an exceptional story. When I came across their petition, I thought of many of my clients. The ones with high-level academic credentials but working as teacher aides, the engineers who work as technicians, and the physicians who pass professional exams but do not succeed in getting internships and instead work as associates to physicians. They are stuck in downgraded job categories because of their inferior professional identities, an outcome of racialization that comes with many subtle and overt reminders of their inferiority, as well as hostility and surveillance.

The meaning of this experience goes beyond financial issues, as the sense of self and self-worth is assaulted and eroded by the pressure to replace a privileged identity with one deemed inferior, and by entrapment in downgraded job categories. This also entails a process of de-skilling. The gradual loss of the professional skills and privileged professional identities they have developed over many years entails grief and a deep sense of loss and powerlessness.

Those who have found a way out of being entrapped in downgraded positions face other challenges to advancing their careers. One of my clients was refused a promotion based on an absurd stereotype of Middle Eastern men being perceived as highly emotionally volatile and explosive. He was told that his Middle Eastern background would interfere with his performance because of his "emotional vulnerability." Many of these racialized professionals do not have other buffers, or the class privilege to protect them from serious mental health problems and the racial impact of professional exclusion (Andrews 2020).

Ndlovu (2017) reflects on Fanon's conceptualization of white institutions as two mutually exclusive zones, one for racialized professionals and the other for white professionals. The zone assigned to the racialized professionals is like an impoverished desert with nothing to offer for nourishment, while the other zone has an abundance of opportunities. These mutually exclusive zones constituted within elite white institutions may help differentiate "imposters" as colonial perceptions of racialized professionals from a syndrome caused by some unknown psychological deficiency. My clients were locked into impoverished zones and were acutely aware of being perceived as imposters, but they vigilantly resisted internalizing these perceptions. They felt their competence was doubted and their character suspected, and they were denied the opportunities to feel belonging. They themselves did not experience self-doubt, but used their creativity for coping; however, they could not avoid the impact of being treated as imposters.

Fanon (1967) observed how the colonized African endured colonial hostility: "I slip into corners and my long antennae pick up the catchphrases strewn over the surface of things...I slip into corners, I remain silent. I strive for anonymity, for invisibility. Look, I will accept the lot, so long as no one notices me" (116). My clients' awareness and ability to develop acute vigilance and threat detection is well described as antennae by Fanon. This capacity helped them cope with the dangers expressed through the exchange of glances between their colleagues, the whispered gossip, and the glaring gazes of their supervisors. Here, I must do some self-disclosure. The stories of the glaring gazes of my clients' bosses resonated with my experiences of being targeted by one of my bosses. She tried to intimidate me with persistent criticism, and insulted me by asking the office secretary to monitor the administration of the questionnaire for my performance evaluation. My clients and colleagues, many of whom were white, were generous and often evaluated me positively. My boss accused me of influencing them. Like my racialized immigrant professional clients, I also worked very hard and yearned for anonymity, because being noticed always meant exposure to hostility. The hostility was coercion, to replace a meaningful professional identity with an inferior identity.

This coerced replacement of the old professional identity with an inferior identity is experienced as a loss of self, entailing a deep sense of grief and longing for belonging. Since a professional identity plays a prominent role in the perception of the self and its worth, it gains salience in relationships with others as well. Memories of how the old self was received by others haunt individuals in the midst of hostilities they experience. Memories of being nurtured remind them of the loss and absence of the space that provided nurturance. My clients talked about their yearning to find that space, their struggle to recreate it, and the powerlessness they experienced, as there was no space that offered access to opportunities for nurturance. The struggle and disappointment led to exhaustion, an unbearable degree of anxiety, and confusion about who they were. Fanon (1967) describes this state of mind as an estrangement from self. I believe that this estrangement from self can entail self-doubt, which may be interpreted as imposter syndrome by Euro-American psychology. It is not unusual for this psychology to hold the oppressed responsible for their own oppression and individual pathologies, rather than their oppressive context (Duran 2019; Fanon 2004).

Racialized professionals experience a constant undermining of their culture and status beyond the professional space. One example is a client who lost her son who was being treated in the hospital. The lack of support offered to her and her family was explained as the hospital's inability to do anything for them in the face of the family's "shame-based culture." The client was rendered silent by the hospital's psychologist, whose authoritative diagnosis of the situation shifted the burden of responsibility to the traumatized family, thus erasing the reality of the marginalized. The emotional pain caused by such treatment also gets diagnosed and distorted as a psychological deficit by such psychologists, instead of them understanding the external oppressive source of this experience.

The stories from racialized professionals indicate a painful mental state that is also caused by ongoing trauma. The emotional impact of the loss of professional identity and the sense of powerlessness created by being pushed into inferior professional roles are rarely mentioned in the literature on overseas-trained professionals. The literature from most industrialized countries and the World Health Organization (WHO) have identified that immigrants—but not those from Europe and the US—have a health advantage in comparison to residents of the host country upon arrival. This HIE (Healthy Immigrant Effect) deteriorates over the years, however (Ali, McDermott, and Gravel 2003; Beiser 2005; McDonald and Kennedy 2004; Newbold 2005). This dispels the myth embedded in colonial ideology about the threat that racialized immigrants pose to Canadians by bringing disease from the so-called Third World; however, the literature has not provided much help in determining the cause of HIE deterioration.

The literature acknowledges the immigration and settlement process as highly stressful (Levitt, Lane, and Levitt 2005; Robert and Gilkinson 2012), and acknowledges the significance of the social determinants of health for relief from stress, but ignores exposure to institutional and interpersonal racial discrimination as risk factors. According to this literature, the causes of the deterioration of HIE include acculturation and cultural differences, language proficiency, unemployment and underemployment, and discrimination. Statistics Canada's 2023 Canadian Mental Health and Access to Care Survey (MHACS) reporting on 2022 data has observed higher rates of psychosis in certain groups that face overt discrimination and has identified women and skilled workers as more vulnerable to the deterioration of their mental health. Overall, the research literature I went through raised questions, rather than providing the conclusive evidence I needed to substantiate my observations and to enable me to overcome self-doubt in the process of writing this chapter. The inconsistency in the conclusions of this literature interfered with my effort to find confirmation of the legitimacy of what I wanted to present. I also found gaps, such as the impact of interlocked subjectivities and the underemployment of skilled workers. I did not find any research on the treatment of the foreign-trained racialized immigrants who manage to enter and work in elite white institutions. Research on the mental health consequences of the loss of professional identity and on work experiences would have given insight into the deterioration of the health advantage. This gap in exploring reasons for HIE deterioration does not make much sense, considering the vigour with which we screen immigrants (Beiser 2005).

Despite the gaps, I have found some of the explanations this literature offers to be quite useful, albeit needing further exploration. For instance, underemployment, unemployment, and discrimination were identified as risk factors, while skilled workers were seen as more vulnerable to stress. These explanations can serve in developing a conceptual framework to explore gendered and racial discrimination-based occupational segregation in Canada, conceptualized by Galabuzi (2004) as an economic apartheid constructed to keep Canada white. This apartheid, according to Galabuzi, not only violates the constitutional rights of racialized people enshrined in the *Canadian Charter of Rights and Freedoms* (1982), but also disrupts the stability of society and the mental and physical well-being of those people. Beiser (2005) sees this economic apartheid as a leading cause of poverty in the racialized population and of the escalation of inequality. The outcome of the economic apartheid is that exalted citizens are set apart from others. The analysis of the occupational segregation that Beiser (2005) provides explains the alienation that racism causes for those experiencing discrimination. Galabuzi (2004) sees the economic apartheid as a parallel to slavery, and attributes to it the prosperity enjoyed by privileged Canadians. This apartheid has historical roots and is deeply embedded in colonial relations, causing what Fanon (2004) conceptualizes as alienation.

Racialized Professionals and the Post-9/11 War on Terror

I will now discuss how the post-9/11 War on Terror and the COVID-19 pandemic have had serious consequences for racialized professionals. 9/11 sent a powerful shock wave throughout the world. The fear of Islamic fundamentalism was a powerful force, as terrorist attacks loomed large worldwide. However, the response to this threat was markedly different than the response to attacks elsewhere. The Global North immediately enacted security measures. The US was enraged and immediately started to wage a war against terrorism. Its allies were also furious, and with their help a coalition was formed to attack Afghanistan. That country was still struggling with the aftermath of the war that Russia had waged, and the incessant and ruthless air and ground attacks destroyed whatever was left. This was followed by an attack on Iraq. The War on Terror was also fought at home. The US Homeland Security Act of 2002 (DHS, n.d.) and other initiatives were put in place to keep an eye on suspected citizens and visitors, mostly Muslims and Arabs. Canada followed suit and joined the US in the War on Terror by introducing security initiatives, such as Bill C36 and other legislative pieces that granted sweeping powers to law enforcement institutions (Bahdi 2003). This had an enormous impact on Muslim and Arab Canadians, including through arbitrary detentions and strict scrutiny at airports and border crossings, and in public spaces. Racial profiling, albeit not legally sanctioned, was widely used by police and the Canadian Security and Intelligence Service (CSIS).

These measures targeted at Muslims and Arabs also terrorized other racialized citizens, including non-Muslim South Asians. I have witnessed this on many occasions, including in an incident where two young social activists from Saskatoon accompanied me on a railway trip to New York to attend a session of the United Nations' Commission on the Status of Women. They were held up at the border in Quebec, while I was allowed to go through. They went through excruciating interrogation for hours, and missed the train. They managed to make it to the session but were exhausted and terrified. They were South Asians, not Muslims, and were born and raised in Canada. Their experience illustrates how skin colour becomes what Bahdi (2003) refers to as race as a proxy to threat. This is critical in colonial relations. The fear invoked by the theory of replacement reflects this proxy, and this fear has been a part of white consciousness since the arrival of South Asians in Canada in 1903. For a thorough critique and debunking of replacement theory, see Obaidi, Kunst, Ozer, and Kimel's (2022) work. Also, replacement theory discusses how part of white consciousness is the misperception of foreign-trained racialized immigrants and citizens as imposters, which is prevalent in elite white institutions. The salience of this proxy increases or decreases in response to what goes on in a specific context, but it never gets erased in the collective consciousness of a country shaped by colonialism. Sadly, its intensity increases when a crisis emerges.

The COVID-19 pandemic illustrated this fear of racialized immigrants. According to Das Gupta and Nagpal (2022), South Asian Canadians were disproportionately affected by COVID-19 in terms of the loss of jobs and livelihood and exposure to high risk of infection, as they were concentrated in essential services. The death rate of this population was the highest, and the distress caused by these dynamics led to serious mental health problems. Their losses were discounted, while their cultural traditions, including multigenerational households, were blamed for the spread of the virus. For example, Gupta and Nagpal (2022) discuss how Sikhs in Ontario were blamed for spreading the infection by ignoring the health protection initiatives at their cultural events. This blame concealed very high poverty rates, substandard housing, and work in highly risky jobs such as essential services and other sectors that do not provide paid sick leave. South Asian Canadians constituted 18 percent of the people who lost jobs because of COVID-19. These conditions are also medically acknowledged as high-risk factors in the deterioration of mental health. The broader contextual issues are not incorporated into Canadian mental health discourses and ethical guidelines, particularly in psychology and psychiatry, which often dismiss the mental consequences of racialization in both normal and crisis periods (Gupta and Nagpal 2022).

The strategy of decontextualizing the emotional state of powerless racialized citizens maintains the power relations that benefit the dominant group. Instead of incorporating contextual oppressions and realities, a "colonial habit" deeply rooted in colonialism justifies the treatment of the colonized as objects and inferior subjects, through multiple narratives of genetic deficit and inherent inferiority that lead to the inability to function effectively (Duran 2019; Fanon 2004). Although formal enslavement and colonialism have ended for South Asians in Canada, Indigenous Peoples still face colonial occupation and genocide. Notably, many would argue we still have laws that allow, for example, horrendous work conditions that can be said to mimic enslavement practices, for example with immigrant workers as discussed at the beginning of this chapter (Khan 2021). The process of decolonizing psychology has begun. This work has helped develop promising initiatives, such as changing the ethical guidelines of the Association of Psychologists of America by including anti-colonial ethical principles.

Conclusion

In conclusion, the experiences of racialized foreign-trained professionals navigating elite white institutions reveal a systemic pattern of devaluation and misrepresentation. Their struggles, often misdiagnosed as "imposter syndrome" by Euro-American psychology, are rooted in the enduring legacies of colonialism and racism. The narratives shared highlight the trauma of having credentials dismissed, skills undermined, and professional identities forcibly downgraded. This process, compounded by the pressures of post-9/11 security measures and the disproportionate impact of crises like the COVID-19 pandemic, results in a profound loss of self and a deterioration of mental well-being. The decontextualization of these professionals' experiences, which ignores the structural barriers and discriminatory practices they face, serves to maintain the privilege of dominant groups and perpetuate a form of economic and social apartheid. Recognizing the systemic nature of this oppression and challenging the colonial embeddedness of mental health discourses are crucial for fostering equity and justice within these institutions.

References

Ali, Jennifer S., Sarah McDermott, and Ronald G. Gravel. 2003. "Recent Research on Immigrants Health from Statistic Canada's Population Survey." *Canadian Journal of Public Health* 43 (2): 337-360.

American Psychiatric Association. 2022. *Diagnostic and Statistical Manual of Mental Disorders*. 5th ed. Washington: American Psychiatric Association Publishing.

Andrews, Kehinde. 2020. "The Post-Racial Princess: Delusions of Racial Progress and Intersectional Failures." *Women's Studies International Forum* 84 (January-February). https://doi.org/10.1016/j.wsif.2020.102432.

Andrews, Kehinde. 2021. *The New Age of Empire: How Racism and Colonialism Still Rule the World*. Oxford: Oxfam Books.

Bahdi, Reem. 2003. "No Exit: Racial Profiling and Canada's War Against Terrorism." *Osgoode Hall Law Journal* 41 (2/3): 293-322. http://digitalcommons.osgoode.yorku.ca/ohlj/vol41/iss2/7.

Bannerji, Himani. 1995. "Re: Turning the Gaze." In *Beyond Political Correctness: Toward the Inclusive University*, edited by Stephen Richler and Lorna Weir, 220-236. Toronto: University of Toronto Press.

Basran, Gurcharn S., and B. Singh Bolaria. 2004. *Sikhs in Canada: Migration, Race, Class, and Gender*. Oxford: Oxford University Press.

Beiser, Morton. 2005. "The Health of Immigrants and Refugees in Canada." *Canadian Journal of Public Health* 96 (Suppl 2): S30-S44. https://doi.org/10.1007/BF03403701.

Bolaria, B. Singh, and Peter S. Li. 1988. "Colonialism and Labour of East Indians in Canada." In *Racial Oppression in Canada*, 161-184. Toronto: Garamond Press.

Canadian Charter of Rights and Freedoms. Part 1 of the *Constitution Act, 1982*. Schedule B to the *Canada Act 1982* (UK), 1982, c 11. https://laws-lois.justice.gc.ca/eng/const/page-12.html.

Canadian Research Institute for the Advancement of Women/L'Institut canadien de recherches sur les femmes (CRIAW-ICREF). 2022. "Feminist Response to the Global Rise of Right-Wing Extremism: A Summary." Ottawa: CRIAW-ICREF.

Clance, Pauline R., and Suzanne Ament Imes. 1978. "The Imposter Phenomenon in High Achieving Women: Dynamics and Therapeutic Intervention." *Psychotherapy* 15 (3): 241-247.

Das Gupta, Tania, and Sughanda Nagpal. (2022). "Unravelling Discourses on COVID-19, South Asian and Punjabi Canadians." *Borders, Boundaries, and the Impact of COVID-19 on Immigration to Canada* 16 (1). https://journals.library.brocku.ca/index.php/SSJ/article/view/3471.

Duran, Eduardo. 2019. *Healing the Soul Wound: Trauma-Informed Counseling for Indigenous Communities*. 2nd ed. New York: Teachers College Press.

Fanon, Frantz. 1967. *Black Skin, White Masks*. Translated by Charles Lam Markmann. New York: Grove Press.

Fanon, Frantz. 2004. *The Wretched of the Earth*. Translated by Richard Philcox. New York: Grove Press.

Fernando, Suman. 2017. *Institutional Racism in Psychiatry and Clinical Psychology: Race Matters in Mental Health*. Berlin: Springer International.

Galabuzi, Grace-Edward. 2004. "Social Exclusion." In *Social Determinants of Health: Canadian Perspectives*, edited by Dennis Raphael and David Langille, 235–251. Toronto: Canadian Scholars' Press.

Hamer, Forrest. M. 2006. "Racism as a Transference State: Episode of Racial Hostility in the Psychoanalytic Context." *The Psychoanalytic Quarterly* 75 (1): 197–224.

Khan, Ahmar. 2021. "2 Medical Experts Allege Harassment, Bullying, Exploitation at U of O." *CBC News*, August 12. https://www.cbc.ca/news/canada/ottawa/harassment-bullying-allegations-university-of-ottawa-international-medical-experts-1.6136229.

Levitt, Mary, Jonathan Lane, and Jerome Levitt. 2005. "Immigration Stress, Social Support, and Adjustment in the First Postmigration Year: An Intergenerational Analysis." *Research in Human Development* 2 (4): 159–177.

McDonald, James Ted, and Steven Kennedy. 2004. "Insight into Healthy Immigrant Effect, Health Status and Health Services Use of Immigrants to Canada." *Social Science and Medicine* 59 (8): 1613–1627.

Ndlovu, Siphiwe. 2017. "The Concept of Alienation in the Work of Fanon." PHD diss., University of KwaZulu.

Newbold, K. Bruce. 2005. "Self-Rated Health Within Canadian Immigrant Population and Health Immigrant Effect." *Social Science and Medicine* 60 (6): 1359–1370. https://doi.org/10.1016/j.socscimed.2004.06.048.

Obaidi, Milan., Jonas Kunst, Simon Ozer, and Sasha Y. Kimel. 2022. "The 'Great Replacement' Conspiracy: How the Perceived Ousting of Whites Can Evoke Violent Extremism and Islamophobia." *Group Processes & Intergroup Relations* 25 (7): 1675–1695. https://doi.org/10.1177/13684302211028293.

Robert, Anne-Marie, and Tara Gilkinson. 2012. *Mental Health and Well-Being of Recent Immigrants in Canada: Evidence from the Longitudinal Survey of Immigrants to Canada*. Ottawa: Citizenship and Immigration Canada. https://www.canada.ca/content/dam/ircc/migration/ircc/english/pdf/research-stats/mental-health.pdf.

Said, Edward W. 1979. *Orientalism*. New York: Vintage Press.

South Asian Studies Institute, University of the Fraser Valley. 2022. "History of South Asians in Canada: Timeline." southasiancanadianheritage.ca. https://www.southasiancanadianheritage.ca/history-of-south-asians-in-canada/.

Statistics Canada. 2023. "Canadian Mental Health and Access to Care Survey (MHACS)." September 22. https://www23.statcan.gc.ca/imdb/p2SV.pl?Function=getSurvey&SDDS=5015.

US Department of Homeland Security (DHS). n.d. "Homeland Security Act of 2002." https://www.dhs.gov/homeland-security-act-2002.

5

Blurred and Bright Boundaries

Reflexive Appraisals of Pakistani Canadian Home and Host Religions and Cultures

SARAH SHAH

Introduction

Feminist organizing invites collaborators and co-conspirators to find common ground in addressing avenues for mutual liberation. While religion has been utilized by oppressive groups to subjugate the marginalized, it has also been a multifaceted resource for marginalized groups organizing and resisting oppressive forces. Given the instrumental role of religion in immigrant integration (Karam 2019), how religiosity may play a role in immigrant identity, then, is an important aspect to consider for feminists engaged in activism, academia, or community building.

To investigate the social contours of diasporic Muslim narratives on home and host religions and cultures, I interviewed a purposive sample of forty-six Toronto-based Pakistani Canadian Muslims, a group for whom "identity work is unavoidable" (Latif et al. 2018, 614). In this chapter, I demonstrate how religious approach is related to the ways that immigrants exiting contexts of religious hegemony frame home and host religions and cultures (see Shah 2022 and 2023 for details about sample and data collection). I found that the exclusivist reflexive Muslim participants (henceforth "exclusivists") perceived sharp differences between Canadian and Pakistani cultures and Islams, with a clear preference for Canadian Islam. Inclusivist reflexive Muslim participants (henceforth "inclusivists"), in contrast, did not frame Canadian Islam and culture as better than Pakistani Islam and culture. Before turning to these findings, I briefly review the literature on diasporic Muslim ethnic boundaries and immigrant identities.

Religious Reflexivities and Ethnic Boundaries

Migrant religious minorities are pushed from "taken-for-granted" categories toward religious reflexivity (Brubaker 2012), or critical engagement with religious identities and practices, in a racialized social process. Diasporic Muslims are an apt case for interrogating minority religious reflexivity because of the current era of Islamophobia, which renders Muslims a systematically disadvantaged minority group. With the rise of right-wing populism, diasporic Muslims, including those in Canada, are facing increasing levels of violence (Meyer 2018).

When Muslims migrate from Muslim-majority countries to non-Muslim majority countries—or from contexts of Islamic hegemony (Cesari 2014) to Christian hegemony and Islamophobia—their previously taken-for-granted religious identity and practice become a marker, as they are thrust into a racial formation process (Omi and Winant 2015) and categorized as "Muslim" by both non-Muslims and other "Muslims" (Brubaker 2012). They experience this process most clearly when they are confronted by boundaries (Alba 2005). In the case of Muslim communities in Canada, the rise of Islamophobia and ongoing construction of "Muslim exceptionalism" (Kazemipur 2014) indicates that boundaries are becoming brighter. When confronted by these boundaries through experiences of Islamophobic discrimination, among other interactional situations where Muslims feel othered, Muslims are pushed "to reactively assert a Muslim identification," and to "account not only for themselves as Muslims, but also for what others say or do as Muslims" (Brubaker 2012, 3). Thus, as boundaries become brighter, "'Muslim' is increasingly reflexively embraced rather than simply taken for granted" (3).

In this chapter, the concept of reflexivity is extended by pluralizing the term, rejecting the idea of a uniform reflexivity in which Muslims engage. Extant literature indicates that diasporic Muslim social experiences and locations are diverse (Cheruvallil-Contractor 2018; Mac an Ghaill and Haywood 2018; Lamont and Collet 2013), and that even within homogenous samples, individual reflexive engagement with religion is structured by sociodemographic subjectivity (Kadirov, Allayarova, and Boulanouar 2016; Kazi 2018). Drawing on this growing body of scholarship, I apply a sociological lens to interrogate the dialectical relationship between the social institutions (race and religion) that these social actors draw on for identity formation. As such, racialized religious minority group identification, and perceived threats to that minority group, coincide with bright boundaries (Alba 2005) and reinforce authority-focussed, rigid approaches that inform how individuals frame religion and culture. This coincides with an exclusivist approach to Islam, discussed further in the chapter. On the flipside, the lack of perception of boundaries that exclude one's minority group relaxes the impulse to seek authority-focussed approaches, allowing for more fluid understandings of both religion and culture. This coincides with an inclusivist approach to Islam, discussed in the following section.

Religious Approach and Immigrant Identity

The context that individuals frame their reflexivity as emerging from matters, as divergent patterns coincide with these contexts. There are two contrasting patterns: Muslims as a minority group (insecurity), and Muslims as a diverse group (security). Focusing first on insecurity, when individuals are confronted by discrimination that they perceive as threatening to themselves or their minority group, they seek out a legitimate authority to reinforce their identity, and this legitimacy is leveraged from the institution being used to mark them as "other." When race is used to mark a minority group as "other," then race-based ideologies are leveraged by the minority group to reclaim a legitimate identity (e.g., Espiritu 2001).

Given that in both academic and public discourse, "Muslim," rather than geographic origin, is increasingly used as the primary category to mark the "other," "Muslims" are turning to Islam for identity legitimacy. Adding to this is the tendency for minority groups who imagine themselves as a community to reinforce out-group exclusion when confronted by perceptions of inter-group conflict. For example, while studies on *diasporic* Muslim religiosity demonstrate "selective moral traditionalism" (Rayside 2011; see also Ajrouch 2004), Muslims in non-migratory settings demonstrate different patterns (see Shah, Acevedo, and Ruiz 2017 for similar findings about Christian minorities in a Muslim-majority context). Thus, insecurity bolstered by perceptions of belonging to a threatened minority coincides with orthodoxy, and exacerbates perceptions of inter-group conflict while brightening boundaries.

When individuals are brought to reflexivity through other means, for example, not because of perceptions of discrimination and inter-group conflict, but because of motivations to understand or articulate within-group diversity or inter-group similarity, then these individuals are not tasked with claiming legitimate authority and can embrace inclusivist approaches. There are two patterns of this inclusivist reflexivity. First, globalization is making Muslim reflexivity possible and increasingly prevalent in Muslim-majority contexts (Brubaker 2012), and those contexts are structured by Islamic hegemony (Cesari 2014). This can be observed, for example, in the migration of Muslims from their countries of origin to oil-rich nations that are home to Muslim-majority populations. Thus, when reflexivity is initiated in Muslim-majority settings, reflexivity takes on an inclusivist approach to Islam—one not relying on one true authoritative form, and accepting of multiple types of Islams (see also Khan 2018). The second route is in the migratory setting, where individuals are exposed to diverse Muslim communities and appreciate religious pluralism, as demonstrated with the current sample (Shah 2022, 2023).

This contrasts sharply with individuals drawn to exclusivity, with "Muslim-as-other" immigrant experiences. And since individuals with inclusivist approaches to Islam do not perceive themselves as "other," or as being "othered," they also do not perceive inter-group conflict. Thus, individuals with inclusivist approaches either perceive blurred boundaries or none at all, while those with exclusivist approaches perceive brighter boundaries and sharp differences. Exclusivists often perceive these differences with moral indignation, since, given their exclusivist approaches, they frame only one way—their own way—of religious belief and practice as correct. Inclusivists, however, view multiple approaches to Islam as correct. Additionally, while inclusivists do not perceive bright differences between Canadian and Pakistani Islam, nor between Canadian and Pakistani culture, exclusivists do.

Pakistani and Canadian Islam and Culture

In this section, I describe the social patterns related to the reflexive religious approaches by drawing on qualitative data from forty-six interviews with Pakistani Canadian Muslims. All reflexive participants, both exclusivist and inclusivist, framed their Islams as compatible with "Canadian values" (see Shams 2017, for comparable findings within Muslim American organizations). Further, the exclusivists also framed Islam in Canada as *the* true Islam compared with the "cultural" Islam in Pakistan (cf. Rozario 2011). Unlike the inclusivists, who shied away from making comparisons even when asked directly, exclusivists saw "huge differences" between Pakistani and Canadian Islam. While exclusivists disdained Pakistani Islam, the inclusivists did not. Likewise, while exclusivists framed Islam in Pakistan as cultural, their inclusivist counterparts framed Islam in Muslim-majority contexts as convenient, given Islamic hegemony (Cesari 2014, 11).

For example, Rahim, an inclusivist and first-generation Canadian, described his experience of religiosity in Pakistan and Dubai, two Muslim-majority contexts, and compared that experience to his practice in Canada. Like many other first-generation inclusivists, Rahim had lived in non-Pakistani Muslim-majority contexts, allowing his exposure to Islam in diverse Muslim contexts. He described critically reflecting on Islam in the Canadian context:

> In Pakistan, I didn't give religion much thought...Eating halal was never something that would come up there, because everything was halal, and we didn't have to talk about it. So *you'd just sort of go with the flow there*. In Dubai, it was sort of the same. Everyone had their own level of religiousness. *No one questioned anyone about it either*. Whatever people did, they did. In both Pakistan and Dubai, we had the *luxury* of being in Muslim countries, so in months like Ramadhan, *you'd get special hours and special treatments like that. Moving to Canada, you lose all those privileges*. Ramadhan was particularly a fun time in Dubai because there would be a lot of nighttime activities, and it was a very different environment there. *You would feel more part of the community...* Coming here and living alone in Canada, I had to define what I want to do by myself, on my own. During my university years, Jehovah's Witnesses would come to my door, and [myself] being naive and mild mannered and soft spoken, and being nice, I wasn't able to tell them to not bother me, so I ended up engaging with them way more than I wanted to. It ended up being repeated visits with them. *That forced me to keep thinking about what is my religious understanding of Islam, do I want to progress it further, do I want to read the Quran more in depth and find out more for myself, or am I happy with the way I am?* (emphasis added)

Rahim described "going with the flow" in Muslim-majority contexts, and being comfortable with the convenience of being "part of the community," where "no one questioned anyone about" their religious beliefs and practices. But in Canada, Rahim felt he had lost "all those privileges," and described having repeated visits and conversations with non-Muslims, which caused him to reflect on his relationship with and practice of religion. Rahim's framing of Islam as convenient in Muslim-majority contexts reflects the pattern for inclusivists.

Likewise, Elyas, an inclusivist and first-generation Canadian, framed the hegemony of Islam in Pakistan as a convenience. When asked to compare the way Islam is practiced in Pakistan and in Canada, he avoided making the comparison by stating instead:

> To be honest, the way I was brought up and the way my family is, the way my elders are, they told us—they taught us, "You have to be a human first, and then you will be a Muslim. If you're a good human, you're a good Muslim."...I lived in the Middle East, and so did my family. We have certain respect for all religions—I don't know how it came up—but we have respect for Jews, Christians, Hindus—because we were living with them. And being from the Middle East, I have so many Sikh friends, Filipinos, Christians, Catholics, Protestants, Roman Catholics, so it's like Islam is—the good part about Pakistan is that you will find a *masjid* anywhere you want to. Over here, you have to search for the nearest mosque to pray *jumma* [Friday congregational prayer]. That's a bit annoying. But the rest of it is—practicing Islam is basically practicing humanity. So if you can practice humanity in Pakistan [you can do it in] Canada, that's about it.

In his response, Elyas highlighted a respect for all religions, and downplayed the differences between Islam in Pakistan and Canada, although he noted that practicing in Canada could be "a bit annoying." Compare this response with that of Faiza, an exclusivist. When asked about the difference between Pakistani and Canadian Islam, Faiza said:

> In a way, it's not as tamed, to practice Islam here. In Pakistan, the religious and cultural boundaries are very blurred, so a lot of practices and rituals got adapted and are so informed by cultural and societal practices that *they're almost non-Islamic* for the fact that *they are so history-based and ancestor-based*. I feel like here—although in some [Muslim] houses that is still the case, you do things because you were told to do it that way. But *I feel like you're not as influenced here because when you do your own research here, in Islam, you'll find the true Islam*, you'll find evidence. You're not *pressured* into believing what has been handed down. I feel like, in that way, it's better to be a Muslim here than it is in Pakistan. I've met my cousins and other family in Pakistan, and I feel like, for them, the idea of Islam is completely skewed. (emphasis added)

Faiza saw clear differences between the Pakistani and Canadian Islams, and framed the former as "completely skewed" while the latter was "the true Islam."

Like Faiza, Sonia was also an exclusivist. However, she was also a first-generation Canadian, and thus, unlike Faiza, she grew up in Pakistan and had come to Canada with her husband and children. Nevertheless, Sonia had an exclusivist approach to Islam, and her reflexivity had emerged from migrating to a Muslim-minority context. She stated: "When you're in the States—or in any other country other than your origin—you want to keep the religion." Sonia highlighted the concern that other exclusivists echoed, around being Muslim outside of a Muslim-majority context and having to make an extra effort to "keep the religion." And while, logically, this would imply that Pakistani Islam is somehow superior to Canadian Islam, Sonia, like other exclusivists, made it clear that she thought Canadian Islam was better than, and different from, Pakistani Islam, and placed that difference directly within the fear of threat to diasporic Muslim identity and practice:

> Interviewer: Is there a difference in how Muslims practice in Pakistan and Canada?
>
> Sonia: Huge difference. The difference is that here, when we need guidance, we have access to our imams, if we cannot understand something in the Quran or Hadith. But in Pakistan, when people need to look for guidance, they don't think that way. They think the Quran is something very difficult to understand, it's old... But here, if I have a question, I call the mosque. I can talk to the imam, and I get my answer. And not just that, I get references from them, what they are using to support their answer, with this kind of opinion. They're really open in Canada. They don't just tell me things according to one *fiqh* [Islamic ruling], they tell you, "this *fiqh* or that *fiqh*, these are the answers, and you should follow your own *madhdhab* [Sunni school of thought]."
>
> Interviewer: Why do you think there is that difference?
>
> Sonia: Being different—over *here, we are trying to preserve ourselves* and *we don't have that threat in Pakistan, because everyone looks the same*. Everyone knows and shares the same religion. (emphasis added)

Despite Sonia acknowledging the easier access to imams and religious resources in the Canadian context, she still framed religious practice as a struggle, as did other exclusivists. While exclusivists framed Islam in Canada as something they had to strive for, to incorporate it into their lives, inclusivists did not describe the same struggle.

Though inclusivists recognized that Islam might be "easier" in Pakistan given Islamic hegemony, they also recognized how Islam could be easier in Canada when taking gendered practices into account. For example, when Nadia, an inclusivist and first-generation Canadian, described her immigration and religious experiences, she mentioned:

> In some ways, [practicing Islam is] actually easier here because—so when we were in Dubai, yes, it's a Muslim country, and you're living in a Muslim environment. But, for example, going to the masjid was not a normal thing for women there. Some of the masjids don't even have spaces for women. Here, just about every masjid has a space for women. So, it's much easier to go for Friday prayers. Women's-only classes are also much easier here than in Dubai. From that perspective, it's actually much easier to practice religion.

Although, like other inclusivists, Nadia recognized that Islam in a Muslim-majority context (Dubai) provided a "Muslim environment," she also noted that practicing in Canada was easier because gendered religious practices, like male-only masjids, are not taken for granted as norms in Canada.

While inclusivists and exclusivists differed in how they framed Pakistani and Canadian Islams, both groups recognized reflexivity as somehow intrinsic to "Canadian Islam." This was sometimes more of a feeling that participants could not quite express in words. For example, Jameela, an exclusivist, was married to Jaffer, an inclusivist. Although they were both reflexive, Jaffer's earlier immigration had allowed him more time to engage reflexively with Islam compared with her more recent post-marital arrival. And while they approached Islam differently (e.g., exclusivist vs. inclusivist), she framed the difference between her religiosity and that of her husband's as being the reflexivity in Canada, which, she stated, did not occur in Pakistan:

> I think, over here, there are so many seminars to help you with the problems of this society. When you're growing up, when you're a young person, you have a lot of problems. So, there are seminars, there are *maulanas* [religious scholars] you can reach out to directly. Even a girl can reach a maulana! But over there, if you have any problems, it wasn't like that. It's not like you can reach a maulana. The person you can talk to is an *alima* [female religious scholar], and I don't know how to describe it, but it is different. *I think people are more open about stuff here, like about how they practice Islam and how they always want to talk about Islam. Over there, we weren't so open about it. Over here, they make kids understand what Islam is.* Over there, we were just told, "You have to do this." Kids here understand, we talk about it, and we don't force them...So, there you're forced to do Islam, and here—I mean, you're not forced, but they don't give reasons of why you have to do this. Here, they give you reasons...I think Jaffer is way more mature in Islam than I was when I came here. I thought Islam was very tough—you have to do this, these are the rulings. But now, over the past three years, I've realized it's not tough, it's not hard, it's a very easy religion. There are ifs and buts and how and what to do. Jaffer thinks Islam is easy, and he practices it that way. I took it as tough, and [as] you have to do these rulings. (emphasis added)

Like Sonia, Jameela framed Islam as not as "tough" as she had initially presumed it to be when she was still in Pakistan, because in the Canadian context, she had critically reflected on religion and become more "mature." She also noted that Islam in Pakistan is taken for granted, and like Sonia, she named the inaccessibility of guidance from (male) scholars for women-identified Muslims. Instead, she framed Islam in Canada as reflexively approached, since "people are more open" to talking about "how they practice Islam and...always want to talk about Islam," and as "they make kids understand what

Islam is" and in turn, "kids here understand, we talk about it, and we don't force them."

Similarly, the inclusivists also framed "Canadian Islam" as reflexive. Like the exclusivists, they might have found it difficult to express this in words, but unlike exclusivists, they avoided comparing Canadian Islam with Pakistani Islam. Luqman, unlike other inclusivists who avoided making comparisons, named "Canadian Islam" voluntarily when reflecting on his gratitude for his father's struggle and sacrifice in immigrating to Canada. However, like other inclusivists, he still avoided generalizations:

> Luqman: [My father's immigration experience] is amazing stuff. I don't want to minimize that at all by saying, "Oh, I want to practice the Canadian Islam." I still really respect everything that they do and their values and what they stand for, too.
>
> Interviewer: You mentioned Canadian Islam. What is that?
>
> Luqman: (*hesitates*) It's a combination of everything. Right. Isn't it just people from different ethnic backgrounds sort of—I don't think it's been completely defined yet.
>
> Interviewer: What is it to you?
>
> Luqman: It's a mix of hopefully what's good in every culture, and what's good and what's bad, who knows, but just more open-minded, inclusive.
>
> Interviewer: What makes it "Canadian"?
>
> Luqman: The diversity of it. It's not just—it's everyone.
>
> Interviewer: What is not Canadian Islam?
>
> Luqman: When you go to a masjid that's purely Somalis or purely Pakistanis or purely Arabs.
>
> Interviewer: OK, what is Pakistani Islam, or what is Saudi Islam or Somali Islam? And how does that contrast with Canadian Islam? You mentioned something about being open-minded. So, do you think that perhaps the version of Islam that is accepted or thought of or practiced in other countries is not as open-minded as it is here?
>
> Luqman: Probably not.
>
> Interviewer: Why do you think that?

Luqman: I don't have any basis to think that—now that you're asking, I realize I don't have any reason to say that it wouldn't be.

Interviewer: But what made you first think that? It doesn't have to be true, but it's an assumption you seem to have come across?

Luqman: I think it goes back to the way I was raised—instead of just having a conversation, [like] "Hey, let's just look this up—is there any different point of view on this subject?" [That didn't happen.] I never once asked my parents where—or if there was a disagreement, [it never happened that] someone would open a book and say, "Let's just look at the different ways that you can look at this, and then decide on what the best way to do it is."

Like Jameela, Luqman framed Canadian Islam as "open-minded," and as incorporating critical engagement with Islam through research ("let's just look this up"; "someone would open a book") and discussion ("is there any different point of view on this subject?"). Luqman framed Canadian Islam as not only reflexive, but also inclusivist, as he stated that Canadian Muslims could "look at the different ways" to look at religious and social issues—although this was not a common narrative for inclusivists, especially those who frequented masjids. Unlike Jameela, and other exclusivists, Luqman described Canadian Islam as diverse, reflecting the context in which the inclusivists framed their reflexive approach to Islam. This contrasts with the exclusivists, as mentioned, who framed their reflexivity as emerging in a Muslim-minority context—like Sonia, who stated, "We are trying to preserve ourselves and we don't have that threat in Pakistan, because everyone looks the same."

Conclusion

Within a constellation of identities of Muslim, Canadian, and Pakistani, in this study the exclusivists aligned themselves with a religious-based identity while negotiating or even distancing themselves from the latter two cultural identities (see Table 5.1). The exclusivists framed Canadian Islam and Muslims as superior to

Pakistani Islam and Muslims, and their superiority as emerging from their "cultureless" Islam. As such, in positioning themselves within the racial hierarchy, one strategy they used for accessing proximal whiteness was to reject adherence to Pakistani culture by positioning their identity as cultureless Muslims, rather than as Pakistani Muslims. Karam (2019) also notes this trend among Muslim Americans, who "strategically assimilate" by "consciously craft[ing] a de-ethnicized interpretation of Islam and hence a Muslim American identity" (390). I found that this form of strategic assimilation—of taking on a de-ethnicized religious identity—manifested for all exclusivists in the current study, regardless of which immigrant generation they belonged to. However, I did not find this form of assimilation among the inclusivists.

Table 5.1. Religious and Cultural Framings by Religious Approach

Framing	Exclusivist reflexive Muslims	Inclusivist reflexive Muslims
Islam/Culture in Canada	Acknowledged resources were easier to access, especially for women, but framed religious identity as threatened. Framed "Canadian Islam" as reflexive and correct.	Acknowledged loss of religious hegemony, but framed practice as easier given women's access to religious resources. Framed "Canadian Islam" as reflexive and multicultural.
Islam/Culture in Pakistan	Dismissed religious beliefs and practices as culturally tainted.	Recognized religious hegemony within culture and social institutions as a privilege.
Identity	Identified as Muslim only, creating distance from Pakistani and Canadian identities. Framed identity categories as brightly separated.	Identified as Pakistani Canadian Muslim, embracing aspects of all three identities. Framed categories as overlapping, with no clear separation.

In contrast with the exclusivists in this study, the inclusivists did not frame Canadian and Pakistani Islam or Muslims as starkly different, even when asked to make direct comparisons. They recognized a difference between the Islams based on reflexivity—that Canadian Islam is reflexive while Pakistani Islam is typically not—and that they critically self-reflected about their religiosity, something they valued, but they still framed Pakistani Islam as just another way to approach Islam, rather than as corrupt or wrong. Compared with the exclusivists, inclusivists embraced aspects of all their identities, a novel finding not well-represented in scholarship.

The ways in which immigrant cultural and religious identities form are of interest to feminists, as research indicates that, for second-generation women especially, the desire to pursue a pure, culture-less Islam coincides with the desire to emancipate themselves from restrictive customs that they view as cultural baggage that their first-generation parents (wrongly) imbued into religion (Ballard 2006). Therefore, living in a non-Muslim majority context is a benefit (not a barrier) when it comes to parsing "authentic Islam" from cultural practices (Kahani-Hopkins and Hopkins 2002, 292).

Within the family, for individuals with less power or authority because of family structure—including children vis-à-vis parents, and women vis-à-vis men—religion is a useful resource that can empower those seeking to resist non-religious based (e.g., cultural) authority (Rozario 2011). According to some diasporic Muslims, especially diasporic Muslim women, Islam grants women more honour, respect, and rights than it does men (Kibria 2008). In the current study, both inclusivist and exclusivists critiqued Pakistani culture for lacking the gender equality that they believed to be inherent in Islam. However, while the inclusivists still appreciated and respected Pakistani Islam as well as Pakistani culture, exclusivists framed Pakistani Islam as cultural and Pakistani culture as an impediment to "true" Islam. These framings played a role in their identities, as inclusivists embraced being Pakistani, Canadian, and Muslim, while exclusivists distanced themselves from ethnic identities. This has implications for South Asian feminist organizing.

Furthermore, while both inclusivists and exclusivists critiqued Pakistani culture for lacking the gender equality that they believed to be inherent in Islam, a separate analysis reveals that only inclusivists, particularly inclusivist men, engage in gender liberatory practices while exclusivists hold fast to gender rigidity (Shah 2022, 2023). This finding is ironic given the way exclusivists distanced themselves from the Pakistani identity, while inclusivists did not. This finding also has implications for alliance building across genders.

The findings presented in this chapter highlight the complexity of post-immigration identity formation relating to ethnicity and religion. South Asian feminists seeking to create representative activist networks and communities or to theorize and study the experiences and realities of immigrants in the South Asian diaspora may want to include religious representation. Given that some—namely, exclusivist—Muslims identify with their religious affiliation rather than their ethnicity, religious inclusion would facilitate finding common ground in feminist activism for mutual liberation.

References

Ajrouch, Kristine J. 2004. "Gender, Race, and Symbolic Boundaries: Contested Space of Identity Among Arab American Adolescents." *Sociological Perspectives* 47 (4): 371-391.

Alba, Richard. 2005. "Bright vs. Blurred Boundaries: Second-Generation Assimilation and Exclusion in France, Germany, and the United States." *Ethnic and Racial Studies* 28 (1): 20-49. https://doi.org/10.1080/0141987042000280003.

Ballard, Roger. 2006. "Popular Islam in Northern Pakistan and its Reconstruction in Urban Britain." In *Sufism in the West*, edited by Jamal Malik and John Hinnells, 160-186. London: Routledge Taylor & Francis Group.

Brubaker, Rogers. 2012. "Categories of Analysis and Categories of Practice: A Note on the Study of Muslims in European Countries of Immigration." *Ethnic and Racial Studies* 36 (1): 1-8. https://doi.org/10.1080/01419870.2012.729674.

Cesari, Jocelyne. 2014. *The Awakening of Muslim Democracy: Religion, Modernity, and the State.* Cambridge: Cambridge University Press.

Cheruvallil-Contractor, Sariya. 2018. "The Right To Be Human: How Do Muslim Women Talk About Human Rights and Religious Freedoms in Britain?" *Religion and Human Rights* 13 (1): 49-75.

Espiritu, Yen Le. 2001. "'We Don't Sleep Around Like White Girls Do': Family, Culture, and Gender in Filipina American Lives." *Signs* 26 (2): 415-440.

Kadirov, Djavlonbek, Nilufar Allayarova, and Aisha Wood Boulanouar. 2016. "Transformation as Reversion to Fitrah: Muslim Māori Women's Self-Transformation through Reflexive Consumption." *Journal of Business Research* 69 (1): 33-44.

Kahani-Hopkins, Vered, and Nick Hopkins. 2002. "'Representing' British Muslims: The Strategic Dimension to Identity Construction." *Ethnic and Racial Studies* 25 (2): 288-309.

Karam, Rebecca A. 2019. "Becoming American by Becoming Muslim: Strategic Assimilation Among Second-Generation Muslim American Parents." *Ethnic and Racial Studies* 43 (2): 390-409. https://doi.org/10.1080/01419870.2019.1578396.

Kazemipur, Abdolmohammad. 2014. *The Muslim Question in Canada: A Story of Segmented Integration*. Vancouver: UBC Press.

Kazi, Taha. 2018. "Religious Television and Contesting Piety in Karachi, Pakistan." *American Anthropologist* 120 (3): 523-534.

Khan, Arsalan. 2018. "Pious Masculinity, Ethical Reflexivity, and Moral Order in an Islamic Piety Movement in Pakistan." *Anthropological Quarterly* 91 (1): 53-78.

Kibria, Nazli. 2008. "The 'New Islam' and Bangladeshi Youth in Britain and the US." *Ethnic and Racial Studies* 31 (2): 243-266.

Lamont, Sarah, and Bruce Collet. 2013. "Muslim American University Students' Perceptions of Islam and Democracy: Deconstructing the Dichotomy." *Equity & Excellence in Education* 46 (4): 433-450. https://doi.org/10.1080/10665684.2013.838126.

Latif, Ruby, Wendy Cukier, Suzanne Gagnon, and Radia Chraibi. 2018. "The Diversity of Professional Canadian Muslim Women: Faith, Agency, and 'Performing' Identity." *Journal of Management & Organization* 24 (5): 612-633. https://doi.org/10.1017/jmo.2018.18.

Mac an Ghaill, Mairtin, and Chris Haywood. 2018. "Performance and Surveillance in an Era of Austerity: Schooling the Reflexive Generation of Muslim Young Men." *British Journal of Sociology of Education* 39 (2): 166-181. https://doi.org/10.1080/01425692.2017.1418293.

Meyer, Carl. 2018. "Attacks Against Canadian Muslims and Other Hate Crimes Are Surging." *Canada's National Observer*, November 29. https://www.nationalobserver.com/2018/11/29/news/attacks-against-canadian-muslims-and-other-hate-crimes-are-surging.

Omi, Michael, and Howard Winant. 2015. "The Theory Racial Formation." In *Racial Formation in the United States*. 3rd ed. New York: Routledge/Taylor & Francis Group.

Rayside, David. 2011. "Muslim American Communities' Response to Queer Visibility." *Contemporary Islam* 5 (June): 109-134. https://doi.org/10.1007/s11562-011-0157-8.

Rozario, Santi. 2011. "Islamic Piety Against the Family: From 'Traditional' to 'Pure' Islam." *Contemporary Islam* 5 (June): 285-308.

Shah, Sarah. 2022. "Black and White or Shades of Grey: Religious Approaches and Muslim Marital Conflict." *Social Compass* 69 (1): 113-132. https://doi.org/10.1177/00377686211020567.

Shah, Sarah. 2023. "Religious Reflexivities." In *Oxford Research Encyclopedia of Religion*. Oxford: Oxford University Press. https://doi.org/10.1093/acrefore/9780199340378.013.882.

Shah, Sarah, Gabriel Acevedo, and Andrea Ruiz. 2017. "Contextualizing Events in Imagined Communities: Pre- and Post-September 11th Egyptian Attitudes Toward Non-Arabs and Jews." *Sociology of Islam* 5 (4): 1-29. https://doi.org/10.1163/22131418-00504002.

Shams, Tahseen. 2017. "Visibility as Resistance by Muslim Americans in a Surveillance and Security Atmosphere." *Sociological Forum* 33 (1): 73–94. https://doi.org/10.1111/socf.12401.

6

Exploring Diasporic Indo-Caribbean Identity Through the *Ms. Marvel* Series

SAFIYYA HOSEIN

AS A RESEARCHER OF MUSLIM SUPERHEROES, I chart the rise of the Pakistani American Muslim superhero Kamala Khan through an anti-racist feminist lens in this chapter. South Asian feminisms inform my political and intellectual work as a space that helps me problematize prevailing representations of Muslims in popular culture, which tends to portray them as Middle Eastern and male. Additionally, my work on Muslim superheroines allows me to destabilize dominant discourses of Muslim women as oppressed. And my focus on South Asian narratives lets me spotlight the heterogeneity of the Muslim world. This chapter situates South Asian feminisms in Indo-Caribbean identity, thus challenging hegemonic notions of diasporic South Asian identity as a non-resident South Asian representation.

This chapter will explore Kamala Khan's representation as a *mohajir* (immigrant),[1] through an autoethnographic lens informed by my experience as an Indo-Caribbean Muslim woman living in Canada. I connect the series' representation of the Indo-Pak

Partition to my ancestors' own migration to Trinidad as indentured labourers. I also relate the matrilineal connection in the character's story to my great-great-great-grandmother's own, giving context to the history of indentureship. Finally, I connect Kamala's mohajir experience to my own, because we have both been regarded as "inauthentic" by different South Asian communities. In her case, she encounters this belief in Pakistan, whereas with me, I experience this among non-resident South Asians.

Overview

The summer of 2022 saw a major landmark for South Asian Muslim representation in popular culture. The legendary media conglomerate Disney launched the first Muslim superhero for the Marvel Cinematic Universe (MCU), Kamala Khan (aka Ms. Marvel). As a Pakistani American and Avenger (crime-fighting superhero group member) in the comic books, Kamala has been a force to reckon with since her series debuted in 2014, later becoming a *New York Times* bestseller and Hugo winner. Originally, the *Ms. Marvel* comic book title was a short-lived series in 1977 that followed the adventures of a blonde and blue-eyed Air Force pilot named Carol Danvers, who currently stars in the MCU's expanding slate of films as the superhero Captain Marvel. In a bid to diversify its cast of characters in 2013, Marvel Comics announced that they would revamp the Ms. Marvel superhero once again by referring to her as one of their "legacy heroes"—only this time the revamp would be a Pakistani American teenage girl in the titular role of Ms. Marvel (Chung 2019). Originally written by American Muslim convert G. Willow Wilson and edited by Pakistani American Muslim editor Sana Amanat, *Ms. Marvel: No Normal* debuted at number 1 the month it was released, making Kamala a popular superhero in comics since then (Diamond Corporate Network 2014).

The *Ms. Marvel* TV show marked a significant departure from the comics by changing Kamala's superpowers and omitting key plot points. However, the most significant of these changes was its level of exposure to South Asian Muslim culture and how it connects to Kamala's representation. As a scholar of Muslim superheroes, I found Kamala's South Asian Muslim representation to be refreshing, because it highlighted her ancestral culture. For instance, in the comic book, characters speak Urdu, wear South Asian clothes, and attend *mehendis* (a pre-wedding celebration). The TV series expanded on this representation by cultivating the character's South Asian Muslim identity much more than the comic ever did.

This point is best described through the representation of Kamala's great-grandmother, Aisha, and her experience in the Indo-Pak Partition of 1947. Partition—as it is called in the South Asian diaspora—was raised only once in a single issue of the comic book of Kamala's now eleven-year run, at the time of writing. At the time I considered this to be a remarkable advancement in the character's representation, because it distinguished her clearly as a South Asian Muslim in an industry that often equates Muslim representation with Arabs. Partition was featured much more in the TV series. It served as a focal point in the plot, which spanned multiple episodes, culminating in an entire episode devoted to it. The Partition episode places Kamala back in time, where she saves her grandmother from being lost in an Indian train station that is headed for Karachi, Pakistan. This act ends up preserving the continuation of her family line.

Indentureship History

Although an exhaustive account of East Indian migration to Trinidad and the indentureship system cannot be provided in this chapter, it is important to give a brief description of what it entailed, as relayed by a definitive history book from Trinidad, the aptly titled *The Book of Trinidad*, written by Gérard Besson and Bridget Brereton (2010). After the emancipation of 1838, which saw freed Blacks leave the sugar plantations, farmers were in dire need of workers and used their clout with the British government and local authorities to secure a new "scheme to bring immigrant labourers from many parts of the world" (Breson and Brereton 2010, 264). After some trial and error, Indian labourers became the preferred choice. According to Breson and Brereton, "the overwhelming majority of the immigrants were simple rural folk from the traditional communities of village India, accustomed to hard work and poverty and deeply attached to the land and all its routines" (265).

The Book of Trinidad also contains excerpts from older texts, including a passage about Indian immigrants from *Guide to Trinidad* by J.H. Collins, written in 1886. Collins details the nature of the indentureship system, stating: "The Coolies are bound for five years, receiving free lodgings, medicines, and medical attendance with twenty-five cents per day wages...at first, immigrants who served ten years were granted ten acres of Crown land, then this was changed to a grant of five acres with a bonus of £5, now they receive nothing" (as cited in Breson and Brereton 2010, 276). The online *Caribbean Atlas* also has a variety of statistics on Indian indentureship. Most of these labourers came from Uttar Pradesh and Bihar between 1845 and 1917 (the years of indentureship), and 85 percent were Hindu while 14 percent were Muslim (Caribbean Atlas 2013). Breson and Brereton state what many of us of Indo-Trinidadian origin know: by the time indentureship ended in 1917, the Indians were a strong part of the cultural fabric. Further, "as they were gradually transformed from immigrant labourers to settlers, the Indians contributed a great deal to their new society by practicing their rich diversity of religious and cultural forms" (Breson and Brereton 2010, 266). In this case, the authors are referring to the multiple "temples and mosques...towns and estate settlements, and Hindu and Muslim festivals," as well as "Indian dance, music, and songs" that enriched Trinidadian cultural identity (266).

The Representation of Partition in the *Ms. Marvel* Comics

Partition was first represented in the comics as part of the *Ms. Marvel* volume *Civil War II*. The first issue contains the historical memory of Kamala's maternal great-grandparents' migration from India to Pakistan after British rule ended in South Asia (Wilson and Alphona 2016). It starts off with Kamala's great-grandfather, Kareem, loading a set of belongings onto a cart while trying to convince his elderly father and expectant wife (who is pregnant with Kamala's grandmother) that they have no choice but to leave home. One of the reasons he gives for leaving is an arson attack on a nearby mosque that burned to the ground with its imam inside, alluding to the mass riots and sectarian violence that broke out during Partition. The issue is ripe with many Urdu words and phrases, substantial even for the *Ms. Marvel* series. The series had previously featured many Urdu words, thus driving home the point of Kamala's distinctive South Asian Muslim heritage through language. After Kamala's great-grandmother, Aisha, speaks to her father-in-law in Urdu, she says the phrase "Lord of the Worlds" in English, meaning that she is asking for guidance from God because she is conflicted about leaving her homeland of India to give birth to her child in an unknown country. This phrase is notable because it comes from the prayer *Sura Fatihah*, which Muslims are taught to recite in Arabic; but interestingly, Aisha doesn't say it in Arabic.

When Kareem asks Aisha if she's ready to start the journey, she responds: "No, I'm not. I don't want to have our child thousands of miles away from everything I've ever known...I want to stay here, Kareem" (Wilson and Alphona 2016, 28). This is important, because it also reiterates Kamala's mohajir identity by relaying the anxieties many immigrants feel about moving to an unknown place where they know no one. Aisha soon sees a shooting star and gains the resolve to move to Pakistan. Soon after, Aisha's father-in-law starts reciting the *angrezi* (English) poet Keats, poetry that Kamala's great-grandfather Kareem refers to as "nonsense" (29). The implication here is a not-so-subtle resentment of the British colonialism that Indians endured for two centuries, which inspired the independence movement that racked Indian politics during Partition. To drive the point home, Kareem asks his father to instead recite the poetry of the Indian poet—and future Nobel Prize winner—Rabindranath Tagore, again connecting the family to a core South Asian identity. As the family gets ready to leave, Aisha's internal monologue continues, in which she discusses selling her jewelry and hiding the money in her wedding bangles, so that she and her child can start a new life if she is separated from her husband. One of the last images of this scene is a close-up of the bangles—which the reader now sees are the bangles that Kamala wears with her superhero costume.

Representations of Partition in the TV Series

Although the comic issue exploring Partition is short but meaningful, the TV series' exploration of it goes into much greater detail about Kamala's family's migration to Pakistan. In the first episode, Kamala's family receives a package from her *nani* (maternal grandmother) that contains a bangle. This item later unlocks her superpowers, effectively transforming her into a superhero. In Episode 2, Kamala's father tells Kamala's sister-in-law, Tyesha, about how his wife, Muneeba (Kamala's mother), lost everything during Partition when they fled to Karachi. He relates a story about Kamala's then-toddler grandmother, Sana, losing her mother, Aisha, at the train station. Sana miraculously makes her way to her father, Hasan (name changed from the comic), by following a trail of stars that lead her back to him. Incidentally, this is the last the family ever sees of Aisha.

In Episode 3, the introduction takes us back in time to British-occupied India circa 1942, notably around the time that Mahatma Gandhi launched the "Quit India" movement. This movement led to both India's independence and the creation of the state of Pakistan. In this episode, we see Kamala's great-grandmother, Aisha, alive and well and searching for the exact same bangle in a Hindu temple. One of Aisha's companions makes a remark about the British looting the temple twice over, alluding to the large theft of valuables that the British confiscated before leaving India for good, including the world's largest diamond, the Koh-I-Noor. Outside, British forces try to beat down the temple door, which begins to collapse, prompting Aisha and her companions to split up. Right before it collapses, the audience is brought back to the present day, with a cliffhanger hovering around Aisha's survival.

Aisha is of significance throughout the series, even in the present day. We see this through Kamala's questions about her great-grandmother to her mother, her nani, and some gossiping aunties who think that Aisha was a disgrace for abandoning her family. Episode 3 also sees Kamala having a vision of a train coming toward her. Soon after, her grandmother encourages her to come visit Karachi with her mother so that they can all figure out the vision together. Episode 4 shows Kamala and her mother travelling to Karachi to meet her eccentric grandmother. When Kamala takes a tour through the city with her cousins, they point out the first neighbourhood where Karachi's oldest residents settled when they came from India. Kamala later leaves them to investigate the train station. This episode also sees Kamala battle Aisha's companions from 1942 in the present day, before one of them attempts to stab her. She instead hits the bangle Kamala is wearing, transporting Kamala back in time to an Indian train station with trains heading to Karachi during Partition.

In the same episode, Kamala's grandmother also speaks to her in the present about Partition and the mohajir identity. She says she is still learning about herself, having been born in India but possessing a Pakistani passport, with the border in between both countries "marked with blood and pain" (Ali 2022a, 25:27). She further states that, "People are claiming their identity based on an idea some old Englishman had when they were fleeing the country" (25:32). Perhaps the line may have been clumsily written, but I felt that it was really meant to speak to the traumatic effects of British colonialism.

The fifth episode is entirely devoted to Partition. It opens to Kamala's great-grandfather, Hasan, giving a spirited anti-colonial speech to a crowd of onlookers in his village in British-occupied India. We also see Aisha running from a British soldier, who she fights off before she ends up on Hasan's rose patch and takes a nap. Most of the episode shows their love blossoming, resulting in the birth of their child, Sana, Kamala's grandmother. Eventually, they make the decision to flee to Karachi after they hear radio reports of ensuing violence, which distresses Hasan. There is also a notable scene where their Hindu neighbour comes by to offer goods to the couple before Hasan dismisses him, leading the neighbour to say that he is "playing into the British's hands" (Ali 2022b, 10:27). Hasan responds by saying that no one has bought his goods or his wife's milk because they are Muslim. This is important because it discusses the level of animosity Muslims were treated with leading up to their mass migration.

After spotting one of her companions, who are now the show's villains, Aisha convinces Hasan that they are not safe and must leave for Pakistan. She tells Hasan about them before they arrive at the train station. Having spotted the main villain, Najma, as they head to their train, she hands Sana off to Hasan. She then abruptly runs off to find Najma, who kills her for "betraying" them. In the ensuing panic to get on the last train to Karachi, Sana, who is a toddler, runs away from her father to try to find her mother. Kamala—who has been transported back in time at this point—finds a dying Aisha, who begs her to find Sana. Using her powers, Kamala helps Sana get back to Hasan by creating a trail of stars. Realizing that it is she who has saved her family, Kamala is then transported back to the present. However, before this happens, she sees her great-grandfather and grandmother board the last train to Karachi.

The Partition storyline was a key plot point in the comics that was then strongly developed in the TV series by its showrunner, British Pakistani screenwriter Bisha K. Ali. This helped to tether Kamala more closely to the South Asian Muslim identity. The introduction of the *Ms. Marvel* episodes is the same introduction we see in every MCU film, which is an iconic assemblage filled with footage of Marvel's superheroes in full colour. In Episode 5, however, the assemblage is in black and white, accompanied by an old Urdu song, "*Tu mera chand mei teri chandni*" (meaning "you are my moon and I am your moonlight"), by Shyam and Suraiya from the 1949 Pakistani film *Dillagi*, which comes from the Partition era (Kardar 1949). This iconic song from *Dillagi*, a romantic tragedy, is a foreshadowing of the episode, which details Kamala's great-grandparents' doomed love after being separated at the border. The episode opens with a news clip from that era about India's independence from the British, notably showing the first Indian prime minister, Jawaharal Nehru, and Pakistan's founder and first governor general, Muhammad Ali Jinnah. It also shows the *Ms. Marvel* title in several South Asian languages. Factors such as these only serve to solidify the character's distinctive South Asian (particularly Pakistani) history, as well as mohajir identity. Kamala's mother later grows up in Karachi before she and her husband emigrate to New Jersey, making this a second migration on her mother's side of the family.

Much of the series follows in the footsteps of Kamala's first writer, G. Willow Wilson, who created a matrilineal superhero line in Kamala's family for the comic book series. The TV series further develops this matrilineal theme by finding moments of tension and bonding between all three generations of mothers and daughters, alluding to the intergenerational trauma all three of them face. Showrunner Ali herself acknowledged this theme in an interview with Marvel, when she discussed "Kamala healing her matrilineal line" (Paige 2022). She went on to state, "It felt different and new, and we haven't seen this before, and it's speaking to power in women…and also the beauty of being able to see your parents as people and who had to survive a thing. These women had to survive a thing, and that gets in the way of their relationships, and Kamala can be the one to piece all of that back together and heal everybody." In the interview, Ali also acknowledged these characters' intergenerational trauma, and the lingering effects Partition has on them. Kamala's ability to heal her matrilineal line on the night her family boards a train heading for Karachi, in a story about South Asian Muslim women, is refreshing in its own way. This is because we almost never see matrilineal power when it comes to Muslim women's representation in Western film. Instead, we often see them characterized as women who are dominated and abused by an unrelenting patriarchy.

The TV show adds depth to other comic book plot points and themes as well—namely, Kamala's visit to Pakistan. In the comic book, she makes the trip to stay with her grandmother for some time. The comic book *nani* gives her the nurturing and care she needs, and Kamala leaves Pakistan having resolved to face the issues she was struggling with in the US. This issue is also the trip where Kamala meets the Pakistani male superhero, the Red Dagger, who is also in the TV show. He makes several comments insinuating that she is not an "authentic" Pakistani. Again, this is a build-up of more comic book themes, considering the fight both characters had on a recent trip Kamala made to Karachi in the comic book anthology, *Marvel Voices: Identity #1*, where Red Dagger called Kamala a "self-hating Pakistani" (Pirzada 2021). These issues around her authenticity as a South Asian are further addressed in the TV series, where Kamala is called an "ABCD—American Born Confused Desi" (Ali 2022a, 14:05) by her cousin in Episode 4.

An Autoethnographic Reading of Ms. *Marvel*

Kamala's family's second migration was of particular interest to me because it was one that I related to, having had my South Asian ancestry marred with a first traumatic migration out of India through my mother's line during British rule, when my family was moved to Trinidad to become indentured labourers. Later, my family moved to Canada, the way many other Indo-Trinidadians have done, a phenomenon we know as the second migration. The accusations Kamala faced as an "inauthentic" South Asian when she visited Karachi made her even more relatable to me, when I considered the many ways Indo-Caribbean people are treated in North America within the larger South Asian community, members of which often boldly tell us that we are in fact not South Asian, even though we are known as "Indian" back home because of our South Asian ancestry.

Dispassionate accounts of indentureship do not capture the stories passed down in families from their dearly departed loved ones who endured the traumatic realities of indentureship. My mother's side has much older roots in Trinidad than my father's side, and it is the story of my mother's great-great-grandmother, Ramjanee, that is the most riveting. According to the family, my great-great-great-grandmother had an argument with her mother-in-law before she packed up her belongings and left for her mother's house with her two children. On the way, she was tricked by the British into boarding a boat to the West Indies, although at the time she thought that she was simply going to another part of India to work. I often question what the fight was about, and whether Nani Ramjanee was in fact kicked out of her in-laws' home as opposed to leaving there of her own accord. What I do know is that she ended up in Trinidad, indentured to work on a sugar plantation for several years while looking after her two children with no spouse. Based on the research conducted by my relative Shamshu Deen (1998), who is the foremost genealogist in Trinidad for East Indian migration, it appears that indentureship traumatized Ramjanee deeply. She would often try to prevent her grandchildren from giving affection to her daughter, Najeebun. I suspect she did not think it wise for them to become too attached to someone. Her faith in God seemed shaken as well, seeing that she was ambivalent to religious practice.

This stood in stark contrast to her daughter, Najeebun, my great-great-grandmother, who was one of the earlier *hajjins* (Muslim women who perform the *hajj*) in Trinidad, and certainly a woman of significance in Trinidadian Muslim history because she mobilized Muslim women into becoming a regular part of mosque life. As many older members of the community have noted, Najeebun travelled to villages and towns throughout the country after she returned from the hajj, teaching Muslim women prayers and anything else pertaining to women and Islam that she knew about.[2] In the process, she helped them become a bigger part of the mosque community. I think this was particularly instrumental, considering that my knowledge of Muslim women in mainland South Asia is that many don't attend mosque. In Trinidad, however, Muslim women play an active role in Muslim organizations and mosque life and have for a very long time. Trinidad has a National Muslim Women's Organization that is accepting of Muslim women with a diverse set of beliefs, and most *jamaats* (Muslim assemblies) have a ladies' group. This isn't a surprise when you consider Najeebun's own history, which, like Ramjanee's, shows her as surprisingly independent for a woman of her time. Najeebun's marriage to my great-great grandfather, Emamally, was arranged. He was much older than her, and they had met on the sugar plantation she worked at in Trinidad. After Najeebun and Emamally became prosperous, they paid for a passage to Saudi Arabia to perform the hajj pilgrimage with their ten-year old son, Ahmed. However, when the ship docked at Jeddah, Emamally collapsed and died. As the story goes, Najeebun, with her son, buried her husband in the desert close to a palm tree and tied her *ohrni* (scarf) to it should relatives make the voyage in later years and want to visit his grave. She then performed the pilgrimage with her son and left for India, where she lived for about two years, from 1911 to 1913.

When I was a child, I was told that Najeebun had found her old village and reunited with her father. But according to Deen, she lived in inns for several years and was supported by my great-grandfather, Eniath, who would send her money whenever he could. I also learned that Ahmed was a sickly individual who found the sweltering Indian weather too much to bear, and so often spent time swimming in the rivers to keep himself cool. He wasn't officially diagnosed with asthma, but he may have suffered from it because he had regular respiratory issues. After several years, Najeebun boarded a boat with Ahmed and left for Trinidad. The voyage weakened Ahmed so much that by the time they arrived, he was especially frail.

The story goes that when they arrived at the capital, Port of Spain, it was late, and the last train was leaving for the night. Desperate to get on that train, Najeebun tried to rush to it, trying her best to keep Ahmed with her. But he was too ill to get to the train quickly enough, and they watched it leave without them. The moment was particularly devastating for her because she had nowhere to go for the night and was left on the street with a very ill son. As fate would have it, a relative, Boodoo, went to the train station around the same time, and they were both saved. Apparently, it was common for the Indians in Trinidad to have a welcoming person meet incoming indentured labourers at the port, where the train station was also located. Many were already past their indentureship and had settled in Trinidad. They would often go to the port to see if anyone they knew from back home had landed, or if anyone from the part of India that they came from had arrived. Boodoo took them to his home, where Najeebun took care of Ahmed for the night, even going so far as to cradle him in her arms. Ahmed passed away a month later in the comfort of his own birth home (my ancestral home), and people from all over the country attended the funeral, amazed by the story and deeply saddened for his mother, who had endured so much loss on her voyages.

Overlaps With My Story

There is so much to unpack here in these migration stories, which inspired emotion—even nostalgia—in me when I saw Kamala's family's migration story. The Partition episode showed Kamala's great-grandparents separated at the border, which made me think of my great-great-great-grandparents, who were also separated in the ancestral migration story that took our family to Trinidad. These losses due to the effects caused by British colonialism stirred a great sadness in me. Kamala's Urdu-speaking great-grandparents, living in a small simple home in a village where they tended their crops, made me think of my own ancestors. Kamala's life in New Jersey, undoubtedly privileged compared to that of her ancestors, made me think of mine here in Canada. I walked away from this series with an intense nostalgia. When I was a child growing up in Trinidad, I lived in the suburbs with my parents, which was a far cry from the small towns in which they grew up. My parents were from the first generation that became more Westernized, and with that came urbanization. My parents met when they were students at the University of the West Indies and had a love marriage. My grandparents' generation tended to retain the more traditional practices, and the small towns that my parents grew up in had a stronger sense of community than the suburbs did. My parents still kept strong links with their hometowns, and I even attended the local elementary school in my mom's town.

This led me to feel a kinship with older Indians who still ate with their hands, wore *ohrnis* on their heads, and even knew (and sometimes conversed in) the older tongue. Therefore, when I saw Kamala's great-grandparents, it felt like a portal into my past. I didn't see much religious practice in the series, but I thought about the South Asian Muslim practices that my community only practiced in my childhood—before many started adopting Arab practices, which always felt too foreign to me and led me on a secular path. It also wasn't like we were immune to any effects of Partition in Trinidad. There were states of emergency in the "Muslim" towns during Partition, and there was even a shootout in my mother's town, indicating just how much Indo-Trinidadians still react to

Indian politics in the present day. Furthermore, the micro-aggressions Kamala endures from Pakistanis about her lack of authenticity made her relatable to me as an Indo-Caribbean woman who has always been told I am "not Indian," despite my ancestry and Indo-Caribbean culture. But in a strange way, it also gave me a sense of closure, considering that many of those who have said as much probably deal with the same issues among people from the motherland, making their statements, frankly, amusing.

Conclusion

This chapter has achieved several aims. First, I explored the *Ms. Marvel* series through an autoethnographic lens by examining its plot themes related to Partition considering my own ancestors' migration to Trinidad as indentured labourers, giving historical context. Additionally, I connected the matrilineal themes explored in the TV series to my great-great-great-grandmother's story. I also related Kamala's experiences of being regarded as "inauthentic" to my own experiences with the South Asian community here in Canada. As a scholar of Muslim superheroes who has explored Kamala dispassionately in my work, the series felt personal to me for all these reasons.

Notes

1. The term "mohajir," literally migrant, is widely used in historical and popular culture in Pakistan to refer mostly to Urdu-speaking people who migrated during Partition from India to Pakistan and their descendants.
2. These stories are part of our oral history, passed on by my own family members and members of the Muslim community, and recounted to me in my own conversations with Shamshu Deen. For instance, my paternal great-grandmother talked about when Najeebun came to her village.

References

Ali, Bisha K. 2022a. *Ms. Marvel*. Season 1, episode 4, "Seeing Red." Directed by Mira Menon. Released June 29, on Disney+.

Ali, Bisha K. 2022b. *Ms. Marvel*. Season 1, episode 5, "Time and Again." Directed by Sharmeen Obaid-Chinoy. Released July 6, on Disney+.

Besson, Gérard, and Bridget Brereton. 2010. *The Book of Trinidad*. 3rd ed. Port of Spain, Trinidad and Tobago: Paria Publishing.

Caribbean Atlas. 2013. "The Experience of Indian Indenture in Trinidad: Arrival and Settlement." http://www.caribbean-atlas.com/en/themes/waves-of-colonization-and-control-in-the-caribbean/waves-of-colonization/the-experience-of-indian-indenture-in-trinidad-arrival-and-settlement.html.

Chung, Erika. 2019. "Ms. Marvel: Genre, Medium, and an Intersectional Superhero." *Panic at the Discourse: An Interdisciplinary Journal* 1 (2): 5–16.

Deen, Shamshu. 1998. *Lineages and Linages: Solving Trinidad Roots in India*. Charlieville, Trinidad and Tobago: Print-Art Services.

Diamond Comic Distributors. 2014. "Top 100 Graphic Novels: October 2014." http://www.diamondcomics.com/Article/156090-Top-100-Graphic-Novels-October-2014.

Kardar, Abdur Rashid, dir. 1949. *Dillagi.* Lahore: Kardar Productions.

Paige, Rachel. 2022. "'Ms. Marvel': Bridging the Generational Gap Between Kamala, Muneeba, Sana, and Aisha." Marvel, July 6. https://www.marvel.com/articles/tv-shows/ms-marvel-kamala-khan-generational-gap.

Pirzada, Sabir. 2021. "Seeing Red." In *Marvel Voices Identity #1*, 21–25. New York: Marvel Entertainment.

Wilson, Willow, and Adriana Alphona. 2016. *Ms. Marvel*, vol. 6. New York: Marvel Comics.

7

Female Terrorism in the West

The Case of Rehab Dughmosh

KANWAL KHOKHAR

ALTHOUGH THE WAR ON TERROR has "officially" ended with the reinstatement of the Taliban in Afghanistan and the withdrawal of Western forces from that country, its neighbour to the east, Pakistan, continues to face repeated attacks from extremist militants acting in the name of skewed and repressive interpretations of Islam. Terrorism, in fact, remains a daily threat in the imaginations and lives of average people and continues to pervade the lives of diasporic Pakistanis as an ongoing unease about the welfare of their loved ones "back home." Despite repeated declarations by the Pakistani state that countering extremist violence is a top priority, the low effectiveness of contemporary preventive measures continues to be a source of unease and distress (Saeed 2023). In this chapter, I add to the contemporary research on countering violent extremism (CVE), especially that which points to the gender-blind nature of most existing research on the topic (Saeedi and Fransen 2018). This chapter argues that mainstream representations of female radicalization and terrorism are simplistic and problematic, both in the media and scholarly literature.[1] Specifically, the simplistic understandings of the motivations of female radicalization to violence (RTV) are detrimental for

CVE initiatives; and, conversely, recruiters of extremist groups benefit from the gaps in our knowledge and leverage this problematic discourse. Through an analysis of a Toronto incident, it is argued that there are immense disconnects between existing terrorism literature and the realities of gendered radicalization and deradicalization processes in the Western world. To effectively address the problem of female terrorism, research must readily engage in gendered analyses from the perspective that women cannot be denied agency and are real threats and prone to RTV, just as men are believed to be. The purpose of this research is not to provide a comprehensive overview of the existing literature on female terrorism, but rather to critically engage with contemporary understandings of females in extremist settings and identify the discrepancies between our knowledge base and the changing realities of global terrorism. In doing so, this research calls for a more multifaceted and nuanced understanding of female radicalization and CVE initiatives, particularly for Muslim women living in the West.

Notably, discussions of radicalization nestled within South Asian feminisms are pertinent, because although there is a lack of nuance in the literature on female radicalization, the discourse—or lack thereof—impacts South Asian women, particularly those living in the West. This chapter dissects the experiences of a Muslim woman living in the West, and includes the targeted recruitment of young women living outside South Asian regions, whose "South Asianness" often remains at conflict with their identities in the West and is a fundamental aspect of their radicalization. South Asian feminism is a political and intellectual space for this work, as it allows for creatively challenging patriarchal and postcolonial ideas of gender and identity. Specifically, the representation of immigrant, Muslim, and South Asian women is needed within criminological and national defence research. South Asian feminisms offer my voice a prospective space within this arena.

While acknowledging the gaps that exist in the male-centred research, the first section of this chapter examines the prevailing research on female terrorism and the gendered considerations of radicalization, and critiques the problematic assumptions and generalizations concerning females in this space. The second section provides an overview of the case of Rehab Dughmosh, a Canadian woman charged with terrorism offences.[2] This section examines the language used in news and academic articles to describe Dughmosh's case, and investigates other known cases of female terrorists, ultimately illustrating the juxtapositions between Dughmosh's case and dominant representations of female terrorism. This analysis proves helpful in understanding where the disconnects in our knowledge exist and what gaps need to be addressed. The final section discusses the policy implications of the research, explores the benefits of furthering research on female terrorism, and provides suggestions for developing and implementing effective CVE initiatives.

Representations of Female Radicalization

It is important to note that radicalization and terrorism are both contested terms in the literature (Streigher 2015). Radicalization should not be understood as a necessary precursor for violent extremism or acts of terror (CSD 2016, 8). For the purposes of this chapter, RTV or violent extremism are used to refer to instances when women have adopted ideologies and/or demonstrated actions in support of terrorism.

Women engaging in terrorism is not a contemporary phenomenon. While there has been an increase in the number of women engaging in terrorism across the globe, women have historically been involved in violent action for an array of causes and radical groups (Bloom 2011a; CPRLV 2016). Both left- and right-wing extremist groups have had substantial female participation. For instance, women played significant roles in anarchist groups throughout the nineteenth and twentieth centuries, just as they were involved in Palestinian and left-wing and radical groups throughout the 1960s to 1980s. They have played various roles in nationalist groups that have resorted to violence, and demonstrated noteworthy involvement in militant Islamist groups since the 1990s (Bloom 2011a; CPRLV 2016). Notably, over the past decades the role of women has evolved extensively in Islamist groups that conventionally excluded women from participation in activities outside the domestic realm, due to conservative and religious ideals (CPRLV 2016); however, conventional literature from an Islamist point of view has not focussed on the role of women.

Contrary to early research and stereotypes surrounding terrorism, female terrorists are not rare or "exceptions to the rule" (Windsor 2020). Referring to the early 2000s, Nacos (2005) points out that people react with an extreme level of shock and horror whenever women commit acts of terror. Her study was published in 2005, and literature since has repeatedly concluded that female terrorism has increased and is continuing to do so; yet, more than a decade later, people still react with sentiments of shock, as if female terrorists are rare. Bloom (2011a) cautions that women have killed hundreds of individuals and injured thousands more, dozens of women have attempted violent acts and failed, and hundreds are being trained for the future. It is crucial to recognize that, contrary to the general representation in the media and in early literature, female terrorists are not rare or misfits. In fact, women are resilient and are more determined in their missions as they prove themselves in male-dominated organizations, compared to men who are concerned with their self-image, masculinity, and strength (Sixta 2008, 268; Kostes 2015). Female terrorism is thus a pertinent and complex phenomenon that deserves attention.

Some research has noted that, over time, the nature of women's involvement in terrorism has changed from playing invisible roles to very visible and front-line operational roles (Bloom 2017; Malik 2018). In fact, in various countries, the percentage of women since 2002 has exceeded 50 percent of operatives (Bloom 2011a). However, the diversity of roles that women play in terrorist organizations has not been fully recognized in the existing literature (Bloom 2011a, 6). This shift in roles has resulted in terrorist organizations recognizing that women are a powerful tool, beyond procreation. Women are targeted and recruited for various tasks, including as operatives to carry out missions, because women have proven to be most effective in achieving maximum destruction (Kostes 2015, 48).

Interestingly, while it is true that some terrorist groups treat women as mere tools for a greater cause and fail to consider them as equals, many female terrorists have assumed leadership roles with significant positions of power across the globe (Kostes 2015, 247; Streigher 2015). The variances in assumed roles can be explained by the different cultures in which the organizations are based. Despite these differences, women are involved in terrorist organizations in increasing numbers, and this increase strengthens and benefits the terrorist groups (Kostes 2015, 247). For example, women are stealthy, can easily pass checkpoints, and can get closer to targets because people do not expect to see women as terrorists. The motivation to utilize women thus becomes tactical, because they can avoid detection and also receive eight times more media coverage than men, an attractive feature for terrorist organizations as it awards them more exposure (Bloom 2017; Kostes 2015). Since women are stereotyped as nurturing individuals, which juxtaposes with the image of conventional terrorists, female terrorists are perceived as being harder to make sense of than men who fulfill the exact same acts or roles. Terrorist organizations use this double standard to their advantage, as they are aware that female terrorists will prompt overreactions by the public and government (Kostes 2015). It must, however, be acknowledged that all forms of violent offending—including terrorist violence—are disproportionately male domains. Nonetheless, despite women's participation, the general perception remains that women are not political or violent creatures (Shute 2013).

The post-9/11 era proliferated radicalization studies as states became obsessed with national security and CVE. The focus became understanding the motivations behind radicalization. However, the literature was predominantly male centred, because females did not fit the terrorist profile. There was some emerging research on female radicalization, although much of that research is now outdated. For example, Nacos (2005) looked at the portrayal of female terrorists in the media and noted similar patterns in the news coverage of women in politics and in terrorism. This research provided an exceptional analysis of gendered stereotypes that exist in the media about both non-violent and violent political actors, and concluded that there is no evidence that male and female terrorists are fundamentally different in terms of their recruitment, motivation, and ideological dedication. Although this seemingly strengthens the argument that female terrorists, like male terrorists, are common and capable of violent action, it ignores the specific gendered motivations and processes of recruitment behind female radicalization and provides a simplistic understanding of females in this space. Other studies on men participating in various forms of RTV have failed to examine the "masculine character of their subjects," implying that the gender factor is only an issue where radicalized women are the subject (CPRLV 2016, 34). The Centre for the Prevention of Radicalization Leading to Violence (CPRLV) (2016) points to the fact that the gendered perspective on women's radicalization paths takes into consideration that there is an inherent tension between sexist mechanisms of subordination and certain forms of agency that cannot be denied. Early radicalization research was not able to accurately address this tension. Moreover, women have been looked at as a homogenous group in the existing literature, and while some emerging research has recognized that we must look at differences between women, there has been no research done on variations across groups of women that emphasizes that the process of RTV involves multiple facilitators that vary by individual, group, type of belief, and context (National Institute of Justice 2015).

More recent research has assumed a feminist approach that has acknowledged women's involvement in RTV; however, public discourse has not recognized their agency or assigned them the ability to be actors and participants in their own right (CPRLV 2016; Shute 2013; Sixta 2008). Feminist literature has provided a better understanding of paths to radicalization for women, by deconstructing them as victims of a patriarchal society but also giving importance to their capacity to act. Since violent women transgress traditional gender norms, their violence is often excused as they are depicted as harmless victims. For example, the first reaction toward women who go to Syria and Iraq is to label them as "jihadi brides" going for sexual jihad reasons. This is problematic, because it not only denies these women's agency but also reduces awareness of the number of women who choose to join jihadist groups, viewing them as mere enslaved individuals and naive young girls (Navest, De Koning, and Noors 2016, as cited in CPRLV 2016, 22). On the contrary, recruiters of terrorist groups appeal to Western Muslim women by convincing them that women are equals and will be awarded more value and respect than the West offers them; and they appeal to women's ambitions by promising that their educational backgrounds and skills are needed within the organization. Thus, women do not simply leave to become "jihadi brides"; rather, they see an opportunity to become a part of and contribute to a larger cause.

Research has also argued that women are motivated by their emotions, while male terrorists are inspired by religion, nationalism, or the desire to take part in combat as an occupation (Bloom 2011a, 8). This is problematic, as subsequent literature must either build upon those ideas or disprove them, which involves a considerable amount of effort and friction. Other early studies argue that women's political motivations are less central to their radicalization compared to those of men, and assign an emotional explanation by labelling women as hysterical, while proposing that men plan their attacks thoughtfully with rationality (Cone 2016; Nacos 2005; Sixta 2008). This view exudes inherent sexist assumptions that women are less complicated than men and are unable to control their emotions, and strips women of their political motivation while excusing their behaviour (Bloom 2011a).

In 2011, Bloom's book *Bombshell: Women and Terrorism* proved to be an influential body of research, with its summary of women's involvement in terrorism as motivated by what the author labelled as the four R's: Revenge, Redemption, Relationship, and Respect. Bloom (2011b) explained that revenge for the death of a loved one is most often cited as the reason for women's involvement in terrorism, while attempting to redeem themselves for past mistakes through martyrdom, instead of facing the honour code of their societies, is another pervasive explanation (12). Familial relations to men in terrorist groups or marriage into such groups has served as the strongest predictor of women's engagement in terrorism. Finally, according to Bloom (2011b), women want the respect of their community, and by engaging in violence they can prove that they are as committed as the men to their society's cause. Bloom also added an additional R for rape, because there have been instances of sexual exploitation of women to coerce them into terrorism in countries like Iraq (17). These reasons are most often cited as key factors in women's involvement in terrorism and have been adopted by many subsequent scholars in research initiatives. However, the extent to which this research is applicable to Western or immigrant women engaging in terrorism is unknown, as their realities involve a host of differing factors and identities.

Media Coverage

Just as the portrayal of female terrorists in early research has been problematic, media portrayals remain of particular concern for several reasons. First, when a female carries out a violent act, the media focuses heavily on emotional explanations for their violence, stating that women are acting out of passion due to the loss of a loved one, or are blinded by their grief (Bloom 2011a, 8). Second, the general perception of women in extremist settings has been as perpetual victims. When women are examined as perpetrators, stereotypes of women as the puppets or victims of men are perpetuated (Bloom 2011a, 7). These popular perceptions also exclude the network of women who participate behind the scenes, and their involvement and motivations remain unknown and misunderstood. Further, assuming that men force women into terrorism is out of touch with the reality of women's motivations, which are often multifaceted and a complex mix of personal, political, and religious factors (CPRLV 2016; Malik 2018). Media coverage in the West also perpetuates these issues by searching for alternative explanations for women's participation in terror. This process completely contrasts with the coverage male suicide bombers receive, even while women show they are just as predetermined and lethal as their male counterparts (Bloom 2011a).

Further, different framing patterns are important to note in terrorism news, as they influence public perceptions and reactions. The news tends to frame acts of terror committed by women in episodic terms, by highlighting and dwelling on them (Nacos 2005). Not only is this of tactical benefit for terrorist organizations, but episodic framing also translates into people supporting more punitive measures against terrorists in reaction to the sensationalized news. This makes it difficult to implement policies that address the root causes of terrorism. Also notable is the media's tendency to dwell on the physical appearance, facial expressions, and choice of clothing of female terrorists, especially when these aspects contrast with the image of a traditional terrorist (Cone 2016). The media also describes the physical appearance of male terrorists; however, the context is different, as aspects of their appearance are used specifically in relation to their actions. For example, when the physique of a male is described as skinny, it is used as a precursor to the individual being able to climb out of a small window. On the other hand, female terrorists' hair colour is mentioned, even if it is only remotely visible; if they are attractive, it is stated; and their choice of clothing and/or preference in makeup is described (Nacos 2005, 439).

When women terrorists are "pretty," the media narratives wonder about their marital status and question family connections and backgrounds, in attempts to explain their violent actions (Nacos 2005). This tendency is also seen in scholarly literature, where the backgrounds of female terrorists receive more attention than those of male terrorists. Family connections often bleed into another stereotype about female terrorists, namely that their participation was for the sake of love, perhaps because they followed a lover or husband, father, brother, or cousin into the hands of the terrorist group. The "love connection" has been a frequent theme in media coverage of female terrorism, when in reality both men and women are influenced in similar ways by relatives, friends, and/or acquaintances (Nacos 2005). These types of depictions reinforce deep-rooted societal perceptions of female terrorism.

The Case of Rehab Dughmosh

The case of Rehab Dughmosh is useful in examining the perceptions discussed above. Dughmosh is a Syrian Canadian who, at 32 years old, attacked employees and customers with a golf club while wielding a knife at a Canadian Tire store in Toronto in June 2017 (Blatchford 2017b). In an article titled "The Modern New Face of a Terror Case," Blatchford (2017b) details the facts of Dughmosh's case, stating that she was wearing a headband with Islamic State of Iraq and Syria (ISIS) written on it and was screaming "*Allahu-Akbar* (God is Great)." Dughmosh was originally charged with several assault charges (Blatchford 2017a), before being charged with attempted murder for the benefit of or in association with a terrorist group (Blatchford 2017b). A year prior to the incident, she had left Canada to join ISIS and was intercepted in Turkey and brought back to Canada. Subsequently, Dughmosh was charged with leaving Canada for the purposes of committing a terrorist act, contrary to section 83.181 of the Criminal Code, and with thirteen additional offences, which were all linked and classified to be in association with a terrorist group (Canada News Wire 2017).

In court, Dughmosh refused to cooperate, listen to instructions, or leave her holding cell, while pledging her support for ISIS repeatedly. She refused the services of a lawyer, stated she preferred to waive her right to Canadian citizenship, and threatened that if released she would repeat her actions (Blatchford 2017a). Her behaviour prompted the court to order a psychiatric assessment, and she was found fit to stand trial. The judge insisted that Dughmosh participate in court proceedings without coercion and force. In court, regardless of the question asked through an Arabic translator, Dughmosh replied, "You are all infidels...I do not worship what you worship" (Blatchford 2017b, 2). Dughmosh was also heard saying "hurting me" to the guards holding her arms in a court proceeding. In this particular court appearance, the judge noted that it was the first time Dughmosh had appeared without her *niqab*—a full face covering—and asked court officials to find out if this was her choice. Later in the court proceedings, Dughmosh stated: "I do not forgive them [the guards] for taking off my headdress," revealing that she had been mistreated (3).

Dughmosh's time in court is noteworthy, as it exemplifies the Canadian court system's insensitivity when dealing with culturally sensitive cases and racialized populations. The court displayed a lack of understanding of Dughmosh's radicalization process and motivations. For instance, Blatchford (2017b) wrote that the proceedings were "remarkably considerate, and excruciatingly careful of Dughmosh's rights, for a lousy infidel court" (2). This is a problematic assertion, because the judge merely ensured Dughmosh's basic rights were protected; but the narratives observing this displayed no sympathy. Instead, news articles boasted about the court's generosity with loaded language and overtly mocked the court system for being flexible and considerate in their dealings.

Interestingly, the news articles detailing Dughmosh's case did not pay much attention to her RTV process. It was mentioned that she had separated from her husband earlier that month. She had what can be described as the increasingly typical background of the modern terrorist; she had been inspired by an extremist organization, had experienced limited success in her adopted country, and had gone through a recent major stress, all of which can be interpreted as factors in her radicalization process. However, this process was not given much importance in the media. The news articles did mention when Dughmosh cracked a smile, and described a thick lock of dark hair hanging in front of her face. These portrayals are in line with research that has noted the tendency of media articles to dwell on the physical attributes of female terrorists. Still, contrary to existing research, Dughmosh did not receive sympathy, her violence was not explained by emotional factors, and her background or process of RTV was not investigated. Instead, it was implied that she fit the terrorist profile well and was an entitled woman, perhaps because she was a racialized woman living in the West.

The news articles that circulated at the time of Dughmosh's case and the types of language they used to describe the incident did not parallel the predictions laid out in the literature. In other cases where the accused displayed behaviours similar to those displayed by Dughmosh, they mitigated the court's reaction and rendered the accused unable to stand trial. Dughmosh's violence was not explained away, and she was quickly labelled as deadly and dangerous. In her case, her unusual behaviour and gender should have mitigated the media's response, but instead, she received harsher coverage. Whether this can be attributed to her race, religion, or other characteristics is unclear. The lack of parallels between Dughmosh's case and the literature provides a real-world illustration of the limited understandings of female radicalization and terrorism.

Further, Dughmosh's case exemplifies a particularly challenging aspect of CVE initiatives. The question remains—how do we deal with those who, like Dughmosh, are intercepted and brought back to Canada after attempting to join an extremist organization? Had Dughmosh's RTV been understood and addressed through deradicalization programs, perhaps the Canadian Tire incident could have been avoided. This analysis proves helpful in understanding where the disconnects and gaps in our knowledge exist. For example, the role of the internet was not detailed in Dughmosh's case; however, scholars have pointed out that online radicalization has been known to have significant impact on Muslim women (Windsor 2020). Research has indicated that gender roles impact identity perception, especially when cultural identity and secular identity conflict. While shifts in modern technology and globalization challenge traditional elements of Islam, in non-Islamic secularized cultures a dynamic is developing where Muslim women are increasingly having to balance religious guidance, familial pressures, and practical realities (Cone 2016, 45). This is important, because research has shown that female terrorists often feel that Western culture is intrusive and want to keep their own cultures intact (Sixta 2008). Since Dughmosh's online presence was not detailed in news media, her vulnerabilities to online radicalization remain unknown.

Online recruitment has been noted as a major tool in the hands of terrorist organizations (CSD 2016; CPRLV 2016; Cone 2016; Pearson 2016). In 2004, the first women's jihadist web-based magazine was launched, teaching women how to support men in the field (Shute 2013). In 2011, an al-Qaida magazine provided female readers with advice on matters ranging from beauty tips to suicide bombing (Shute 2013). ISIS was the first terrorist organization to launch a systematic campaign to reach out to women using gender-specific data (Malik 2018). They appealed to women by promising that joining the group would enhance their status as women, and that they would be appreciated and awarded respect in their roles, more than the Western world afforded them, thereby leveraging negative experiences of marginalization (CPRLV 2016). Jihadist propaganda has played a major role in mobilizing young Western women, as those who are ISIS sympathizers are highly active online and on social media as creators and distributors of propaganda (CPRLV 2016).

An important case that caught the attention of scholars was that of Roshonara Choudhry, the first British woman convicted of a violent Islamist attack. The prevailing radicalization theories portrayed her as a "lone wolf" and brainwashed victim of internet indoctrination, without agency (Pearson 2016). Scholars have disagreed with the concept of a "lone wolf," because RTV is inherently a social phenomenon (National Institute of Justice 2015). The internet was an essential factor in Choudhry's radicalization, and she became a symbol of "self-radicalization" (Pearson 2016). Much like Dughmosh, Choudhry was deemed mentally fit to stand trial, and she did not accept the court's jurisdiction (Pearson 2016). Choudhry's case became important because it was portrayed as an exception to the rule. It was understood as deviating from conventional understandings of RTV processes, because Choudhry lacked contacts and her gendered radicalization took place online (Pearson 2016, 9). However, Choudhry should not be considered the exception to the rule, as research has shown that more women are radicalizing online.

Pearson (2016) notes that in 2015 over sixty women and girls left the United Kingdom to join ISIS, and they were believed to have radicalized online. There is a marked lack of up-to-date statistics and information on this. Choudhry's radicalization became of particular interest, because she was deemed an average teenager and exceptional award-winning university student before she carried out the violent attack six months after her initial exposure to radical material online. The rapid nature of Choudhry's RTV displays the importance of responding with CVE and deradicalizing initiatives. Both Dughmosh's and Choudhry's cases, although dissimilar in many respects, exemplify how contemporary realities of terrorism include gendered and religious identity factors that require further investigation.

Policy Implications and Directions for Future Research

Continued research is needed on female RTV, for Western Muslim women in particular and on female terrorism more generally (CPRLV 2016). The issues discussed in this chapter could not be addressed in sufficient depth and should be explored further. Future research should focus on gendered considerations pertaining to RTV, including cultural considerations and differences within women as a group. When variations between women are recognized, research on specific risks and protective factors can be identified for different communities and cultures.

More exploration is needed on how social marginalization experienced by women plays a role in RTV, and on the impacts of the "gendered Islamophobia" experienced by Muslim women, as it operates socially and politically to deny material advantages to Muslim women in the West, ultimately leading to their isolation (Zine 2006). Efforts must focus on ways of reducing hostility and increasing the inclusion of minorities in the West, because terrorist groups strategically use anti-Muslim discourse to increase hostility in Western countries. Further, the emerging phenomenon of Western women and Islamic converts radicalizing online, their multiple identities, and their rejection of Western models of womanhood require further reflection and study (CPRLV 2016).

Most importantly, pathways for women to deradicalize from terrorist organizations need to be developed. The more that is known about the gendered nature of radicalization to violent extremism, the better it can be identified and addressed. Terrorist organizations have recognized the benefits of engaging in gendered recruitment, yet CVE initiatives have not been able to understand female RTV adequately.

Notes

1. The author does not provide a formal definition of terrorism, acknowledging that the term "terrorism" is open to multiple and contested interpretations and used for political and ideological purposes.
2. "In Canada, the definition of terrorist activity includes an act or omission undertaken, inside or outside Canada, for a political, religious or ideological purpose that is intended to intimidate the public with respect to its security, including its economic security, or to compel a person, government or organization (whether inside or outside Canada) from doing or refraining from doing any act, and that intentionally causes one of a number of specified forms of serious harm" (Government of Canada 2022, n.p.).

References

Blatchford, Christie. 2017a. "Entitled Suspect Pleads Not Guilty; Dog-and-Pony Show Goes to Trial in Terror Case." *National Post*, September 21.

Blatchford, Christie. 2017b. "The Modern New Face of a Terror Case." *Star-Phoenix* (Saskatoon), August 22.

Bloom, Mia. 2011a. "Bombshells: Women and Terror." *Gender Issues* 28 (1–2): 1–21.

Bloom, Mia. 2011b. *Bombshell: Women and Terrorism*. Philadelphia: University of Pennsylvania Press.

Bloom, Mia. 2017. "Constructing Expertise: Terrorist Recruitment and 'Talent Spotting' in the PIRA, Al Qaeda, and ISIS." *Studies in Conflict and Terrorism* 40 (7): 603–623.

Canada News Wire (CNW). 2017. "RCMP Charges Woman with Terrorism Offences." July 4: 1.

Centre for the Prevention of Radicalization Leading to Violence (CPRLV). 2016. *Women and Violent Radicalization: Research Report*. Québec: Conseil du statut de la femme. https://www.csf.gouv.qc.ca/wp-content/uploads/radicalisation_recherche_anglais.pdf.

Centre for the Study of Democracy (CSD). 2016. "Understanding Radicalization: Review of the Literature." Sofia: CSD.

Cone, Heather Ann. 2016. "Differential Reinforcement in the Online Radicalization of Western-Muslim Women Converts." PHD diss., Walden University.

Government of Canada. 2013. *Building Resilience Against Terrorism: Canada's Counter-Terrorism Strategy*. Report. Ottawa: Public Safety Canada, Government of Canada. July 27. https://www.publicsafety.gc.ca/cnt/rsrcs/pblctns/rslnc-gnst-trrrsm/index-en.aspx.

Kostes, Lauren N. 2015. "Domestic Violence and American Asylum Law: The Complicated and Convoluted Road Post Matter of A-R-C-G." *Connecticut Journal of International Law* 30 (2): 211–240.

Malik, Nikita. 2018. "Why Do We Underestimate the Role of Women in Terrorist Organizations?" *Forbes*, September 26. https://www.forbes.com/sites/nikitamalik/2018/09/26/why-do-we-underestimate-the-role-of-women-in-terrorist-organizations/.

Nacos, Brigitte L. 2005. "The Portrayal of Female Terrorists in the Media: Similar Framing Patterns in the News Coverage of Women in Politics and in Terrorism." *Studies in Conflict and Terrorism* 28 (5): 435–451.

National Institute of Justice. 2015. "Radicalization and Violent Extremism: Lessons Learned from Canada, the UK and the US." July 28–30. Arlington: US Department of Justice. https://www.ojp.gov/pdffiles1/nij/249947.pdf.

Pearson, Elizabeth. 2016. "The Case of Roshonara Choudhry: Implications for Theory on Online Radicalization, ISIS Women, and the Gendered Jihad." *Policy and Internet* 8 (1): 5–33.

Saeed, Aamir. 2023. "Pakistan's 'First Priority' is Countering Terrorism from Afghanistan, PM Tells UNGA." *Arab News*, September 22. https://www.arabnews.com/node/2378876/world.

Saeedi, Nika, and Rosalie Fransen. 2018. "Violent Extremism Reopens the Conversation About Women and Peace." United Nations Development Programme, March 29. http://www.undp.org/content/undp/en/home/blog/2018/violent-extremism-reopens-the-conversation-about-women-and-peace.html.

Shute, Joe. 2013. "Convert One Woman, You Convert an Entire Family." *Daily Telegraph*, September 28: 23.

Sixta, Christine. 2008. "The Illusive Third Wave: Are Female Terrorists the New 'New Women' in Developing Societies?" *Journal of Women, Politics and Policy* 29 (2): 261–288.

Streigher, Jason-Leigh. 2015. "Violent-Extremism: An Examination of a Definitional Dilemma." In Conference Proceedings, 8th Australian Security and Intelligence Conference, held November 30–December 2, 2015, 5–86. Perth: SRI Security Research Institute, Edith Cowan University. https://doi.org/10.4225/75/57a945ddd335.2.

Windsor, Leah. 2020. "The Language of Radicalization: Female Internet Recruitment to Participation in ISIS Activities." *Terrorism and Political Violence* 32 (3): 506–538.

Zine, Jasmin. 2006. "Unveiled Sentiments: Gendered Islamophobia and Experiences of Veiling Among Muslim Girls in a Canadian Islamic School." *Equity and Excellence in Education* 39 (3): 239–252.

8

Speaking Out About Abuse, Patriarchy, and Misogyny Against South Asian Women

An Examination of Because We Are Girls

PERUVEMBA S. JAYA

Introduction

> In one situation a young woman was being sexually abused by a family member. When the school and family services found out and decided to intervene on her behalf, against the advice of the girl, this girl's life changed for the worse. Her parents now viewed her as sexually suspect and blamed her for the abuse. As a result of the experience she has learned not to reach out for help either within or outside the family and deals with the effects of the abuse on her own. (Handa 1997, 34)

At the outset, I would like to locate myself in the context of this investigation into intimate violence. I am a cisgender woman from India, and part of the South Asian diaspora in Canada. I am also an upper-caste Hindu woman from India and thus in a privileged position in the Indian social system. But in the Canadian context,

I recognize my position as a woman of colour with experiences of sexism and racism, who is aware of the political nuances of South Asian geopolitics. As such, my identity while in India and later in Canada has provided the basis for my understanding of the challenging and sometimes difficult aspects of being part of South Asian feminisms. I further locate myself as a transnational and postcolonial feminist who is also connected by a sense of solidarity to South Asian feminist scholars in the diaspora. Simultaneously, there are also points of disjuncture and contradiction within this larger group, because South Asian feminist diasporic scholars are not a monolithic entity. In this chapter, I focus on the specific experience of three sisters from a Punjabi Indo-Canadian South Asian background in Canada, who were the subjects of a documentary that spotlights their particular experience of sexual abuse and violence within their family.

Because We Are Girls is a Canadian documentary film directed by Baljit Sangra, released in 2019 by the National Film Board of Canada. The film is about Jeeti, Kira, and Salakshana Pooni, three Punjabi Indo-Canadian sisters from Williams Lake, British Columbia, who went public in adulthood about allegations of childhood sexual abuse by a relative. The sisters belonged to an immigrant family, with their parents having migrated to Canada from India, and they stated that they decided to tell their story to protect their daughters as well as other young relatives. I examine this film using the theoretical perspectives of ethnic identity theory (Phinney 1989, 2000, 2003), and locating it within the context of postcolonial feminism (Mohanty 1984, 1991) and a system of entrenched patriarchy.

At the same time, it is important to recognize that constructions of gendered violence in South Asian diaspora communities must be tempered with the need to guard against colonialist and racist victimizing and disempowering, as well as stigmatizing, family violence as a uniquely South Asian phenomenon. This has been discussed in the context of patriarchy and honour (Grewal 2013; Abji and Korteweg 2021). Additionally, the National Film Board of Canada is a government body, and hence some important questions must be raised: what is the process for deciding which documentaries will be chosen to be made or funded? Is the concern to represent immigrant women aimed at highlighting only particular aspects of their lives? Are there films being made about celebrated strong South Asian women who are active in the Canadian landscape, in terms of both polity and other aspects of public life? These questions are worth pondering, in order to acknowledge that representations of South Asian women tend to further the stereotyping of South Asian communities as "backward" and the women as silent victims and acquiescent in their oppression.

While acknowledging the aspect of stereotyping and stigmatizing, and being aware of the dangers of doing so, my goal is to highlight the agency of these women and their challenging of expected normative notions of behaviour and silence. To me, this is the most significant contribution of the documentary. By displaying agency, telling their own story, coming out publicly, and doing so with great courage, the women portrayed in this film challenge the stereotypes of South Asian women as submissive, meek, and not capable of acting for themselves. Hence, while the focus is on the abuse and violence, I propose that the film does this in a manner that privileges the women's stories in their own words and showcases their strength and resilience. To do this, I use a transnational feminist and postcolonial feminist lens and situate the experiences of the women in a particular context framed by their history and their racialized immigrant identities. Adopting these frames, I argue, separates the film from a generic Eurocentric feminist perspective and emphasizes the agency of the women. "Only one percent of women make it to where we are. Whatever happens now, happens" were the words whispered by one of the sisters to the other two, as they waited outside the Supreme Court of British Columbia in Williams Lake on a cold wintry day (Sangra 2019, 00:00:52).

Identity, Inclusion, Joy, Belonging

The film contextualizes the violence against the three sisters within scenes of their childhood culled from home videos, scenes of each of their weddings, colourful ethnic attire and the laughter, joy, and celebration of rituals, religious festivals and visits to the *gurdwara*, and dancing—all of these often juxtaposed with short snippets from old Bollywood movies that might have been made at the time of their childhood and youth. There seems to be an attempt to include glamour, a dream-like quality that conveys a sense of wanting to be like the Bollywood actresses and heroines in the movies, creating a charmed and make-believe world. There is a clear reference to their shared heritage, with a sense of belonging and sense of pride that scholars have associated with some of the benefits of ethnic identity. A sense of identification with a particular ethnic group (Tajfel 1981; Phinney and Rotheram 1987), and a sense of belonging and commitment to core values and beliefs are some of the characteristics of ethnic identity (Phinney 1990, 2000, 2003). Phinney and Ong (2007) write, citing Tajfel and Turner (1986): "Ethnic identity is also an important contributor to an individual's well-being; individuals derive positive self-attitudes from belonging to groups that are meaningful to them" (275).

Aspects of ethnic identity that are important include participation in religious and cultural activities and attitudes toward one's own and other ethnic groups, as well as music and food preferences and patterns of affiliation or friendship. Trimble and Dickenson (2005) refer to this as a ritualistic or stylistic emphasis, which becomes significant when ethnic group members are interacting in areas far from their places of origin. The authors mention that it is an example of situated ethnicity and situated ethnic identity.

Ethnic identity and immigrants' experiences and reception by the receiving society are interrelated, as pointed out by Phinney and colleagues (2001): "Ethnic identity and identification with the new society are related to each other, how these identities are related to the adaptation of immigrants, and how these relationships vary across groups and national contexts" (493-494). In the case of the women in the film, identification with ethnic identity is highlighted as an important aspect of their being part of the Punjabi Indo-Canadian group. This emphasis puts a spotlight on the collective, including the family being above all else. This came to override the women's own safety and comfort, as evidenced by the abuse they experienced.

Patriarchy, Honour, and Shame

> We're daughters, we're not wanted anyway. Since we were little girls, he [their father] made us feel that we are not wanted through punishment, through him not giving us love. Mum said he didn't come home for three weeks when he knew he had a daughter. (Sangra 2019, 01:00:55)

The brother says: "You know, in the Indian culture, it is always the girls. We blame the girls" (Sangra 2019, 39:56). Later, the parents say: "We did say to the girls, 'Why didn't you tell us sooner?' They were scared" (40:14). Basically, they were scared because of what people would think due to the cultural context and milieu.

Postcolonial feminist scholars who grapple with issues of domestic violence within their own communities express caution about the danger of feeding colonial discourses and strategies for dealing with the violence. In discussing issues around patriarchy and honour and shame in South Asian communities, Razack (2007) has pointed to the dangers of using what she terms "culture talk" to both categorize and separate such acts as specific to racialized and culturalized minorities. This results in creating a persona of women and girls who are part of particular cultures and victims of their culture. "The image of 'barbaric' men who perpetuate violence because of culture or religion are conjured in the Canadian imagination as bodies that need to be civilized and controlled" (Mucina and Jamal 2021, 3). This, as examined elsewhere under the discussion of patriarchy by Grewal (2013), creates and separates the South Asian racialized woman as other, and as someone who needs to be rescued by the Eurocentric Western civilizing influence and social narrative, through assimilation. Meanwhile, in calling for more protection and support from within influential sectors of the community for young women facing family violence, scholars such as Mucina and Jamal (2021) emphasize the specificity of honour killing as "a form of violence that is ultimately related to sexuality and embodied transgression, largely impacting women and girls" (3). They describe sexual violence against racialized women and girls as "a key site of contestation over rights—state versus community, secular versus religious, local versus global, and individual versus community and group" (see also Jamal 2015; Mucina 2018).

Transnational feminism rejects the homogeneous and universal construction of women's experiences. Grewal and Kaplan (1994) emphasize the necessity of critiquing the Western model of feminism, as well as deconstructing and pointing out the limitations of a global universal feminism. This is important, as women's experiences in different parts of the world are particular, historical, and contextual, and take into account both the relationship/s of women to their locations and the context of global movements across different countries. Combined with postcolonial feminism, this provides a frame for us to understand and locate the particular experience presented in the film within a particular backdrop. The discourse of universal feminism negates the experience of non-white, non-Western women. But postcolonial feminism provides a way of taking note of the nuances of the female experience, by paying heed to unique and individual experiences, shaped by history, location, place, race, ethnicity, and the colonial backdrop, in understanding the experiences of women, both Western and non-Western (Mohanty 2003; Minh-Ha 1989; Narayan 1997; Anzaldua 1987).

Abuse, Pain, and Anguish

> I was 11 years old. It was my cousin, someone my parents trusted. The day that man came to our house, we were told, "This is your brother. You respect him, you call him '*paaji*.'" The abuse was sexual, and it was emotional. So, there were certain things said so that you stayed in your order [place]...Because we were girls, they could take advantage of us. My dad and uncle really supported him, [and] we gave him that respect. He had full authority over us because he's a male. I thought it happened to me because I deserved it...You can't tell anybody, your mom or sisters. Bad girls get shipped off. (Sangra 2019, 00:11.53)

Through the words of the sisters in individual interviews, as well as collectively and in their interactions with each other and with the children of one of the sisters, they share their stories of anguish and of the sexual assault, in both general and very graphic terms. As young children, they endured this and had to suffer through years of sexual abuse with no help, support, or succour, or intervention from responsible adults and parents. The perpetrator planted in them the thought that they were unworthy and fit for abuse, and that they had somehow brought the abuse upon themselves.

The stories of these sisters resonate with the abundant literature that examines the violence experienced by immigrant women with the coming together of sexism and racism (e.g., Agnew 1996, 1993; Boyd 1999, 1990; Calliste 1996, 1989; Das Gupta 1996; Dhruvarajan 2000; Ng 1993, 1987, 1990; Preston and Man 1999; Preston, Lo, and Wang 2003; Tastsoglou and Preston 2005; Tastsoglou and Miedema 2005). While a patriarchal social structure can be identified, there are many causes of domestic violence, and studies of specific ethnic communities focus on the nexus between patriarchy and racism and abuse (Barnes 2001; Drakich and Guberman 1988; Miedema 1999). Miedema (1999) and Miedema and Wachholz (2000, 2002) identify the interplay of cultural norms and structural oppression as barriers to accessing services. It seems that the problem is exacerbated for immigrant South Asian women. The challenges of settlement and migration, coupled with being dependent on a spouse, have been found to increase vulnerability to stress in relationships. Ayyub's study (2000) found that one out of four South Asian immigrant women in the US had reported domestic abuse, but many may not have opened up about it due to the fear of social stigma. Almost eighteen percent of South Asian immigrants across the world suffer violence at the hands of intimate partners (Hurwitz et al. 2006). Some scholars claim that this figure could be even higher, arguing that the actual rates are between 30 and 40 percent (Finfgeld-Connett and Johnson 2013). This can also be extended beyond intimate partner violence to include violence against women by the extended family in the South Asian immigrant community (Abraham 2000).

Postcolonial feminism provides a way of contextualizing immigrant women's lives in a nuanced way by understanding the complexity of women's experiences. Chandra Talpade Mohanty (1984) critiques Western feminist theory, saying that it creates a "singular 'Third World woman'" (334), as a byword for "underdevelopment, oppressive traditions, high illiteracy, rural and urban poverty, religious fanaticism and overpopulation" (Mohanty 1991, 5-6).

Hamam (2015) states that the presence of (non-Western) women creates a range of different, often incompatible worldviews, writing: "Furthermore, it emphasizes that women's experiences cannot be contained within a single narrative of oppression. In other words, it constructs women's identities and narratives as historically specific yet contestable and changing in interrelated ways. This shows that women in postcolonial cultures are interlocked within plural power axes such as race, class, and gender, all of which constitute their lives and responses" (10). Postcolonial feminism recognizes that not all women's lives and lived realities and experiences are the same, and that we need to recognize differences due to race, class, location, and the particular influences of past colonization and vestiges of colonial discourses. As Hamam (2015) states, "as a result, the presence of (non-Western) women creates a spectrum of realities and worldviews which are similar, different, and incompatible" (10).

Discussions of honour and shame tend to separate and box in South Asian women's experiences, and to perpetuate the Eurocentric gaze. However, such discussions are relevant because they also explain the focus on family honour above all else. This theme is clearly addressed in the documentary, which uncovers how the parents were more focussed on *"log kya kahenge"* (what will people say?), even when it jeopardized the safety and well-being of their daughters.

Rebellion and Confrontation

> My motive was always [that] I didn't want him to do this horrendous debilitating disgusting perverted act on anybody else.

> I didn't want anybody to go through that. I told my aunt in Edmonton first, then hell broke loose...[everyone] thought I was making up a story. (Sangra 2019, 00:29:18)

> You say you support my decision. What support do I need? You never asked us. You ask about us in a superficial way, "Are you okay? Will you have tea?" But not [about] the issue. Daddy knew about it but didn't support us. He would say, "Don't sit beside him." I never did. I was in my room, and he would come and touch me. (Sangra 2019, 01:03:44)

The sisters' mother admits: "We wanted to keep it hidden/under wraps...In 2006, we told you [the daughters], it was no longer hidden." Their father says in denial, and defensively: "I told you to avoid the thing." One of the sisters asks: "Did you confront him and tell him, 'If you touch my daughter, I will do something to you?'" The father says: "You are accusing us. Is there no fault of yours? Did you not have any responsibilities? I had my limitations...I could not be violent." One of the daughters says: "When you say nothing, you condone that action. You didn't help me, Dad." The father says: "When such a situation develops to such an extent, people and society will never understand whose fault it is" (Sangra 2019, 01:14:16). But finally, the mother breaks down and says she is sorry, and the father admits he is proud of their making it (the sexual abuse) public and acknowledges their courage.

The documentary focuses on the courage of the three sisters in taking on their patriarchal family, as well as the entire Punjabi Indo-Canadian community, by becoming vocal and empowered and speaking their truth, by finding their voice and breaking their decades-old silence about what they had undergone as children. There is a powerful scene where there is a confrontation/conversation with their parents and younger brother. They directly accuse their parents of not protecting them, not believing in them, and not standing by them. There are tears and recriminations. The sisters tell their father that they were not safe in their own home, and that he did nothing about it. The parents seem rather embarrassed, but the viewer is left with the feeling that, for them, the dishonour and shame that would have ensued in the larger community—*"log kya kahenge?"*—was their overriding thought; hence they chose to gloss over the crimes of the perpetrator, who repeatedly molested their young daughters in their own home. This part of the documentary is shocking, heart-wrenching, and heartbreaking. The mother relents and apologizes for not being there for them. But through the layers of patriarchy, the sisters and their voices are loud, finally clear and strident after so many years.

Conclusion

The documentary throws light on the misogyny and patriarchy that had such disturbing and horrifying repercussions and created a very permanent impact, scarring the lives of the sisters. However, I think it is important to understand the issue of abuse in the South Asian context in a nuanced way, by looking at how cultural and patriarchal restraints are shaped regionally in different parts of South Asia. Thus, we must take note of matrilineal societies and structures like those of the Nagas in Nagaland or the Nayars of Kerala, wherein women's status and role in society are defined and bounded in a completely separate cultural and social space than in predominantly patriarchal societies. Can we then make any generalizations about South Asian women in Canada, and does this particular experience represent the reality of South Asian diasporic women's gendered lives and experiences?

Patriarchal constructions of society and institutionalized, structural, and deep-rooted patriarchy provide legitimacy for perpetrating violence against women and normalizing such violence. Family members are silenced and co-opted into upholding these very powerful structures and mechanisms of patriarchy. Kandiyoti (1988) illustrates this idea with specific reference to the South Asian context, stating that this patriarchy gets perpetuated and reproduced because, traditionally, in agrarian and agricultural economies the senior men have power and control over the entire family. This mindset carries over transnationally into the space of the Canadian social milieu.

How can entrenched patriarchal systems be overcome when they are deep-rooted and embedded and taken for granted in family structures, as seen in this documentary? What about the disruptions/disjunctures among South Asian communities, such that in this case the Punjabi Indo-Canadian experience may not mirror the experience in all South Asian regions, even just within India? How can this be reconciled with powerful strong female voices in South Asia, from women of influence in many spheres? How do we resolve such contradictions?

And then there is the discussion wherein we can see how patriarchy is not just unique or specific to South Asian communities, but could have been highlighted to further the narrative of the Eurocentric project of rescuing "brown women from brown men." It is very important, therefore, to nuance our understanding by emphasizing that patriarchy is not just being accentuated in the case of racialized bodies. It is not just the preserve of South Asian communities, but has in fact been used as a mechanism to separate South Asian communities and their practices. Thus, I would like to end with this powerful quote from Grewal (2013): "Yet an essentialist notion of the term 'patriarchy' has become naturalized in relation to the 'Global South' (especially Muslim communities) as well as among migrant communities from the Global South in the West. How do we explain the erasure of patriarchy as a concept for the 'West' especially since there is considerable evidence that gender inequalities (not to mention many forms of violence, often fatal) persist also in that same 'West'?" (6).

References

Abji, Salina, and Korteweg, Anna. C. 2021. "Honour-Based Violence and the Politics of Culture in Canada: Advancing a Cultural Analysis of Multiscalar Violence." *International Journal of Child, Youth and Family Studies* 12 (1): 73–92.

Abraham, Margaret. 2000. *Speaking the Unspeakable: Marital Violence Among South Asian Immigrants in the United States*. New Brunswick, NJ: Rutgers University Press.

Agnew, Vijay. 1993. "Feminism and South Asian Immigrant Women in Canada." In *Ethnicity, Identity, Migration: The South Asian Context*, edited by Morton Israel and Narendra K. Wagle, 142–164. Toronto: University of Toronto Press.

Agnew, Vijay. 1996. *Resisting Discrimination: Women from Asia, Africa and the Caribbean and the Women's Movement in Canada.* Toronto: University of Toronto Press.

Anzaldua, Gloria E. 1987. *Borderlands/La Frontera: The New Mestiza.* San Francisco: Aunt Lute.

Ayyub, Ruksana. 2000. "Domestic Violence in the South Asian Muslim Immigrant Population in the United States." *Journal of Social Distress and the Homeless* 9 (3): 237-248.

Barnes, Brittany McCarthy. 2001. "Family Violence Knows No Cultural Boundaries." *Journal of Family and Consumer Sciences* 93 (1): 11-14.

Boyd, Monica. 1990. "Immigrant Women: Language, Socioeconomic Inequalities and Policy Issues." In *Ethnic Demography: Canadian Immigrant, Racial and Cultural Variations*, edited by Shiva Halli, Frank Trovato, and Leo Driedger, 275-296. Ottawa: Carleton University Press.

Boyd, Monica. 1999. "Integrating Gender, Language, and Race." In *Immigrant Canada: Demographic, Economic, and Social Challenges*, edited by Shiva Halli and Leo Driedger, 282-306. Toronto: University of Toronto Press.

Calliste, Agnes. 1989. "Canada's Immigration Policy and Domestics from the Caribbean: The Second Domestic Scheme." In *Race, Class and Gender: Bonds and Barriers*, edited by Jesse Vorst et al., 133-165. Winnipeg: Society for Socialist Studies.

Calliste, Agnes. 1996. "Anti-Racism Organizing and Resistance in Nursing: African Canadian Women." *Canadian Review of Sociology and Anthropology* 33 (3): 361-390.

Das Gupta, Tania. 1996. *Racism and Paid Work.* Toronto: Garamond Press.

Dhruvarajan, Vanaja. 2000. "People of Colour and National Identity in Canada." *Journal Of Canadian Studies* 35 (2): 166-175.

Drakich, Janice, and Connie Guberman. 1988. "Violence in the Family." In *Family Matters: Sociology and Contemporary Canadian Families*, edited by Karen Anderson, 201-235. Scarborough: Nelson Canada.

Finfgeld-Connett, Deborah, and Diane E. Johnson. 2013. "Abused South Asian Women in Westernized Countries and Their Experiences of Seeking Help." *Issues in Mental Health Nursing* 34 (12): 863-873.

Grewal, Inderpal. 2013. "Outsourcing Patriarchy: Feminist Encounters, Transnational Mediations and the Crime of 'Honor Killings.'" *International Feminist Journal of Politics* 15 (1): 1-19.

Grewal, Inderpal, and Caren Kaplan, eds. 1994. *Scattered Hegemonies: Postmodernity and Transnational Feminist Practices*. Minneapolis: University of Minnesota Press.

Hamam, Kinana. 2015. "Postcolonialism and Feminism: An Intersectional Discourse of Reconstruction." *Postcolonial Studies Association Newsletter* 15: 10-12.

Handa, Amita. 1997. "Caught Between Omissions: Exploring 'Culture Conflict' Among Second Generation South Asian Women in Canada." PHD diss., University of Toronto.

Hurwitz, Elizabeth J., Jhumka Gupta, Rosalyn Liu, Jay G. Silverman, and Anita Raj. 2006. "Intimate Partner Violence Associated with Poor Health Outcomes in U.S. South Asian Women." *Journal of Immigrant & Minority Health* 8 (3): 251-261.

Jamal, Amina. 2015. "Piety, Transgression and the Feminist Debate on Muslim Women: Transnationalizing the Victim-Subject of Honor-Related Violence." *Signs: Journal of Women in Culture and Society* 41 (1): 55-79.

Kandiyoti, Denis. 1988. "Bargaining with Patriarchy." *Gender and Society* 2 (3): 274-290.

Miedema, Baukje. 1999. "Barriers and Strategies: How to Improve Services for Abused Immigrant Women in New Brunswick." Research Paper Series 1. Fredericton: University of New Brunswick.

Miedema, Baukje, and Sandra Wachholz. 1998. *A Complex Web: Access to Justice for Abused Immigrant Women in New Brunswick*. Status of Women Canada. https://publications.gc.ca/collections/Collection/SW21-24-1998E.pdf.

Miedema, Baukje, and Sandra Wachholz. 2000. "Risk, Fear, Harm: Immigrant Women's Perception of the 'Policing Solution' to Woman Abuse." *Crime, Law and Social Change* 34 (October): 301–317.

Minh-ha, Trinh. 1989. *Woman, Native, Other: Writing Postcoloniality and Feminism*. Bloomington: Indiana University Press.

Mohanty, Chandra Talpade. 1984. "Under Western Eyes: Feminist Scholarship and Colonial Discourses." *Boundary 2* 12 (3): 333–358.

Mohanty, Chandra Talpade. 1991. "Cartographies of Struggle: Third World Women and the Politics of Feminism." In *Third World Women and the Politics of Feminism*, edited by Ann Russo and Lourdes Torres, 1–47. Bloomington: Indiana University Press.

Mohanty, Chandra Talpade. 2003. *Feminism Without Borders: Decolonizing Theory, Practicing Solidarity*. Durham: Duke University Press.

Mucina, Mandeep. K. 2018. "Exploring the Role of 'Honor' in Son Preference and Daughter Deficit within the Punjabi Diaspora in Canada." *Canadian Journal of Development Studies* 39 (3): 426–442.

Mucina, Mandeep K., and Amina Jamal. 2021. "Introduction to Special Issue: Assimilation, Interrupted: Transforming Discourses of Culture- and Honor-Based Violence in Canada." *International Journal of Child, Youth and Family Studies* 12 (1): 1–12.

Narayan, Uma. 1997. *Dislocating Cultures: Identities, Traditions, and Third-World Feminism*. New York: Routledge.

Ng, Roxana. 1987. "Sexism, Racism, Nationalism." In *Race, Class, Gender: Bonds and Barriers*, edited by Jesse Vorst et al., 10–25. Winnipeg: Society for Socialist Studies.

Ng, Roxana. 1990. "Immigrant Women and Institutionalized Racism." In *Changing Patterns: Women in Canada*, edited by Sandra Burt, Lorraine Code, and Lindsay Dorney, 184–203. Toronto: McClelland and Stewart.

Ng, Roxana. 1993. "Racism, Sexism and Nation-Building in Canada." In *Race, Identity and Representation in Education*, edited by Warren Crichlow, Cameron McCarthy, Greg Dimitriadis, and Nadine Dolby, 50–59. New York: Routledge.

Phinney, Jean. 1989. "Stages of Ethnic Identity Development in Minority Group Adolescents." *Journal of Early Adolescence* 9 (1): 34–49.

Phinney, Jean S. 1990. "Ethnic Identity in Adolescents and Adults: Review of Research." *Psychological Bulletin* 108 (3): 499–514.

Phinney, Jean. 2000. "Ethnic Identity." In *Encyclopedia of Psychology*, vol. 1, edited by Alan E. Kazdin, 254–259. New York: Oxford University Press.

Phinney, Jean. 2003. "Ethnic Identity and Acculturation." In *Acculturation: Advances in Theory, Measurement, and Applied Research*, edited by Kevin Chun, Pamela Balls Organista, and Gerardo Marin, 63–81. Washington: American Psychological Association.

Phinney, Jean, Gabriel Horenczyk, Karmela Liebkind, and Paul Vedder. 2001. "Ethnic Identity, Immigration, and Well-Being: An Interactional Perspective." *Journal of Social Issues* 57, (3): 493–510.

Phinney, Jean S., and Anthony D. Ong. 2007. "Conceptualization and Measurement of Ethnic Identity: Current Status and Future Directions." *Journal of Counseling Psychology* 54 (3): 271–281.

Phinney, Jean S., and Mary Jane Rotheram, eds. 1987. *Children's Ethnic Socialization: Pluralism and Development*. Newberry Park: Sage.

Preston, Valerie, Lucia Lo, and Shuguang Wang. 2003. "Immigrants' Economic Status in Toronto: Stories of Triumph and Disappointment." In *The World in a City*, edited by Paul Anisef and Michael Lanphier, 192–232. Toronto: University of Toronto Press.

Preston, Valerie, and Guida Man. 1999. "Employment Experiences of Chinese Immigrant Women: An Exploration of Diversity." *Canadian Woman Studies/Cahiers de la femme* 19 (3): 115–122.

Razack, Sherene. H. 2007. "The 'Shari'a Law Debate' in Ontario: The Modernity/Premodernity Distinction in Legal Efforts to Protect Women From Culture." *Feminist Legal Studies* 15, (1): 3–32.

Sangra, Baljit, dir. 2019. *Because We Are Girls*. Montreal: National Film Board of Canada. https://www.nfb.ca/film/because-we-are-girls/.

Tajfel, Henri. 1981. *Human Groups and Social Categories*. Cambridge: Cambridge University Press.

Tajfel, Henri, and John C. Turner. 1986. "The Social Identity Theory of Intergroup Behavior." In *Psychology of Intergroup Relations*, edited by Stephen Worchel and William Austin, 7–24. Chicago: Nelson Hall.

Tastsoglou, Evangelia, and Baukje Miedema. 2005. "'Working Much Harder and Always Having to Prove Yourself': Immigrant Women's Labour Force Experiences in the Canadian Maritimes." In *Gender Realities: Local and Global*, special volume of *Advances in Gender Research*, edited by Marcia Texler Segal and Vasilikie Demos, 201–233. Bingley: Emerald Publishing Group.

Tastsoglou, Evangelia, and Valerie Preston. 2005. "Gender, Immigration and Labour Market Integration: Where We Are and What We Still Need to Know." *Atlantis: A Women's Studies Journal* 30 (1): 46–59.

Trimble, Joseph, and Ryan Dickenson. 2005. "Ethnic Identity." In *Encyclopedia of Applied Developmental Science*, vol. 1, edited by Celia B. Fisher and Richard M. Lerner, 415–420. Newberry Park: Sage.

Not All Together

Gender, Sexuality, Class, and Diverse Patriarchies

9

The Names We Carry With Us

Challenging the Omission of Caste and Interrogating Caste Privilege Among South Asian Feminists in Canada

SAILAJA V. KRISHNAMURTI

Names and Feminist Inquiry

The politics of naming and names is a feminist concern. Naming practices are often an apparatus of heteropatriarchal family systems: in many parts of the world, names declare parentage, gender, marital status, ethnicity, and religion. Names can map unequal social relations and signal both marginalization and belonging. Names can diminish, harm, and subordinate, just as they can mark privilege and status. Names are mediated by the state and are part of systems of surveillance, and management, and control. Names connect us to territories and histories. As Anishinaabe writer Patty Krawec (2022) says, "Names are never neutral; they have something to teach us about our history and how we see ourselves in a place. They create a relationship" (12).

For many South Asians, names are intimately connected with histories of caste oppression and privilege across geographies, languages, and religious communities (Patel 2017). There is growing interest among South Asian diaspora feminist activists and academics in the intersecting dimensions of caste, gender, and sexuality. For people whose names are encoded by caste, entering into this work requires a reckoning: when we encounter each other, what do our names make legible, and what might they obscure? What do we choose to share or hide? What histories of domination and oppression do we carry in our names?

A commonly held belief among caste-privileged people in the South Asian diaspora is that casteism has somehow been left in the past. But this is a move to innocence, as Dia Da Costa (2018) writes: "People raised in relatively liberal homes like mine in particular are socialized to evade their caste identity. My Bengali Brahmin socialization is no exception to this rule of liberal casteism. Our relentlessly projected castelessness is a central modality through which we engage in the everyday terror of caste supremacy." The notion of shedding or "forgetting" caste without consequence is a privilege reserved for those who have never felt oppressed by it: caste discrimination persists across South Asia, despite laws preventing religious discrimination (Patel 2020; Sultana and Subedi 2016).

That caste persists in the US or Canada, or that it might take new forms, should not be a surprise. How could such a complex, deeply woven social system *not* follow us into diaspora? Whether we acknowledge it or not, South Asians have brought caste with us to Canada, and we wear it in our passports, professions, and religious practices. South Asian names are both a mechanism of and a metaphor for all the messy ways that people in diaspora encounter, navigate, recognize, and misrecognize each other. Those who were born into diaspora or who migrated as young children might not have the cultural capital or fluency of name recognition that their parents and grandparents might have, but they certainly encounter the vestiges of caste and religious conflict as they interact with other South Asians.

In this chapter, I take a feminist approach to South Asian diaspora onomastics to better understand the histories that our names tell. As a cisgender woman with inherited Hindu caste privilege, I draw on personal narratives about my own name as a heuristic for thinking through these questions. In the first part of this chapter, I provide a brief historical overview of the social encoding of South Asian names, focusing on the relationship between caste and

Hindu tradition. In the second section, I discuss the ways that caste travels, coagulates, and reasserts itself in diaspora, propelled by Hindu hegemony. In the final sections, I consider caste privilege in the context of Canada and South Asian diaspora social justice organizing.

Caste and South Asian Onomastics

> *In my first year of teaching Hinduism in a religion department, a retired Indian professor from another department drops by my office to introduce himself. He is pleased to learn that, like him, my language background is Telugu. He parses my surname and says, "So you are a brahmin." Switching seamlessly to Telugu, he asks, "Mi inti peru emiti?" (What is your house name?), since Krishnamurti doesn't give him the full information he seeks about my family. I suspect he is asking in part because he is wondering about my authenticity as a Hindu and as a teacher of Hinduism. I know that he is a brahmin because his name tells me so; he also leads rituals at the local temple, another indicator of his high caste status. I tell him that my inti peru is Oruganti; this name belongs to my father. He muses for a moment, trying to place it. He asks me my husband's name and occupation.*

From an anthropological perspective, the function of names in any social context is to distinguish individuals from each other, delineate social roles and relations, and mark boundaries of inclusion and exclusion. The ability to decode this information requires local and linguistic familiarity and a degree of cultural capital. In many naming traditions around the world, people combine a personal/individual name and other names that identify one's ancestral family, clan, location, trade, or status. In South Asia, language, region, and ethnicity are often signalled through names. And since many names reflect figures and concepts in religious traditions, South Asians are often able to quickly identify whether someone's religious background matches their own.

Caste brings many more layers of complexity to the parsing of South Asian names. The term "caste" refers to an entanglement of hierarchical systems of social relations that vary across geography and history. In general, caste rules regulate occupation, marriage, and commensality, and access to religious space (Omvedt 2017). Caste names distinguish between those who have access to cultural, religious, and power and those who are oppressed by that power. While the practice of caste tends to be most closely associated with Hindus, casteism and caste-like social hierarchies exist in other religious communities. Depending on cultural and linguistic proximity, South Asians can often guess a person's caste ancestry when they hear their name.

Scholars differentiate between two concepts that are both translated into English as caste: the concepts of *varna*, the Hindu caste groups described in the Vedas, and *jati*, which refers to the many categories of traditional hereditary occupations across South Asia (Rao 2009). Varna and jati have intermeshed in different ways over time. Varna tends to be understood in similar ways across Hindu South Asia. The four hierarchically organized varnas as described in Hindu texts are *brahmin*/priest, *kshatriya*/warrior, *vaishya*/merchant, and *shudra*/peasant. The brahmins, at the top, are considered the most "pure" and closest to divinity, and with each varna that follows, purity and proximity to the divine is seen as further diminished. Caste is understood as hereditary and patrilineal. Those who are born into one of the four varna groups are called *savarna*, or with caste, and they have different levels of access to knowledge and rituals depending on their caste status. Hindu rituals often require a priest—a brahmin man—to oversee them. Hindu temples restrict entry based on caste status. Food practices such as vegetarianism indicate caste boundaries. Hindu marriages traditionally occur endogamously within caste groups (Chakravarti 2018).

Below and outside of the varna hierarchy are those who are called *avarna* or "without caste." This includes Adivasis (Indigenous "tribal" communities) and members of oppressed-caste groups whose traditional occupations demand the most "impure" forms of physical labour in the community, such as tending animals, clearing refuse, managing human waste, and handling the dead. The contemporary term that many in this group have chosen to use is

"Dalit" (Omvedt 2006). Dalit workers experience many forms of marginalization, discrimination, extreme poverty, and violence. Dalit women are vulnerable to sexual abuse and exploitation (Irudayam, Mangubhai, and Lee 2014).

"Jati" is another term translated as "caste," or sometimes as "subcaste." It refers to the myriad names identifying roles and occupations in the community, and unlike varna, this varies across South Asia by language, geography, and religious tradition. Among Hindus, the two concepts of caste roughly overlap, so that jatis tend to be associated with varna status. While only caste Hindus have a varna, many South Asians, including Dalits, have a jati in their ancestry. Jati names and the labour associated with them are handed down through generations. Although naming order and conventions differ from region to region, traditional Hindu names tend to include some combination of a given/personal name and a name identifying family lineage; this might be a patronym, a village or clan name, or a jati name (Jayaraman 2005). As colonial systems of documentation and registration were imposed, jati names or village names often came to function as surnames (Rawat 2016).

Caste can often be parsed by learning someone's full name, if one is familiar with the language or region. For example, Pandit is a common Kashmiri brahmin surname that literally describes an occupation (learned person or priest); Iyer and Iyengar are Tamil surnames that refer to brahmin jatis from different traditions. Jati names like Chamar, Chuhra, or Paraiyar, referring to Dalit or oppressed-caste occupations in Punjabi, Hindi, and Tamil contexts, often become deployed among upper-caste people as insults or epithets (Valmiki 2008; Equality Labs 2018; Noronha 2021). Although only Hindu religious tradition codifies caste in textual tradition, the social practices of caste exist in other religious communities, and these too are mobilized through names and sometimes the vestiges of jati. For example, Muslim names in the region may distinguish between Ashraf, those who claim ancestry from the Middle East, and Arzal Muslims, oppressed-caste Hindu converts from South Asia (Rahman 2016; Alam 2009). While the surnames Singh and Kaur were intended by the Sikh Gurus to eliminate caste differentiation based on names, in practice many Sikhs have continued the use of jati or village names (Sian and Dhamoon 2020). Sikhs from dominant Jat caste backgrounds have discriminated against those they call Mazhabi, members of the community with Dalit ancestry (Ram 2017; Sato 2012). Sara Singha (2022) writes about Dalit Christians in Pakistan who were and still are called by the jati name Chuhra. Sonja Thomas (2018) writes about how caste privilege is inscribed in India's Syrian Christian community. Across these traditions, caste continues to function to distinguish between practitioners who can claim a long ancestral relationship with the tradition, more recent converts, and those who carry oppressed-caste jati names.

Names and naming practices serve as a map to the social locations of South Asians in all these ways. But it is important to remember that while the recognition of names is tied to local forms of linguistic and cultural knowledge, this knowledge has never been temporally or taxonomically static. Some jati occupations are seen as avarna in some regions and as savarna in others. In some regions, the most economically and politically dominant communites are middle-caste groups, as is the case with some Sri Lankan Tamil Vellalars. While an individual from one linguistic/geographical region may know all the local jati names, they might migrate within South Asia to a place where names are less familiar. And of course, there are people who have intentionally chosen to change their names, either to obscure jati and family history or to demonstrate solidarity with others. In his memoir, *Joothan: A Dalit's Life*, Omprakash Valmiki (2003) writes about how he chose to use the surname Valmiki along with other members of his Dalit jati. In his home region in Uttar Pradesh, this name was widely associated with his jati, but when Valmiki moved to Bombay, he was often misread as brahmin. Valmiki recounts a brief romance with a friend's daughter that ended when she learned his caste:

> I said as plainly as I could that I was born in a Chuhra family in Uttar Pradesh.
>
> Savita appeared grave. Her eyes were filled with tears and she said tearfully, "You are lying, right?"

"No, Savi. It is the truth. You ought to know this." I had managed to convince her.

She started to cry, as though my being an SC was a crime. She sobbed for a long time. Suddenly, the distance between us had increased. The hatred of thousands of years had entered our hearts. What a lie culture and civilization are. (113)

While misrecognition might seem to offer some forms of upward mobility, Valmiki's story shows how it can lead to harm and conflict because the oppressive order of caste remains intact.

Caste was codified in colonial administrative processes of record keeping and census taking. The British used information gathered about caste in the management of land, assets, education, and politics. Caste was used as a factor in deciding legal cases, inheritances, and rights. While some brahmin Hindus and elite Muslims had a seat at the table with colonial power, oppressed-caste jatis were marginalized and even criminalized under colonial law. Local police used colonial caste knowledge to surveil and discipline oppressed-caste people, and such practices have continued in present-day policing (Kumar 2012).

Through the work of B.R. Ambedkar, caste discrimination was addressed by the post-independence Indian constitution.[1] An affirmative action program commonly called "reservations" holds positions in schools and government jobs for oppressed-caste people. To manage this program, the government relies on official lists of Scheduled Castes and Scheduled Tribes, which enumerate which jatis are eligible.[2] Such lists create opportunities for education and class mobility for Dalit people, but at the same time they cannot fully capture caste complexity. Some groups feel they have been excluded and should have access to these programs, while others who might be locally perceived to have improved class status continue to benefit from them. Like other equity programs, it is also susceptible to abuse: rumours abound of savarna people falsifying caste certificates to gain access to reserved positions. And yet, those who have converted to Islam or Christianity and changed their names lose their access to these programs, even if they can prove that they have Dalit ancestry (Fazal 2019).

Caste Names in Diaspora

> *My mother's* inti peru*—her "house name" or family name—was recorded as her first name when she emigrated to England after marriage in the early 1970s. Vemuri, the surname of her father and brothers, became her given name on all her official documents and has remained there since. Her maiden name was listed as Rao, a South Indian masculine honorific that was part of her father's personal name. Her married name is Krishnamurti, my father's surname of record. Her own first or personal name, Krishna Kumari, appears nowhere on her official documents. The new name she acquired obscured her language, regional history, gender, and personal identity, but still coded her brahmin caste status. My mother, who at twenty-one had just been married to a man she'd met only once before the ceremony, landed in a new country with no name of her own. This is not an unusual story in diaspora.*

Caste has followed South Asians around the world for centuries, and with it the complexity of meanings that might be recorded, misrepresented, obscured, or erased in a South Asian person's name: histories of ancestral labour, violence, migration, and loss, and stories of pride, heroism, ancestral knowledge, and survival. In the nineteenth century, as indentureship scattered workers across the world, names were among the few possessions that crossed the sea with them—but these were precarious possessions. Colonial record keeping reshaped South Asian names but did not eliminate caste. Documents of arrival and registration confused or omitted caste names, and new names were invented and adopted. As a result, names in the "old diaspora" are often specific to those regions and do not exist in the same form in South Asia, and this made for some possibilities of movement through caste. On the ships, caste names and statuses were intentionally exchanged for others for many reasons: there were those who became "ship brahmins," and there were upper-caste people who chose to hide their caste and/or identity (Jayaram 2006, 148).

Since caste rules are largely governed by boundaries around the sharing of food and bodily fluids, and since cooking, domestic rituals, and sex are gendered spaces, the maintenance of caste boundaries particularly serves to regulate women, marriage, and families (Kumar 2012, 220). In much of the old diaspora, migration through indenture and other labour regimes was dominated by men and sometimes married couples. Single women entering indenture were rare and were particularly vulnerable to exploitation (Hiralal 2016). When they married or bore children, it was often across caste lines. Gaiutra Bahadur (2014) writes about her great-grandmother, Sujaria, who left India for Guyana, gave birth on the ship, and acquired the masculine honorific Bahadur:

> As far as I can tell, Sujaria made it up. It wasn't her name. It wasn't the name of the man she ultimately married in Guiana. And, if the archives are to be believed, she had no husband on leaving India. She conferred a high title on the child of her middle passage, possibly born out of wedlock...As a member of Hinduism's highest caste, Sujaria had the most to lose by crossing the Indian Ocean. This was a forbidden passage, especially for a woman, especially for a Brahmin, and most especially for a Brahmin woman travelling without a male relative. (21)

Writing about the story of his Trinidadian mother and his own name, Andil Gosine (2016) writes about the "name-wrecking" processes of indenture. He notes that colonial naming distortions and the chosen names of indentured workers "simultaneously perplexed and interrupted the caste system":

> It's hardly surprising, therefore, that many indentured discarded names that marked them as less and chose ones that offered a notion of more worthy status. This kind of switching is of course an ambivalent endeavor: It at once indicates the social privileges that a name might confer, but the act of switching works to

> "wreck" the system—in this case, caste—that imbues names with worth..."Gosine," which I was brought up to regard as a Brahmin name, seems an unlikely match for the relatively poor economic and social status of my paternal family. I suspect, but have no evidence yet, that it was one of those names switched by a rebellious indentured laborer. (51–52)

These examples show how caste movement through naming did not signify an erosion of the concept of caste; rather, caste hierarchies were reconstructed. Brahmins, or those who could claim brahmin-ness through an adopted name and a working knowledge of texts and rituals, were often re-centred as religious and community leaders. Brahmins continued to separate themselves from those seen as "low caste"; vegetarianism and abstinence from alcohol persisted as social boundaries. In colonies where indenture was practised, caste practices were reasserted in new configurations as Hindus organized themselves into temple and worship communities, and these continued to shift post-indenture and independence. Throughout the diaspora, anti-Black racism was tethered to casteism, and among Hindus were anti-Muslim beliefs as well. In twentieth-century Trinidad, hereditary brahmins and non-brahmin priests shared leadership of rituals and congregations, although this was sometimes uneasy (Singh 2012). In Mauritius, Hindus organized themselves into associations or committees along sectarian and caste lines (Claveyrolas 2015). In Fiji and South Africa, P. Pratap Kumar (2012) writes, many people changed their jati names in search of upward mobility. But the presence of caste consciousness remained, particularly evidenced by caste-based marriage arrangements and ongoing workplace discrimination. Caste discrimination is an issue of justice everywhere that the diaspora has touched.

Caste in Canada

> *I accompany my father to an appointment at the bank. My father, a retired senior, has been in Canada for more than forty years. The bank representative is a younger South Asian man. He welcomes us into his*

little glass-walled office. "Are you from India?" he asks, smiling. He tells us he came from Delhi to the GTA a few years ago. Looking down at the paperwork, he says, "Ah, Krishnamurti: you are a Tam-Bram!" This is shorthand for "Tamil brahmin." My father, somewhat taken aback, asks, "What makes you say that?" The man says, "When I went to college I stayed in the hostel. You get to know people from everywhere in India, and you start recognizing names." He makes effusive small talk about his college days.

Later, my father says that the man's comment struck him as inappropriate. He says that in his experience, people do not discuss caste in such a direct way in Canada. I realize that I parsed the man's South Asian-ness too. He had a recognizable upper-caste North Indian Hindu name. His accent and his job implied middle-classness. What privilege comes with this kind of mutual recognition and familiarity? What if a client with a different name had walked in, one that the advisor recognized as Dalit or Muslim, looking for a loan or mortgage?

Upper-caste privilege was baked into Canada from the start, entangled in access to British passports, economies of empire, and a racial discourse that allowed upper-caste South Asians to make claims to whiteness (Krishnamurti 2021b, 18). The first wave of South Asian migration before World War I was largely concentrated on the west coast, with a significant population of Punjabi agricultural workers who connected and built communities along caste lines (Verma 2002). Racist policy decisions then staunched Asian migration between 1908 and 1967. The introduction of the points system in Canada and the opening of immigration to skilled Asian immigrants in the late 1960s coincided with a new policy limiting Commonwealth migration to Britain. These changes meant that the new wave of South Asian migrants who arrived in the 1960s–1980s consisted largely of educated English-speaking professional men with families. While many of these arrivals were from India and Pakistan, South Asians also arrived from "old diaspora" locations like South and East Africa, Fiji, and the Caribbean. Some arrived as refugees and exiles from Uganda and Sri Lanka. Across these groups, caste and class privilege and access to English language professional education smoothed the path of arrival. Ajantha Subramanian (2019) shows how in the post-independence period, India's elite engineering college system, the Indian Institutes of Technology (IITs), was dominated by upper-caste, middle-class men. As immigration to North America began to open up, many IIT graduates chose to emigrate: "diasporic mobility emerged as a key tool for a wide spectrum of upper castes looking to secure the conditions of capital accumulation in the face of increasing lower-caste demands for representation within public education and state employment" (264).

This wave of upper-caste immigrants established communities in the prairies and Eastern Canada (Krishnamurti 2021b). A look at the histories of Canada's first Hindu temples and Indian Canadian associations shows that these were dominated by brahmins and those with other upper-caste names. Bhudendranauth Doobay, a brahmin doctor from Guyana, founded the Vishnu Mandir, one of the Toronto area's oldest and largest temples. Two brahmin doctors, Shiv Ram Sharma and Yogi Joshi, founded one of Canada's oldest temples in Auld's Cove, Nova Scotia, in 1972 (Hindu Sanstha 2010; Ramessar 2022). While these early temple spaces claimed to be inclusive of differing beliefs, the leadership was largely upper-caste Hindus. And while early Sikh gurdwaras in Canada might have initially served a variety of caste backgrounds, Dalits who felt excluded established a separate gurdwara in Vancouver by 1981. Dalit and oppressed-caste groups established other distinct communities and places of worship: the Ambedkar Mission (2025) was first established in Vancouver and Toronto in the late 1970s. Several other Ambedkarite Buddhist groups including the Ambedkarite International Mission are present in Canada today.

As South Asian communities have grown in Canada, worship spaces have become more specific and limited in the communities they serve, and caste-based associations have proliferated. Organizations like the Ontario Brahmin Samaj, the Kashmiri Overseas Association (Pandit caste), and the World Brahmin Federation are active in Canada. There are many US and UK based and transnational caste associations as well, like the Kamma Association of North America. Beyond the pretense of a shared cultural context, these groups function to connect families interested in marriage possibilities for their children and to facilitate business networking and professional connections. Marriage and matchmaking remain a significant locus of caste thinking across religious communities. Matrimonial websites like *shaadi.com* offer the ability to search by hundreds of specific caste names.

While upper-caste and dominant-caste people in the South Asian diaspora practise and even celebrate caste in these ways, they are also quick to insist that caste discrimination is not practiced in diaspora, and that its significance is exaggerated. The Hindu American Foundation (HAF) and the Coalition of Hindus of North America (COHNA) insist that caste is not part of Hinduism, and that public attention to it constitutes "Hinduphobia" (Krishnamurti and Sippy 2021). They have advocated against the inclusion of caste in public education, using tactics that are very similar to the Christian right's battle against "critical race theory."

Nonetheless, there is ample evidence that caste practice and prejudice persist across the diaspora, signalled through the vestiges of names and the persistence of social boundaries. Dalit people in diaspora have described great anxiety and fear about their caste being identified, and report ostracization and exclusion when it is revealed (Soundararajan 2022). For some, "not revealing their caste identity offers a modicum of belonging to the hegemonic ethnic community in an otherwise alien country" (Adur and Narayan 2017). In a blog post, Meera Estrada (2021) writes about coming into her own awareness of caste in Canada:

> Growing up in Canada, I'd heard about this system but I actually didn't know what caste I was part of until I was fifteen. I remember as a child telling people "I don't believe in that" when asked what caste I belonged to, echoing a phrase my mother often said in awkward social encounters. It wasn't until my parents revealed we were Dalits, and what that meant, that I understood what lay behind my mother's response. Despite knowing, we kept it to ourselves. My parents heard the casual jokes and denigrating

remarks about lower caste people, even in the diaspora. Already labelled outsiders as immigrants, they didn't want to be stigmatized by their own community too. It then became a secret I also guarded closely. Despite living in Canada, I started to notice caste all around me.

Estrada's story shows how silence around caste has different outcomes for those with and without caste privilege. There is no social consequence to being identified as a brahmin, but being identified as a member of an oppressed-caste group or "outed" as Dalit can bring harassment and harm. Reporting on interviews with Vancouver Dalits, the *National Post* (2013) discussed how participants:

> shared stories of how they were called slur words by fellow Indo-Canadians. One man recounted listening to colleagues, who did not know he was dalit, exchanging crude jokes about dalit women and rape. Another woman recounted how her best friend, a woman from what was considered a higher caste, was divorced by her husband who couldn't stomach their friendship. Activists say some dalits who own businesses are scared of being outed in case customers stop patronizing them. Many change their names.

Recent legal actions and campaigns by Dalit and anti-caste activists have made it clear that caste persists in the diaspora and has real and painful ramifications. Anecdotally, members of Dalit communities have reported workplace harassment and denial of job opportunities. Major public campaigns have been undertaken to address caste-based discrimination in Canada and the US.[3]

While no major legal actions have been filed to date in Canada, the Cisco Systems case in California is a recent example of caste-based harassment that has led to a legal challenge (Soundararajan 2022, 28; Mukherji 2021). More recently, senior manager Tanuja Gupta resigned from Google after being harassed by upper-caste employees who blocked her efforts to organize an event about caste-based discrimination (FCHS Collective 2022).

Naming South Asia in the Diaspora

> *I am in a group supporting Dalit scholars who are being harassed by Hindutva groups. The strategy, as requested by the Dalit scholars themselves, is to specifically approach those whose names are identifiably Hindu to sign a letter from "concerned Hindus." It has not actually been hard to identify potential signatories, as many South Asian academics in Canada have upper-caste Hindu names. Most agree to sign, though some question the strategy. A feminist professor writes to me: "I was born of high brahmin stock but don't identify as such. After all, I did not have a choice...what strange political times we have been forced into."[4] I cannot stop thinking about this statement. Indeed, none of us have a choice in the names we are given, but the consequences of those names are so violently different according to the rules of caste. Does choosing to identify as a non-Hindu, or as an atheist, or as a feminist absolve us of the caste privilege we carry?*

Interrogating caste innocence is not just a matter of parsing personal names, it is about thinking through the coalitional politics of feminist social justice work. In South Asian diaspora activist spaces, there is often a denial of the impact of our names and naming practices—both at the personal level and the coalitional level. The term "South Asian" was initially used by activists in Canada as a way to claim solidarity and affinity with each other (Shakir 2008; Sundar 2008; Ghosh 2013), but in practice this term merely blurs the fault lines of unequal power relations. South Asian sounds inclusive, secular, and non-nationalist, and it points to an ethno-racial category that we believe we share. But a meaningful and inclusive coalition cannot be built unless we are clear about the limits and failures of this category.

"South Asian" provides a kind of alibi: it allows us to pretend that caste is not real, that complex national-historical divisions are not at work, that Islamophobia is not rampant in Hindu communities and in the mainstream, and that Hindu India is not a looming hegemonic presence in the region and in the diaspora. It is a privilege to decide what is and isn't named. Some activists who already feel marginalized in these ways choose not to participate in South Asian spaces (Krishnamurti 2021a). More meaningful interrogation is required of what "South Asian" can do for us, and who it excludes. A critical dimension of this interrogation is naming and thinking through how caste operates in the diaspora. What does it mean to organize in "South Asian" diasporic feminist spaces as a person with a caste Hindu name, even if one does not identify as Hindu? We cannot renounce the histories that come with our names, so we must acknowledge them.

Academics are especially implicated in these questions as teachers, researchers, and producers of knowledge. Da Costa (2018) writes: "Apart from the institutional exclusion of Dalit and anti-caste scholarship through most of my education resulting in my lack of exposure, in retrospect, I suspect that liberal Bengali Brahminism has coded into me a conscious and subconscious draw towards and investment in reputable authors with their legibly upper caste scholar *names* and thus an affective preference for reading their writing—one of the many manifestations of my casteism. What do I do with this knowledge?" Our names occupy intellectual and even physical space when they appear on lists of speakers, membership lists, publications, keynote talks, and conference name tags. When the conference program for the panel on "gender and caste" presents five upper-caste names, what are we really saying about caste? Our names take up space on the panel before we even sit down at the table. Our names precede us into classrooms and job interviews and announce our "diversity" to EDI committees. Caste-privileged people need to directly address how our names and caste histories impact our work as activists and academics, in publications, informal networks, and our citational practices (even, and especially, in a chapter like this one). Ignorance of caste is not an alibi.

Reckoning with Caste in Diaspora

> *My father has always written his name as J. Krishnamurti. The J stands for Jagannathan, and it should be my father's surname. My father's family are Telugu land-owning brahmins who settled in the Tamil*

French colonial region of Pondicherry. Neither my father nor my grandfather used their Telugu inti peru, Oruganti; if they had, my father's name might have been written as O.J. Krishnamurti. Upon emigrating to England, my father's "first name" became Jagannathan, and his "last name" become Krishnamurti, since this is the order in which they were written. Krishnamurti is now my surname. Those who can parse South Asian names might know that Krishnamurti means "form of Krishna" in Sanskrit. If you see Murti, or Moorthy, or Murthy following the name of a Hindu deity, the name is likely to be that of a Tamil, Telugu, or Kannada-speaking brahmin. J. Krishnamurti is also the name of a famous twentieth-century Indian philosopher; the fact that I share my mistaken surname with a brahmin intellectual is itself a marker of caste.

South Asian diaspora feminists must name caste and its intersecting implications as part of our social justice work. Those of us with caste privilege have to think beyond unpacking our invisible knapsacks and making performative identity claims; these are self-serving actions that do nothing to actually challenge casteism. The thinly veiled truth about casteism in the diaspora is that it shapes how we think about anti-Black and anti-Indigenous racism, policing, immigration, and state violence.

Despite the varying narratives and circumstances of our arrival, we as South Asians live and work on this colonized land as settlers and uninvited guests. As Nishant Upadhyay (2019) has shown, casteism is imbricated with anti-Indigenous thinking among some savarna settler South Asians, noting that through "investments and inclusion in the Canadian state, the racialized dominant caste subject learns who the Native is through the discourses of the settler society" (162). Upadhyay shows how the othering narratives of casteism are redeployed in the anti-Indigenous and anti-Black racisms of diaspora, so that privileged caste status and "model-minority" status are interlinked.

Métis scholar Chantal Fiola (2021) writes about the significance of introducing ourselves and reflecting on our histories for building good relations: "Métis, Anishinaabe, and Midewiwin protocol teaches me to first introduce myself so that we may know how we are related through place, clan, family, and spiritual community. Knowing how we are connected helps us understand our roles, responsibilities, and mutual obligations if we aim to be good relatives—whether our ancestors have been here for millennia, settled here in the last few hundred years, or are newcomers who have just arrived" (260).

To be a good relation requires more from me than simply introducing myself as a South Asian, or as someone who is transnationally connected by colonial history and committed to decolonization. Reflecting on "place, clan, family and spiritual community" requires grappling head-on with caste. Tangled up in my name and my family history are long histories of brahmin orthodoxy. My ancestors and my extended family are practitioners of caste. My family has benefitted from caste privilege in myriad ways. I continue to benefit through my access to the academy. There are continuing social benefits to diasporic caste privilege. My name is never used as an insult to me or to other South Asians, although it has been a target of racism in Canada. My name associates me with intellectuals and celebrities; I do not share this name with people who have inherited abject poverty and painful labour. Members of my family in India do not fear harassment from police or from neighbours. Women in my family do not experience violence because of their caste.

Caste is anything but invisible in the diaspora. It predetermines our relations with each other. As I have tried to show through personal reflections throughout this chapter, names are a technology for determining access and privilege. Brahmins recognize other brahmins, and they recognize non-brahmins too. Dalits and oppressed-caste people recognize dominant-caste names. Mazhabis and Ravidassias know who Jats are. Pasmanda Muslims know who Syeds are. It is absurd to pretend that South Asians do not do this—it is the equivalent of the old racist cliché, "I don't see colour." Casteism is an open secret in the diaspora, and diaspora feminists must begin by naming it out loud.

Notes

1. Ambedkar wrote a great deal about caste discrimination in religion and law. *The Essential Ambedkar* (2017) offers an excellent introduction to his writing on this subject.
2. These lists of recognized SC and ST groups are available from the Indian government (see Government of India, n.d.). The reservation system and its history are discussed in Rao (2009) and Subramaniam (2019).
3. The city of Seattle passed a motion against caste discrimination in 2023 (Kaur 2023). In March 2023, the Toronto District School Board passed a motion acknowledging the existence of caste-based discrimination and requesting the Ontario Human Rights Commission to provide a framework for addressing it; a similar resolution was passed by the Brampton City Council in May 2023 (Jagannathan 2023).
4. Private communication, May 2019; name withheld.

References

Adur, Shweta Majumdar, and Anjana Narayan. 2017. "Stories of Dalit Diaspora: Migration, Life Narratives, and Caste in the US." *Biography* 40 (1): 244–264. https://doi.org/10.1353/bio.2017.0011.

Alam, Arshad. 2009. "Challenging the Ashrafs: The Politics of Pasmanda Muslim Mahaz." *Journal of Muslim Minority Affairs* 29 (2): 171–181. https://doi.org/10.1080/13602000902943542.

Ambedkar, Bhimrao Ramji. 2017. *The Essential Ambedkar*. Edited by Bhalchandra Mungekar. First impression. New Delhi: Rupa.

Ambedkar Mission. 2022. "About Us." Buddha Vihara Ambedkar Mission. https://www.ambedkarmission.com/about/.

Bahadur, Gaiutra. 2014. *Coolie Woman: The Odyssey of Indenture*. Chicago: University of Chicago Press.

Chakravarti, Uma. 2018. *Gendering Caste: Through a Feminist Lens*. New Delhi: Sage India.

Claveyrolas, Mathieu. 2015. "The 'Land of the Vaish'? Caste Structure and Ideology in Mauritius." *South Asia Multidisciplinary Academic Journal*. https://doi.org/10.4000/samaj.3886.

Da Costa, Dia. 2018. "Academically-Transmitted Caste Innocence." *Raiot* (blog), August 24. http://raiot.in/academically-transmitted-caste-innocence/.

Equality Labs. 2018. "Caste in the United States: A Survey of Caste Among South Asian Americans." https://www.equalitylabs.org/research/publications-resources/.

Estrada, Meera. 2021. "How I Shed My Shame Around Caste." *Refinery 29*, December 9. https://www.refinery29.com/en-ca/2021/12/10700243/indian-caste-system-in-canada-real-experience.

Fazal, Tanweer. 2019. "Caste, Religion and Recognition: Trajectories of Pasmanda Muslim Movements." In *Change and Mobility in Contemporary India*, edited by Sobin George, Manohar Yadav, and Anand Inbanathan, 117–132. New Delhi: Routledge India.

Feminist Critical Hindu Studies Collective (FCHS Collective). 2022. "Hindu Fragility and the Politics of Mimicry in North America." *The Immanent Frame*, November 2. https://tif.ssrc.org/2022/11/02/hindu-fragility-and-the-politics-of-mimicry-in-north-america/.

Fiola, Chantal. 2021. "Diaspora, Spirituality, Kinship, and Nationhood: A Métis Woman's Perspective." In *Relation and Resistance: Racialized Women, Religion, and Diaspora*, edited by Sailaja V. Krishnamurti and Becky R. Lee, 259–280. Montreal and Kingston: McGill-Queen's University Press. https://doi.org/10.2307/j.ctv1z7kk7j.

Ghosh, Sutama. 2013. "'Am I a South Asian, Really?' Constructing 'South Asians' in Canada and Being South Asian in Toronto." *South Asian Diaspora* 5 (1): 35–55.

Gosine, Andil. 2016. "My Mother's *Baby*: Wrecking Work After Indentureship." In *Indo-Caribbean Feminist Thought: Genealogies, Theories, Enactments*, edited by Gabrielle Jamela Hosein and Lisa Outar, 49–60. New York: Palgrave Macmillan. https://doi.org/10.1057/978-1-137-55937-1_4.

Government of India. n.d. "List of Scheduled Castes: State Wise / UT Wise List of Scheduled Castes Updated Up to 15-02-2024." Ministry of Social Justice and Empowerment. Accessed March 5, 2025. https://socialjustice.gov.in/common/76750.

Hindu Sanstha, Nova Scotia. 2010. "History." December 21. https://hindusansthans.wordpress.com/.

Hiralal, Kalpana. 2016. "Gendered Migrations: A Comparative Study of Indentured and Nonindentured Immigrants to South Africa 1860–1930." *Diaspora Studies* 9 (1): 41–52. https://doi.org/10.1080/09739572.2015.1088613.

Irudayam S.J., Aloysius, Jayshree P. Mangubhai, and Joel G. Lee, eds. 2014. *Dalit Women Speak Out: Caste, Class and Gender Violence in India*. Kolkata: Seagull Books. https://press.uchicago.edu/ucp/books/book/distributed/D/bo19265380.html.

Jagannathan, Shilpashree. 2023. "Brampton Becomes Third Canadian Jurisdiction to Include Caste as a Protected Category." *New Canadian Media*, June 1, 2023. https://www.newcanadianmedia.ca/brampton-becomes-third-canadian-jurisdiction-to-include-caste-as-a-protected-category/.

Jayaram, N. 2006. "The Metamorphosis of Caste Among Trinidad Hindus." *Contributions to Indian Sociology* 40 (2): 143–173. https://doi.org/10.1177/006996670604000201.

Jayaraman, Raja. 2005. "Personal Identity in a Globalized World: Cultural Roots of Hindu Personal Names and Surnames." *The Journal of Popular Culture* 38 (3): 476–490. https://doi.org/10.1111/j.0022-3840.2005.00124.x.

Kaur, Harmeet. 2023. "Seattle Becomes the First City in the US to Ban Caste Discrimination." *CNN*, February 22, 2023. https://www.cnn.com/2023/02/22/us/seattle-bans-caste-discrimination-cec/index.html.

Krawec, Patty. 2022. *Becoming Kin: An Indigenous Call to Unforgetting the Past and Reimagining Our Future*. Minneapolis: Augsburg Fortress Publishers.

Krishnamurti, Sailaja. 2021a. "Grounded Religiosities: Women Navigating Hindu Identity and Social Justice." In *Relation and Resistance: Racialized Women, Religion, and Diaspora*, edited by Becky R. Lee and Sailaja V. Krishnamurti, 19–44. Montreal and Kingston: McGill-Queen's University Press.

Krishnamurti, Sailaja. 2021b. "Race, Representation, and Hindu-Christian Encounters in Contemporary North America." In *The Routledge Handbook of Hindu-Christian Relations*, edited by Chad M. Bauman and Michelle Voss Roberts, 180–192. New York: Routledge.

Krishnamurti, Sailaja, and Shana Sippy. 2021. "Counterview: Not All Hinduism Is Hindutva, But Hindutva Is in Fact Hinduism." *Scroll India*, September 15. https://scroll.in/

article/1005407/counterview-not-all-hinduism-is-hindutva-but-hindutva-is-in-fact-hinduism.

Kumar, P. Pratap. 2012. "Place of Subcaste (Jati) Identity in the Discourse on Caste: Examination of Caste in the Diaspora." *South Asian Diaspora* 4 (2): 215–228. https://doi.org/10.1080/19438192.2012.675726.

Mukherji, Anahita. 2021. "California's Legal Ground in Battling Caste Discrimination Takes Centre Stage in Historic Cisco Case." *The Wire*, March 10. https://thewire.in/caste/cisco-case-caste-discrimination-silicon-valley-ambedkar-organisations.

National Post. 2013. "'We Are Zero': Immigrant Says She Can't Escape Sting of India's Caste System, Even in Canada." October 10. https://nationalpost.com/news/we-are-zero-immigrant-says-she-cant-escape-sting-of-indias-caste-system-even-in-canada.

Noronha, Ernesto. 2021. "Caste and Workplace Bullying: A Persistent and Pervasive Phenomenon." In *Dignity and Inclusion at Work*, edited by Premilla D'Cruz, Ernesto Noronha, Carlo Caponecchia, Jordi Escartín, Denise Salin, and Michelle Rae Tuckey, 489–512. Singapore: Springer. https://doi.org/10.1007/978-981-13-0218-3_17.

Omvedt, Gail. 2006. *Dalit Visions: The Anti-Caste Movement and the Construction of an Indian Identity*. Hyderabad: Orient Blackswan.

Omvedt, Gail. 2017. *Understanding Caste: From Buddha to Ambedkar and Beyond*. Hyderabad: Orient Blackswan.

Patel, Kamna. 2017. "What Is in a Name? How Caste Names Affect the Production of Situated Knowledge." *Gender, Place & Culture* 24 (7): 1011–1030. https://doi.org/10.1080/0966369X.2017.1372385.

Patel, Shaista Abdul Aziz. 2020. "It Is Time to Talk About Caste in Pakistan and Pakistani Diaspora." *Al Jazeera*, December 15. https://www.aljazeera.com/opinions/2020/12/15/it-is-time-to-talk-about-caste-in-pakistan-and-pakistani-diaspora.

Rahman, Tariq. 2016. "Personal Names in Pakistan: Onomastic Beliefs, Naming Practices, and Islam's Influence." *Economic and Political Weekly* 51 (39): 69–73.

Ram, Ronki. 2017. "The Genealogy of a Dalit Faith: The Ravidassia Dharm and Caste Conflicts in Contemporary Punjab." *Contributions to Indian Sociology* 51 (1): 52–78. https://doi.org/10.1177/0069966716677411.

Ramessar, Vernon. 2022. "This Rural N.S. Temple Is One of North America's Oldest, and It's Celebrating Its 50th Diwali." *CBC News*, October 22. https://www.cbc.ca/news/canada/nova-scotia/diwali-hindu-temple-nova-scotia-oldest-50th-anniversary-1.6626250.

Rao, Anupama. 2009. *The Caste Question: Dalits and the Politics of Modern India*. Berkeley: University of California Press.

Rawat, Ramnarayan S. 2016. "Colonial Archive Versus Colonial Sociology: Writing Dalit History." In *Dalit Studies*, edited by Ramnarayan S. Rawat and K. Satyanarayana, 53–73. Durham: Duke University Press.

Sato, Kiyotaka. 2012. "Divisions Among Sikh Communities in Britain and the Role of Caste System: A Case Study of Four Gurdwaras in Multi-Ethnic Leicester." *Journal of Punjab Studies* 19 (1): 1–26.

Shakir, Uzma. 2008. "Demystifying Transnationalism: Canadian Immigration Policy and the Promise of Nation Building." In *Organizing the Transnational: Labour, Politics, and Social*

Change, edited by Luin Goldring and Sailaja Krishnamurti, 67–82. Vancouver: UBC Press.

Sian, Katy Pal, and Rita Kaur Dhamoon. 2020. "Decolonizing Sikh Studies: A Feminist Manifesto." *Journal of World Philosophies* 5 (2): 43–60.

Singh, Sherry-Ann. 2012. "Trinidad Hinduism 1917–1945: Religious Transformation and Identity Construction." In *Indian Diaspora in the Caribbean: History, Culture, and Identity*, edited by Rattan Lal Hangloo, 55–59. Delhi: Primus Books.

Singha, Sara. 2022. "Caste Out: Christian Dalits in Pakistan." *The Political Quarterly* 93 (3): 488–497. https://doi.org/10.1111/1467-923X.13153.

Soundararajan, Thenmozhi. 2022. *The Trauma of Caste: A Dalit Feminist Meditation on Survivorship, Healing, and Abolition*. Berkeley: North Atlantic Books.

Subramanian, Ajantha. 2019. *The Caste of Merit: Engineering Education in India*. Cambridge: Harvard University Press.

Sultana, Habiba, and D.B. Subedi. 2016. "Caste System and Resistance: The Case of Untouchable Hindu Sweepers in Bangladesh." *International Journal of Politics, Culture, and Society* 29 (1): 19–32. https://doi.org/10.1007/s10767-015-9202-6.

Sundar, Aparna. 2008. "South Asia Left Democratic Alliance: Dilemmas of a Transnational Left." In *Organizing the Transnational: Labour, Politics, and Social Change*, edited by Luin Goldring and Sailaja Krishnamurti, 206–214. Vancouver: UBC Press.

Thomas, Sonja. 2018. *Privileged Minorities: Syrian Christianity, Gender, and Minority Rights in Postcolonial India*. Seattle: University of Washington Press. https://muse.jhu.edu/book/81741.

Upadhyay, Nishant. 2019. "Making of 'Model' South Asians on the Tar Sands: Intersections of Race, Caste, and Indigeneity." *Critical Ethnic Studies* 5 (1–2): 152–713. https://doi.org/10.5749/jcritethnstud.5.1-2.0152.

Valmiki, Omprakash. 2008. *Joothan: A Dalit's Life*. Translated by Arun Prabha Mukherjee. New York: Columbia University Press.

Verma, Archana B. 2002. *The Making of Little Punjab in Canada: Patterns of Immigration*. Thousand Oaks: Sage.

10

"You Are Not a Muslim"

Critically Examining South Asian-ness and Religious Politics in the Diaspora

AYESHA MIAN AKRAM

Initial Critical Conversations

In 2019, I had the privilege of being invited by this collection's co-editors to participate in a roundtable discussion on critical diasporic South Asian feminisms at the Canadian Sociological Association's Annual Conference at the University of British Columbia. My doctoral supervisor, one of the co-organizers of the session, invited me to participate due to my Pakistani and Kashmiri heritage.

The invitation surprised me.

Until that moment, I do not recall ever being labelled "South Asian." Muslim, of course. Feminist, yes. Of Pakistani heritage, sure. But South Asian?

I hesitated.

My parents, grandparents, and other ancestors have roots in the South Asian region, with lineage traceable to Kashmir, India, and post-Partition Pakistan. That is my heritage. So why was I hesitant to embrace the label "South Asian?"

Upon reflection, I realized that the reason for my disconnect was because I also belonged to the Ahmadiyya Muslim Community, a community that has been and continues to be targeted through institutionalized persecution across South Asia.

And so, I began to reflect on this discovery, critically and academically.

The Ahmadiyya Muslim Community and Religious Politics in South Asia

The Ahmadiyya Muslim community is a movement within Islam founded in 1889 by Mirza Ghulam Ahmad, who claimed to be the long-awaited Messiah (Al Islam 2025). Although the Ahmadiyya community originated in Qadian, India, today it is a worldwide community with followers spread across continents and from varying racial and ethno-national backgrounds.

Comprising 0.22 percent of the Pakistani population (CREID 2020), members of the Ahmadiyya community have been historically persecuted since before the 1947 Partition of Pakistan from India, enduring legislative restrictions, criminalization of the practice of their faith as Muslims, and a lack of protection as religious minorities. Although this chapter speaks specifically to the Pakistani context, this targeting is not unique to Pakistan but rather is a South Asian sentiment rooted in pre-Partition India and spread to proximal countries such as Bangladesh, India, Malaysia, and Indonesia (Inasshabihah 2020; Noor 2015). Particularly distressing are the growing Islamophobic sentiments promoted by government officials in India (Al Jazeera 2022).

In Pakistan, the state-sanctioned persecution of the Ahmadiyya Muslim community remains a direct violation of the United Nations' 1966 International Covenant on Civil and Political Rights (Rashid 2011). In 1974, the Pakistani Constitution was amended to declare Ahmadis as non-Muslim. In 1984, the issuance of Ordinance XX criminalized Ahmadi Muslims who referred to themselves as Muslim or acted as Muslims, e.g., by reciting the *Kalimah Shahadah* (declaration of faith) or performing *salat* (ritual prayers). Penalties included fines and imprisonment, and consequently this impacted Ahmadi individuals' access to public services, employment opportunities, and official state documentation (CREID 2020). In addition, religious minorities such as Ahmadis, Hindus, Christians, and Shi'ites in Pakistan (CREID 2020) are not entitled to equal protection by the government. Scholars have been documenting and challenging the injustices behind this state-sanctioned persecution (CREID 2020; Gualteri 1989; Kamran 2019; Khan 2015; Qadir 2018; Rashid 2011; Sultana et al. 2015), and yet the discrimination persists today. For example, a recent study of Ahmadi women in Pakistan (CREID 2020) found that they continue to hide their religious identities and remain silent about oppressions, "mainly due to their defenseless position to the anti-Ahmadiyya laws" (217). Living in poverty increases their vulnerability to persecution, as there is no opportunity to seek asylum in another country. The study concluded that poor Ahmadi women in Pakistan "are marginalised, targeted, and discriminated against in all aspects of their lives, including religious, cultural, social, economic, legal, constitutional, and judicial contexts" (218).

The 1974 legislative changes and subsequent effects led to increased violence and threats against Ahmadi Muslims in Pakistan, and with no protection from the government Ahmadi Muslims were not safe, with their lives and livelihoods constantly under attack. This led to the mass migration of Ahmadi Muslims out of Pakistan and into the diaspora, including Canada, the US, the UK, and Germany. Violence against the Ahmadiyya Muslim community in Pakistan persists today. One of many incidents of organized violence was the Lahore Massacre of 2010, where two Ahmadi mosques were attacked by perpetrators with guns and grenades, leading to the deaths of 94 worshippers and injuries to over 120 believers, including children. This massacre remains a painful reminder of the hatred toward Ahmadi Muslims in South Asia, a hatred that continues to follow even those Ahmadi Muslims who have the immense privilege of being able to escape and migrate out of the region.

South Asian-ness and Gender in the Diaspora

In the diaspora, the process of identity (re)formation and racial categorization is complicated and nuanced. The term "South Asian," for example, is much contested as a form of identification (Ghosh

2013). With deeply embedded and conflicting sociopolitical underpinnings, "being South Asian" is not simply a matter of geographical identification. Although as a "visible minority" I check off this category on the Canadian census, the act of lumping together diverse religious, ethno-cultural, and other differences under one label essentializes a multiplicity of overlapping and intersecting but quite distinct communities and masks their inter-group diversity (Patel 2006). Ghosh (2013) writes: "Explicit assumptions of the natural links between 'race,' 'culture' and 'place,' and putting those assumptions into practice in creating macro-cultural regions, simply exposes the deliberateness behind unwitted institutional racism" (38). In other words, the essentialist grouping of this range of diverse communities under one banner is a neocolonial tool of control of and domination over the Other. The homogenized "South Asian" experience, as is captured through the category of "South Asian" in the census, "uncritically replicate[s] Anglo-American ethnic categories" as both a visible minority grouping and an ethnic origin (40). Therefore, identifications with this label remain complicated and contested, signifying the disconnect between institutionally prescribed labels and self-identified associations, or contestations between "imposition and internalization" (42).

South Asian second-generation youth who grow up in the diaspora, in particular, face additional challenges with the label (Shariff 2008), as they are multiply positioned between globalization and white settler nationalism (Park 2011). With their "brown skin," they may struggle with whether to "brown it up" or "bring down the brown," and with determining how to understand and advance their ever-shifting South Asian identities differently and strategically in diverse sociopolitical spaces (Sundar 2008, 251). For example, Sundar (2008) found that second-generation South Asian youth "actively negotiate different aspects of their environments and make deliberate, strategic choices about how to express their identities in ways that help them achieve both material/economic goals (e.g., access to resources, securing employment) and/or emotional/psychological goals (e.g., gaining legitimacy or a sense of belonging)" (265).

As a South Asian Ahmadi Muslim in Canada, especially as one who practices hijab and visibly identifies as Muslim, I am primarily recognized as Muslim. When Canadians look at me, they do not see "Ahmadi" or even "South Asian"; they see "Muslim." I am recognized through the masculinist Orientalist gaze that pre-defines and pre-constructs Muslim women in the West (Jamil and Rousseau 2012; Razack 2018; Thobani 2021, Zine 2006). In a post-9/11 context, Muslims are "highly visible as suspect figures," and followed by fear and suspicion as they navigate their multiple subject positionings in the diaspora (Jamil and Rousseau 2012, 383). Violent acts of hate, such as the murder of the Afzaal family in London, Ontario in 2021 and the Quebec City mosque shooting in 2017, which led to the death of six worshippers, and the violence inflicted upon hijab- and *niqab*-practicing women across the nation are reflective of deeply rooted anti-Muslim sentiments in Canadian society. The "gendered Islamophobia" experienced by Muslim women constructs them as "signifiers of differences" in the diaspora, constructed at the nexus of disavowal and desire (Zine 2006, 9). Muslim women then navigate complicated racialized and gendered politics, with the possibility for feminist praxis emerging in the nexus between gendered Islamophobia and fundamentalist ideological patriarchies.

Transnational feminist theories are particularly useful in understanding how gendered identities are rooted in migratory and transnational processes in the diaspora. This is perhaps why so many scholars studying Muslim women and intersections between religion, secularity, cultural politics, and feminist subjectivities situate themselves in this field (Jamal 2005b; Mahmood 2016; Razack 2018; Zine 2004). Transnational feminism focuses specifically on "how patriarchies are recast in diasporic conditions of postmodernity—how we ourselves are complicit in these relations, as well as how we negotiate with them and develop strategies of resistances" (Grewal and Kaplan 1994, 439). What draws me to transnational feminism is the usefulness of connecting transnational structures of heteropatriarchy, racism, and neoliberalism with local subjectivities, particularly subjectivities that both transgress borders and boundaries and exist within liminalities and ambiguities (Ku 2019). The transnational feminist imagery of "scattered hegemonies" (Grewal and Kaplan 1994) is particularly poignant for illustrating the local contextualization of transnational structures of marginalization.

I keep the work of these scholars in mind as I embark on a critical unpacking of how my own questioning of a South Asian identification is directly related to the Pakistani declaration of Ahmadis as non-Muslim, and how intergenerational fears and anxieties around my community's persecution have impacted me in the diaspora.

Intergenerational Fears and Anxieties in the Diaspora

My family was one of the families that migrated out of Pakistan shortly after the 1974 constitutional amendments. My mother's family arrived as uninvited settlers on Indigenous lands on the coast of Cape Breton Island, Nova Scotia in 1976. Their connections with the Ahmadiyya community remained strong, and growing up in Alberta, I have powerful memories of regularly attending Ahmadi mosques across North America for Friday prayers, Eid prayers, meetings, children's classes, educational competitions, and national conventions.

Fear of persecution remained an integral part of my childhood narrative. Although we grew up within a tightly knit Ahmadiyya community, those anxieties still followed me throughout personal and professional spaces and relationships. Conscious of the violence in South Asia and aware of the immense privilege that had allowed us to escape direct persecution in Pakistan, we remained vigilant. I recall many instances of being cautioned when making a new Pakistani acquaintance—"What do they think about Ahmadis? Are they allies or not?" As I began to engage in activism around anti-Muslim racism during my undergraduate and graduate programs and began networking with other Muslim advocates, even as we rallied together to challenge Islamophobia in our classrooms and communities, I couldn't help but wonder: what will happen when they find out that I'm an Ahmadi Muslim? In a corresponding analysis (Mian Akram 2022), I reflect on an incident where I was invited to be a research assistant on a project exploring diverse Muslim communities. Even though I experienced no direct threat, the more I became involved in the project, the more I became fearful that my family or I would be targeted, leading to my resignation from the team. I was fearful that the anti-Ahmadi thinking that had led to the Pakistani law that said "you are not a Muslim" would transcend borders and root itself in South Asian mindsets in Canada, leading to similar expressions of threats, harassment, and violence. "Be careful," my parents warned.

To make sense of this experience, I turn to Hirsch's (2008) concept of "postmemory," which elucidates how second generations make connections to powerful, "often traumatic, experiences that preceded their births but that were nevertheless transmitted to them so deeply as to seem to constitute memories in their own right" (103). This postmemory, reflective of an intergenerational imparting of trauma and fear, can be a pivotal source of identity and decision-making for future generations in the diaspora. Hirsch writes: "Postmemory's connection to the past is thus not actually mediated by recall but by imaginative investment, projection, and creation. To grow up with such overwhelming inherited memories, to be dominated by narratives that preceded one's birth or one's consciousness, is to risk having one's own stories and experiences displaced, even evacuated, by those of a previous generation. It is to be shaped, however indirectly, by traumatic events that still defy narrative reconstruction and exceed comprehension. These events happened in the past, but their effects continue into the present" (107).

My fears, rooted in intergenerational trauma not experienced by me personally but by my elders, affected me differently in the diaspora. As a descendant of Pakistani Ahmadis, and never having lived in Pakistan myself, I was directly removed from the direct violence and targeting experienced by my elders. I experienced it as an ever-present caution, even when no tangible threat was present. Remembering the violence and fear with which my family and other community members left their homes and lives in Pakistan, I constantly debate whether to disclose my identity as an Ahmadi Muslim to others. This feeling is especially prevalent in settings where I know that many South Asians will be present, as I fear that transnational anti-Ahmadi sentiments may be firmly embedded in diasporic South Asian community members' mentalities. This selective disclosure does not equate to concealment or lying; rather, it reflects a visceral coping strategy, rooted in my elders' trauma and born out of intergenerational experience and caution.

When I was growing up, I heard from my parents about Pakistani acquaintances in Canada who had stopped all contact after they found out my parents were Ahmadi. I carried this with me as I moved to a new city and started making friends, including one who also happened to be Pakistani Muslim. Although I met her through professional networks, we started to become good friends. We bonded well, like soul sisters. As we started to meet more often for chai or lunch, throughout our time together, I would always be thinking in the back of my mind, *What's going to happen when she finds out I'm an Ahmadi? I don't want to lose this amazing friendship.* One day, I mustered the courage to bring up the fact that I'm Ahmadi in one of our conversations—I believe in reference to which mosque I was attending. I eagerly watched her face for any sign of contempt or fear. Nothing happened. We continued our conversation that day, and as our friendship continued for many years through pregnancies and motherhood and spending time collectively with our families, I think of how much I would have lost had I hesitated to continue this friendship out of fear of reproach or repercussion. Her friendship, this extremely positive association that challenges all my intergenerational traumas and anxieties, is a lesson for many reasons. The disclosure of my Ahmadi-ness, far from being a source of fear or anxiety, provided a source for a deep female friendship, having shared something with her that I hesitated to share with so many others. I have realized that although I must still be cautious and practise deliberate disclosure on a case-by-case basis, I should also be careful not to prejudge all Pakistanis and South Asians as possessing anti-Ahmadi sentiments.

And yet, there is much evidence of transnational anti-Ahmadi sentiments originating in South Asian homelands and seeping into diasporic contexts. Research on South Asian communities in Toronto has revealed that South Asian non-Muslims "have reservations towards them [Ahmadi Muslims]," signifying that religio-political tensions in the homeland have carried over and impact their everyday identities in the diaspora (Ghosh 2013, 48). Nijhawan's (2016) study of Ahmadi youth in Toronto has revealed the restrictions they face on Canadian university campuses, such as hostility toward Ahmadi events on campus, and not being permitted to use the same prayer mats as non-Ahmadi Muslims in prayer spaces. Take also as an example Mahershala Ali's Best Actor win at the 2017 Academy Awards for the film *Moonlight*. Ali, an Ahmadi Muslim convert, was widely celebrated as the first Muslim actor to win an Oscar. And yet, this momentous occasion was contested by Pakistanis who claimed that since Ali is not considered a Muslim according to Pakistani law, he cannot be called a Muslim Oscar winner, just an Ahmadi Oscar winner (Imtiaz 2017). These examples of anti-Ahmadi sentiments in North American contexts signal that state-sanctioned persecution in Pakistan remains engrained in South Asian mindsets in the diaspora.

Research continues to deepen our understanding of the intergenerational experiences of Ahmadi Muslim youth and women in the diaspora. These studies focus on Ahmadi women's experiences of diasporic agency in the US (Ahmed-Ghosh 2004); Ahmadi youths' experiences of ontological security in Scotland (Botterill et al. 2020); and German and Canadian Ahmadi youths' experiences of violence and memory (Nijhawan 2016). Yet there is much opportunity for the continued advancement and amplification of Ahmadi Muslim women's and youths' voices in academia, in continuing to investigate the impacts of intergenerational postmemory on transnational identities.

Mobilizing Within and Across Critical Diasporic South Asian Feminist Spaces

Contested diasporic labels leave much opportunity for forging new understandings and new coalitions across politico-religious divisions in the homeland, and for creating spaces of support, community, and belonging that challenge the hegemonic and masculinist notions of South Asian-ness, which continue to perpetuate divisiveness from the homeland. It is within these spaces that I am also able to find a critical intellectual space for further exploring South Asian feminisms.

The transformative potential of the critical South Asian feminist space generated by this network relies on critical scrutiny of interrelated structures of oppression in South Asia and the diaspora that challenge the erasure of identities. This requires that we respect differences, build solidarities, and ultimately challenge the hegemonies that seek to continue the marginalization of religious minorities through rigid heteropatriarchal politico-religious discourses. As Pakistani feminist scholars Shaheed and Mumtaz argued, feminists must both "acknowledge the degree to which women's lives and their identities, are shaped by religion" and "oppose the pressures on women to conform to prescribed versions of Islam" (as discussed in Jamal 2005a, 64). This is how we centre multiply marginalized voices in discussions around creating a solidaristic critical South Asian feminist community in the diaspora. This means forging spaces for "more collaborative feminist praxis among Muslim women" that strategically integrate multiple oppressions and challenges and build strategies and solidarities for political resistance (Zine 2006, 21). This is how we do the work of advancing our compassion for and solidarities with one another. This is how we do the work of seeking justice for our own communities and for one another's communities.

The invitation to join this network of critical South Asian feminists by participating in the roundtable discussion in 2019 and our continued conversations have been instrumental for me in finding a space to unpack and think academically and critically—to reflect on my journey, my family's history, and the intergenerational impacts and influences on Ahmadi generations in the diaspora. This critical reflection has led to my realization of how powerfully South Asian religious politics have shaped my politics as a feminist, educator, and scholar, without me even realizing. Connecting with other South Asian feminist scholars, learning of the struggles and injustices faced by their communities, and finding a sense of shared justice and solidarity have been unexpected, important, and transformative aspects of my development as a scholar and feminist. As a feminist community coalition member—a coalition that has shared space and power—it has been a relief for me to be able to share and speak in these spaces. I spent so much time fearful of disclosing, and after disclosing so publicly as part of this network, I have fundamentally shifted how I think about "South Asian-ness." Writing this chapter and finding support from critical South Asian feminists in the diaspora across these conditions of continued marginalization have led to a (critical) reclamation of this identification for myself. I offer this chapter as a means of stimulating other such conversations around belonging, solidarity, and community within South Asian feminisms. There is still much more work to do.

References

Ahmed-Ghosh, Huma. 2004. "Portraits of Believers: Ahmadi Women Performing Faith in the Diaspora." *Journal of International Women's Studies* 6 (1): 73–92.

Al Islam. 2025. "Ahmadiyya Muslim Community." https://www.alislam.org/ahmadiyya-muslim-community/.

Al Jazeera. 2022. "Qatar, Other Muslim Nations Condemn India Over Anti-Islam Remarks." June 6. https://www.aljazeera.com/news/2022/6/6/qatar-other-muslim-nations-condemn-india-over-anti-islam-remarks.

Botterill, Kate, Peter Hopkins, and Gurchathen Sanghera. 2020. "Familial Geopolitics and Ontological Security: Intergenerational Relations, Migration and Minority Youth (In)Securities in Scotland." *Geopolitics* 25 (5): 1138–1163. https://doi.org/10.1080/14650045.2018.1512098.

Coalition for Religious Equality and Inclusive Development (CREID). 2020. *Violence and Discrimination Against Women of Religious Minority Backgrounds in Pakistan*. CREID Intersections Series. Brighton: Institute of Development Studies. https://doi.org/10.19088/CREID.2020.003.

Ghosh, Sutama. 2013. "'Am I a South Asian, Really?' Constructing 'South Asians' in Canada and Being South Asian in Toronto." *South Asian Diaspora* 5 (1): 35–55. http://dx.doi.org/10.1080/19438192.2013.724913.

Grewal, Inderpal, and Caren Kaplan. 1994. "Transnational Feminist Cultural Studies: Beyond the Marxism/Poststructuralism/Feminism Divides." *Positions: East Asia Cultures Critique* 2 (2): 430–445. https://doi.org/10.1215/10679847-2-2-430.

Gualtieri, Antonio R. 1989. *Conscience and Coercion: Ahmadi Muslims and Orthodoxy in Pakistan*. Montreal: Guernica Editions.

Hirsch, Marianne. 2008. "The Generation of Postmemory." *Poetics Today* 29 (1): 103–128. https://doi.org/10.1215/03335372-2007-019.

Imtiaz, Saba. 2017. "The Muslims Who Aren't Celebrating Mahershala Ali's Oscar Win." *The Atlantic,* February 28. https://www.theatlantic.com/international/archive/2017/02/mahershala-ali-muslim-ahmadi-pakistan/518091/.

Inasshabihah, Inasshabihah. 2020. "Women and Advocacy: Study of the Ahmadiyya Community in Tasikmalaya." *Ijtihad* 20 (2): 191–210.

Jamal, Amina. 2005a. "Feminist 'Selves' and Feminism's 'Others': Feminist Representations of Jamaat-e-Islami Women in Pakistan." *Feminist Review* 81: 52–73.

Jamal, Amina. 2005b. "Transnational Feminism as Critical Practice: A Reading of Feminist Discourses in Pakistan." *Meridians* 5 (2): 57–82. https://doi.org/10.1353/mer.2005.0008.

Jamil, Uzma, and Cécile Rousseau. 2012. "Subject Positioning, Fear, and Insecurity in South Asian Muslim Communities in the War on Terror Context." *The Canadian Review of Sociology* 49 (4): 370–388. https://doi.org/10.1111/j.1755-618X.2012.01299.x.

Kamran, Tahir. 2019. "The Making of a Minority: Ahmadi Exclusion Through Constitutional Amendments, 1974." *Pakistan Journal of Historical Studies* 4 (1–2): 55–84. https://doi.org/10.2979/pjhs.4.1_2.03.

Khan, Amjad Mahmood. 2015. "Pakistan's Anti-Blasphemy Laws and the Illegitimate Use of the 'Law, Public Order, and Morality' Limitation on Constitutional Rights." *The Review of Faith & International Affairs* 13 (1): 13–22. https://doi.org/10.1080/15570274.2015.1005918.

Ku, Jane. 2019. "Journeys to a Diasporic Self." *Canadian Ethnic Studies* 51 (3): 137–154. https://doi.org/10.1353/ces.2019.0024.

Mahmood, Saba. 2016. *Religious Difference in a Secular Age: A Minority Report*. Princeton: Princeton University Press.

Mian Akram, Ayesha. 2022. "Navigating Triple Consciousness in the Diaspora: An Autoethnographic Account of an Ahmadi Muslim Woman in Canada." *Religions* 13 (6): 493. https://doi.org/10.3390/rel13060493.

Nijhawan, Michael. 2016. *The Precarious Diasporas of Sikh and Ahmadiyya Generations: Violence, Memory, and Agency.* London: Palgrave Macmillan.

Noor, Nina Mariani. 2015. "In Search of Peace: Ahmadi Women's Experiences in Conflict Transformation." *Ijtihad* 15 (1): 61–82.

Park, Hijin. 2011. "Migrants, Minorities and Economies: Transnational Feminism and the Asian/Canadian Woman Subject." *Asian Journal of Women's Studies* 17 (4): 7–38. https://doi.org/10.1080/12259276.2011.11666115.

Patel, Dhiru. 2006. "The Maple-Neem Nexus: Transnational Links of South Asian Canadians." In *Transnational Identities and Practices in Canada*, edited by Vic Satzewich and Lloyd Wong, 150–163. Vancouver: UBC Press.

Qadir, Ali. 2018. "Doors to the Imaginal: Implications of Sunni Islam's Persecution of the Ahmadi 'Heresy.'" *Religions* 9 (91): 1–17. https://doi.org/10.3390/rel9040091.

Rashid, Qasim. 2011. "Pakistan's Failed Commitment: How Pakistan's Institutionalized Persecution of the Ahmadiyya Muslim Community Violates the International Covenant on Civil and Political Rights." *Richmond Journal of Global Law & Business* 11 (1): 1–42.

Razack, Sherene H. 2018. "A Site/Sight We Cannot Bear: The Racial/Spatial Politics of Banning the Muslim Woman's Niqab." *Canadian Journal of Women and the Law* 30 (1): 169–189. https://doi.org/10.3138/cjwl.30.1.169.

Shariff, Farha. 2008. "Straddling the Cultural Divide: Second-Generation South Asian Identity and *The Namesake*." *Changing English* 15 (4): 457-466. https://doi.org/10.1080/13586840802493100.

Sultana, Kishwar, Muhammad Asif Rana, Nadia Imtiaz, Chelsea Soderholm, and Beena Sarwar. 2015. *Exploring Ahmadi Women's Voices.* Denver: Women's Regional Network.

Sundar, Purnima. 2008. "To 'Brown It Up' or to 'Bring Down the Brown': Identity and Strategy in Second-Generation, South Asian-Canadian Youth." *Journal of Ethnic and Cultural Diversity in Social Work* 17 (3): 251-278. https://doi.org/10.1080/15313200802258166.

Thobani, Sunera. 2021. *Contesting Islam, Constructing Race and Sexuality: The Inordinate Desire of the West*. London: Bloomsbury Academic.

Zine, Jasmin. 2004. "Creating a Critical Faith-Centered Space for Antiracist Feminism: Reflections of a Muslim Scholar-Activist." *Journal of Feminist Studies in Religion* 20 (2): 167-187. https://doi.org/10.2979/FSR.2004.20.2.167.

Zine, Jasmin. 2006. "Between Orientalism and Fundamentalism: The Politics of Muslim Women's Feminist Engagement." *Muslim World Journal of Human Rights* 3 (1): 1-24.

11

Queerness and Muslimness in the Lives of South Asian Muslim Women in the Diaspora

MARYAM KHAN

Introduction

In this chapter, I undertake critical discourse analysis on the use of the "Queer South Asian Muslim Woman" (QSAMW) identity, examining in particular its discursive constructions in extant literature hailing from the Global North.[1] The analysis discusses the implications of dominant discursive constructions on the identities and lives of QSAMWs by arguing for the use of critical praxis—for unpacking and unlearning static discursive constructions from transnational, intersectional feminist, and Islamic liberatory perspectives (Collins 2009; Collins and Bilge 2016; Esack 2018; Gopinath 2005). I conclude with personal reflections from my own subject position as a racialized QSAMW, contending that queer life in actual practice offers more flexibility in identity negotiations and nuanced agency and resistance vis-à-vis liminal spaces.

My Subject Position

I am a racialized queer Muslim ciswoman of South Asian heritage with a disability. My parents have their origins and familial connections in Bangladesh, India, and Pakistan, and emigrated to Canada in the 1970s. Over the years, in both personal and professional circles, my understandings and experiences of South Asian-ness and South Asian feminisms have been tumultuous, due to the competing normative expectations and ideals that clash and co-exist within these worlds. Politically and intellectually, I have a love/hate relationship with the discursive traditions wherein at times I belong, and then I don't. Straddling an insider/outsider concurrent status within these worlds is taxing. I am an insider due to discursive identity categorizations related to origins and ethno-cultural connections, and an outsider due to queerness, Islamic feminism, and approaches to Islam. I situate this work following my lived experiences, at the margins and in the liminal spaces (which can fracture easily and are constantly shifting) that exist tenuously, in between fragile worlds of representation, identity, and experience. The porous and cyclical flow *to* and *from* representation, identity, and experience have rendered, for me, a constant state of flux saturated in discomfort, pain, healing, and joy. I locate this work as a cyclical representation of this.

Method

Critical discourse analysis examines how discourses operate—how things get said; how constructions and connections are made between ideas, identities, and bodies; and how technologies and mechanisms of power feature in discursive constructions—and unearths the underlying historical, cultural, and sociopolitical currents that help construct realities and identities, and inform experiences (Van Djik 1997; Van Leeuwen 1993). Discourses can present as objective and neutral—something existing beyond human modes of communication and understanding (Yazdannik, Yousefy, and Mohammadi 2017). To illustrate this point, by putting together or unifying "Muslim" and "terrorist," popular media and literature have inextricably tied together and fused one discourse into another. The constant seeing, hearing, and reading of this has resulted in the configuration of "Muslim terrorist," which inevitably has made Muslim a signifier of terrorism in the imagination of many (Ahmed 2011).

Bifurcating Discursive Identity Constructions

South Asian, Muslim, queer,[2] and woman—all are contested hegemonic categories related to identity, experiences, and geographic affinities and connections. The aforementioned terms can lead to discursive inclusion and exclusion in a variety of intersecting ways that are configured historically, geographically, socially, culturally, and politically (Loomba and Lukose 2012; Roy 2012; Jha and Kurian 2018; Lee and Krishnamurti 2021). For example, hegemonic discourses of Muslim and Muslim-ness locally and globally are commonly attributed to a Sunni-centred paradigm, while ignoring, silencing, and punishing Muslims who are Ahmadi (Tanveer 2020). In most diasporic Muslim communities and Muslim majority nation-states, prejudice and violence against Ahmadi Muslims is rampant (Gualtieri 2004).

Ghosh (2012) offers that diasporic South Asian identities are twofold. One feature is that they are socially constructed "through various symbiotic modes of power: historic, economic, cultural and political" (38). Secondly, diasporic identities have a spatial dimension, whereby "the diaspora is usually associated with a geographical space" (38). The term "South Asian" in Canada is predominantly used to refer to people and regions in the Global South, like Bangladesh, India, Pakistan, and Sri Lanka, but is not necessarily referring to the people and regions of Guyanese, Trinidadian, and Mauritius heritage (Ghosh 2012). I am using South Asian as an expansive, fluid, discursive construction, which can refer to regions, heritage and descent, affinity, traditions, and ways of being in multiple intersecting ways anchored in the historical and sociopolitical, cultural contexts of the evoker. I am relying on the invoker of South Asian-ness to determine for themselves their identities, religions, food, traditions, and so on based on their unique religious, spiritual, sociopolitical, cultural experiences and orientations.

Global North research on queer South Asians tends to focus on the identity negotiations and lived experiences of males (Jaspal 2012; Jaspal and Siraj 2011).[3] Most research coming out of Canada, the US, the UK, and Australia has mixed gender, ethno-racial, and sectarian sampling with some trans women and ciswomen experiences, yet is mostly dominated by cismale queer identities and experiences (Rahman and Valliani 2016).[4] There is some research on the experiences of queer South Asian women, with a focus on Hindu queer and feminist lived negotiations of identity, religiosity, and spirituality (Krishnamurti 2021). Patel (2019) conducted a qualitative study with nine queer South Asian women in Toronto and uncovered experiences of rejection, racism, and othering evident in the larger queer community, grounded in hegemonic discourses of antithesis between South Asian-ness and queerness. Importantly, there is a dearth of qualitative research solely dedicated to understanding the experiences of diasporic QSAMWS.[5] Extant scholarship on queer Muslims, including the QSAMW identity and life, features mostly problematic conclusions arising from the mix of cisgendered and pro-heterosexual expectations and roles; fears and negotiations of dominant religious, ethno-racial, cultural, familial and societal realms; queering of Islam and the rise of queer Islam; some reconciliation of identity facets; and the overall navigation of intersectional identities and experiences of isolation and discrimination in the Global North (Al-Sayyad 2010).

One popular theme featuring in the studies is the constant navigation of identity versus practice, for example, QSAMWS wrestling with the application of contemporary identity labels to explain same-sex relations and attractions to oneself, families, and communities of belonging (Yip 2008). A critique of identity labels is that these do not succinctly capture the real-life nuances of friendship, love, relations, and camaraderie between women and among their varying relationships (e.g., lesbian and bisexual labels convey particular performances in the Global North; see Siraj 2018). Another theme is far-reaching and compounding gendered ethno-cultural and religious expectations, such as heterosexual marriage and procreation, or performing as a good South Asian Muslim woman in familial and public domains to maintain the family honour (respect) in diasporic communities. Many participants in the analyzed studies referred to the popular South Asian adage "What would people say!" in reference to respect, standing, and reputation in the larger diasporic communities when the conversations were steered to queerness, being too Western, coming out, and the fulfillment of cultural norms.[6] As I will discuss, there is an emergent cluster of intersectional and affirmative-centred research and scholarship on the lives and identities of QSAMWS, which is starting to shift common static assumptions about Islam, Muslim women, sexuality, race, ethnicity, and gender identity and expressions.

Emphasizing Notions of Fear, Shame, and "Cultural" Rejection

The first set of dominant discursive constructions that emerge in the narratives of QSAMWS are of rejection, and feature the violence and shame experienced in South Asian Muslim families and communities. Participants discussed at length their experiences in the larger queer communities and society, of racism, othering, and distress from not succumbing to the use of identity labels that promote coming out in loud and performative ways and navigating the closet. For example, Nargis, an Indian participant residing in South Africa who took part in Kugle's (2014) qualitative research with some QSAMW participants,[7] recalled the violence and struggles with strict familial, cultural, and ethno-racial-religious norms and obligations:

> My mother hit me a lot. She was the one who beat me up, not my father...letting her hit me, because I know she's aggressive. So she was bashing me around my ears, [and] I wasn't talking, I wasn't crying, I wasn't screaming, nothing. Then my father got crossed because I wasn't saying anything! "You're not even saying you're sorry! You're not even asking for *mu'af* (pardon)! You're not even crying!" I only said it because he said that, so I said, "I'm sorry I'm sorry, forgive me." So I basically had to go around and ask my whole family for forgiveness...for being who I am. (59-60)

Yip's (2008) study explored the ways Pakistani lesbian and bisexual Muslim women search "for legal and cultural citizenship," which the author argued are "inextricably linked to that [search] for intimate/sexual citizenship" (99).[8] On this quest, the participants faced a plethora of adversities, such as societal prejudice for not assimilating; pressure to get married; racism from the larger community; and homophobia within normative practices of Islam. There was nothing related to peace, support, and acceptance received from Muslims or South Asian Muslim families and communities. Siraj (2018) conducted a qualitative study with two lesbian Pakistani Muslim women in the UK. The participants were extremely fearful about sharing their sexual identity and coming out to family and friends. Due to fear of reprisal from family and friends, the participants upheld "cultural norms and values [which] overshadowed the importance of their sexuality" (37). Siraj's (2011) earlier work with a Scottish Muslim lesbian interviewee mainly emphasized the adversities of living a QSAMW life, more so than the resistance and agency evident in her sole participant's life story. Throughout the article, the interviewee's oppression and marginality were reported as resulting from her South Asian culture, community, Islam, and family of origin. The participant's suicide narrative is the biggest transcript excerpt in the study, followed by a smaller section on the interviewee's self-acceptance of her sexual identity as no longer conflicting with her Muslim identity. The meager space dedicated to the interviewee's agency and her deployment of social and self supports is trivialized in a few sentences. In doing so, her life story is predominantly identified as marginality focussed.

Even though Siraj's (2016a, 2026b) later research with queer South Asians tends to shift away from centralizing the marginal aspects of a QSAMW intersectionality, there is little critical exploration of the discursive constructions of UK cultural values around gender and sexuality (as pro-choice, freedom, openness) in opposition to South Asian, mainly Pakistani, Muslim cultural values (as patriarchal, restrictive, confining). In not disturbing these, the power and pull of the mutually exclusive tropes reign and account for the UK's long-standing historical colonial and now imperial relationship with Pakistani, Bangladeshi, and Indian diasporic subjects, which invisiblizes the roles that secularism and Orientalism play in the construction of the "forever Muslim other" (Said 1978; El-Tayeb 2011, 2012).

Finding Faith in Community

This theme covers examples of QSAMW activism (use of religious and spiritual resistance grounded in piety) within ethno-racial, religious, social, and political communities of belonging. QSAMW activism was not about loud protests with placards; it was demonstrated through refusals and subversions of norms, as well as processes of unpacking, unlearning, and re-learning taken-for-granted or dominant perspectives of Islam, queerness, and South Asian-ness, actively challenging restrictive identity categories through everyday acts and practices. Most studies revealed that after their initial discomfort with identifying as QSAMWs, the participants were able to reconcile faith and sexuality by engaging in self and collective (through queer Muslim support groups) exploration of the Qur'an and *Hadith*.

For example, Siraj's (2016b) study with five Muslim lesbians (three Pakistani, one Indian, and one Arab) found that Islam was an integral aspect of the women's lives, and the women did not abandon Islam or their sexuality. Siraj (2016b) noted that "sexuality and religion were mutually complementary not contradictory. Islam acted as a source of support and guide but at the same time offered the women a framework with which to understand the world and their position within it" (193). Siraj (2012) also conducted research with five British Muslim lesbians (four Pakistani and one Indian) affiliated with Imaan, a UK 2SLGBTQ+ Muslim support group. The participants struggled with normative Islam's staunch stance on queerness and felt rejected, which led to them distancing themselves from religious practices and suppressing their sexual desires. Some participants were able to reconcile their faith and sexuality through an emphasis on "human aspects of religion" and finding "the meaning behind religion" (Siraj 2012, 460). For example, Zyan, a Pakistani Shia queer

Muslim woman, asserted the following when referring to the story of Lut: "If you read it [the Qur'an] yes...if you read it as it is interpreted or translated traditionally then yes but if you read it closely it doesn't really specify which sins they are punishing. I believe it's promiscuity" (Alvi and Zaidi 2021, 14). Sometimes the women won the battle against bi-trans-homophobic clergy, mosque culture, and sermons in their immediate communities, while at other times, some women practiced celibacy, did not engage in same-sex relations, and compartmentalized faith and sexuality. When they were made aware about dominant Islam's beliefs on queerness (in coming out to self, friends, and family), QSAMWS relied upon their intersectional lived experiences to challenge and subvert spiritual and religious norms. For example, in Al-Sayyad's (2010) study, one QSAMW, Meena, discussed her experiences with dominant and static understandings of Islam: "I used to feel like I had to pick one or the other (Islam or having relationships with women)...It's not something that anyone talks about, but you just know same-sex attractions and relationships are not allowed. You just know this...I used to be like that, you know, those people who pray and pray and pray that they will be straight, but not anymore" (378).[9]

Khan and Mulé's (2021) qualitative research with fourteen queer Muslim women included five South Asian participants. Nafisa, a Bangladeshi queer woman, problematized contemporary understandings and expectations related to queer identity development and discourses of coming out in the Global North: "When I decided to come out, I was contemplating many things. Can I and do I want to fit into the mainstream white queer community? Do I want to suppress all these parts of myself and all this history that I have just so I can fit into this homogenized white gay community? Do I want to hear hateful things from the dominant Muslim community?" (154).

Siraj's (2018a, 2018b) research with seven British Pakistani closeted lesbians found that the women resisted conforming to Western hegemonic norms about coming out (they did not privilege the sexuality facet of their identities in a normative sense). Instead, their emphasis was placed on living out their intersectional identities (culture, race, sexuality, and so on) in a way that did not jeopardize cultural and familial norms (family reputation and upholding cultural mores around heterosexuality). Yip's (2005) research study with mostly South Asian British non-heterosexual Muslims (twenty women and twenty-two men) examined reconciliation strategies that resisted normative understandings of Islam and Muslims. For instance, religious texts were read as guidelines and not as the ultimate authority. Secondly, the scriptures were placed in their historical, socioppolitical, and cultural contexts. Jamila, who identified as a queer woman, and Shazia and Hasima, who identified as lesbians, discussed their understanding of the approach to sexuality in the Qur'an, and also non-scriptural sources. The women had deployed *ijtihad* (reasoning or coming to an understanding of matters related to faith) to come to an understanding of the Qur'an and Islam. Similarly, Kugle's (2014) five sexually and gender diverse Muslim women participants provide excellent examples of resisting and subverting the normative through activism (associated with support groups) and individual and collective jihad (to resist against oppression) and ijtihad, as well as remaining steadfast in the beliefs around God, and fostering the pluralistic spirit of Islam. For example, Tasmila, a Pakistani UK lesbian, asserted, "As for my faith, it has always kept me going. It has given me the strength to oppose racism, sexism, and all other *isms*" (45).

Yip and Khalid (2010) conducted in-depth interviews and focus groups with seventeen, mostly gay, 2SLGBTQ+ Muslims from the UK and North America. They had a handful of female participants. The study explored how 2SLGBTQ+ Muslims navigated their "perceived" antithetical identities, to trace their relationship with Allah (God) and practices of spirituality. Yip and Khalid's case study concluded that one can not only maintain both a 2SLGBTQ+ identity and Muslim identity, but can also maintain "meaningful spiritual paths and spaces where the acceptance and love of Allah are found" (83). A lesbian participant, Asmeh, believed that her sexuality was a vital part of her being and existence. The authors argue that the participants had keen insights on the concept of "oneness," that which highlights a solidification of self with the Creator and in all functions of being a human (90). In Islamic doctrine, the concept of *tawhid* (the oneness of God) is considered a core article of faith (Wadud 1999). The lesbian participants demonstrated a strong connection and commitment to Islam by drawing on Islamic principles for spirituality, and provided examples of resistance and deployment of agency, and of subverting conventional religious practices and redefining Muslim-ness. For instance, Amreen "would never step out of the house without reciting a combination of Qur'anic verses" (Yip and Khalid 2010, 98). Another participant, Raminah, wanted to foster her relationship with God through *salat* (prayer), even when on her period; she also offered salat beside her partner, who identified as a trans man. The subversions of daily practices like salat, and how and with whom they are performed, allow for alternative avenues of being a Muslim, and allow devotion for the Creator to surface.

Discussion

Empirical research presents a mere time-and-space snapshot in the lives of QSAMWS, which is couched in the interactions and contexts between the researcher and their interlocutors. In many ways, research resurrects and preserves dominant discursive constructions. For readers to mitigate this is to take conclusions "with a grain of salt" and consider the cultural, sociopolitical, and historical contexts of these powerful discursive texts.[10] One cannot, and should not, argue with the lived experiences (of adversity) for QSAMWS, as there exist robust bi-trans-homophobic attitudes and expectations of continuities of cisgender roles, cisheteropatriarchy, and compulsory heterosexuality roles in South Asian Muslim diasporic communities. This unfortunately constructs South Asianness and Muslim-ness as static, and silences the queer-friendly poetry, practices, and perspectives (notably Sufi) evident in South Asian regions throughout history (Kugle 2002; Vanita 2002). The proliferation of research and scholarship on liberatory, progressive, and feminist approaches to Islam and the Qur'an (Esack 2018) have started to change attitudes and (albeit slowly) the conversation in QSAMW circles, from "You are South Asian Muslim so you cannot be queer" to "Okay, some South Asian Muslims can be happily queer"

(Alvi and Zaidi 2021). The in-between gradations of discursive identities and nuanced real-life everyday experiences through intersectional approaches are now being featured more prominently.

Research on sexual and gender minorities tends to centre marginality, and for racialized individuals and communities such tendencies escalate (Cyrus 2017). Gopinath (2005) eloquently argued and unfurled the ethno-cultural, historical, and religious amnesia experienced by South Asian diasporas in longings for an idealized notion of homeland (where girls are girls attracted to boys, and boys are boys attracted to girls). In this longing, Gopinath (2005) argued, queerness is de-centred; yet, it re-centres when the queer bodies and expressions surface in varying discourses (e.g., media, language). Some of the authors cited in this chapter have made it clear that qualitative research and small sample sizes cannot be generalized to represent all QSAMWS. However, the power of *what* research *says* is still exercised in creating reality-based data. In this way, research can be guilty of creating or adding to discourses about "cultural Others" that are measured according to norms existent in North America and Europe, which speaks to the power "exercised in discourse" (Mohanty 1988, 64). Another way to mitigate this in research is to dedicate robust space to intersectional analyses, agency, norms navigation, and aspects of resistance. Scholars have called for more affirmative representations and more balanced-yet-flexible discursive constructions of Muslim women.[11]

As a QSAMW, I have received some supportive responses from South Asian and Muslim family and community members in relation to queerness, while also receiving some generous backlash for living a QSAMW life. Either/or categories of identities and experiences erase the "and" in the "Queer and South Asian and Muslim and woman" configuration, which intersectional perspectives can highlight (Collins 2009; Collins and Bilge 2016). Growing research is documenting affirmative Muslim familial responses and attitudes as accepting across various diasporic Muslim ethno-racial communities (Khan and Mulé 2021). I want to be clear and say that intersectional marginalities, for example, are systemic, and involve communities of origin and dominant understandings of Islam that are *real* and that do exist in the lives of QSAMWs. Yet, so do resistance and agency.[12] Ahmed (2006) reminds us that as "lesbians, inhabiting the queer slant may be a matter of everyday negotiation...the everyday work of dealing with the perceptions of others, with the 'straightening devices' and the violence that might follow when such perceptions congeal into social forms" (107). Such acts of daily living subvert traditional notions of sex and gender and end up creating new (slanted) possibilities for gender and sexuality to emerge.

A strategy offered by Liinason's (2020) "queer livability" framework can be useful. The "queer livability" framing argues that "everyday experiences" contain refusals, resistance, and subversion, which are "expressed through collective forms of action, carving out spaces for queer livability within multiple constraints" (113). The everyday life experiences of QSAMWs cannot solely be classified as inherently marginal and as victim to intersecting oppressions. Daily interactions are an ongoing negotiation, transpiring amidst the shifting sands of social, cultural, historical, and political plains that require expert skills (i.e., managing the closet, identity labels, expansive understandings of queerness and its performance, concealments and sharing, the separation of identity politics from practices of same-sex love and attractions, and experiences of pain, joy, success, and failures). Examples of individual and collective resistance and action, such as one's relationship to the Creator, fostered through the self and couched in queer Muslim communities, constitute the non-normative, sexual self, which leads to an alternate understanding of the Divine and Muslim-ness.

Conclusion

This critical discourse analysis reveals the complexities inherent in the QSAMW identity, highlighting the limitations of static discursive constructions. Empirical research, while valuable, captures only a fleeting moment, often perpetuating dominant narratives and failing to fully represent the nuanced realities of QSAMW lives. The lived experiences of adversity are undeniable, given the prevalence of bi-trans-homophobia and rigid cisheteropatriarchal expectations within South Asian Muslim diasporic communities. However, these challenges do not negate the agency and resistance demonstrated by QSAMWs, who navigate liminal spaces with flexibility and resilience. The growing body of scholarship on liberatory Islamic perspectives, coupled with increasing affirmative familial responses, signal a shift toward more inclusive understandings of queerness within these communities.

Ultimately, the everyday lives of QSAMWs cannot be reduced to a narrative of marginality and victimhood. Instead, they are characterized by ongoing negotiations, subversions, and the creation of "queer livability" within multiple constraints. Intersectionality allows for a deeper understanding of the "and" in the QSAMW identity, acknowledging the systemic marginalities while also recognizing the agency and resistance inherent in daily living. By focusing on intersectional analyses, agency, and resistance, research can move beyond simplistic representations and offer a more balanced and nuanced understanding of the QSAMW experience, acknowledging the dynamic interplay between identity, faith, and lived reality.

Notes

1. I have relied on empirical studies conducted with South Asian diasporas in English, and in primarily English-speaking parts of the globe like Canada, the US, Australia, and the UK.
2. Following Gayatri Gopinath (2005), queer and queerness speak "to a range of dissident and non-heteronormative practices and desires that may very well be incommensurate with the identity categories of 'gay' and 'lesbian'" (11). Here, I am also relying on the invoker's use of queerness as it fits within their lived experiences and identities. The term "queer" is also characterized by a non-adherence to normative constructions and understandings of gender and sexuality, which inherently "slants" the constructions and makes them different.
3. Notably, in UK literature, the term "Asian" is used interchangeably with "South Asian" to denote diasporic identities that have originated from Bangladesh, India, and Pakistan. In Canada and the US, for the most part, common parlance is South Asian.
4. Here, I want to be inclusive and make sure to denote that Sufism is not a sect of Islam but is considered an approach. Whereas sects of Islam are Shia, Sunni, etc., Sufism does not count as a sect.
5. See independent researcher Asifa Siraj's (2016b, 2018) empirical UK studies on a mostly South Asian participant pool discussed in detail in this chapter.

6. Culture is a nebulous concept and is informed and sustained by many constantly shifting pieces (ideologies, ontologies, epistemologies, beliefs, values, subject position, histories, and such). See the works of Stuart Hall (1973, 1991, 1992, 2005). My use denotes the dominant said and unsaid expectations, fantasies, ideals, and norms in traditional South Asian Muslim families and communities. Every South Asian Muslim family is unique, so not all expectations and norms will be the same (i.e., there will be differences in socioeconomic status, age, family unit dynamics, and so on). For example, in my family of origin, the unsaid expectation of sharing *everything* with family openly (personal and professional particulars) is the norm. And withholding any information (friends, plans, private thoughts) can lead to disagreements and suspicions of turning "Western," fostering a lack of trust.
7. Kugle (2014) conducted fifteen oral history interviews (four lesbians, nine gay men, one FTM trans person and one MTF trans person), with mostly racialized (some were of South Asian heritage) Muslim LGT activists from the Netherlands, South Africa, Canada, the US, and the UK.
8. Yip (2008) used data on lesbian and bisexual, predominantly South Asian, Muslim women from his 2005 study (discussed as well) and the work of Safra Project and Iman, two 2SLGBTQ+ support groups in the UK.
9. Al-Sayyad's 2010 qualitative research was comprised of twelve diasporic participants, most of whom were Arab queer Muslim women. The study had one South Asian participant, Meena.
10. See the works of Foucault (1972), Hall (1991, 1992, 2005), and Hunter (2002) for particular theoretical and practical strategies for challenging the status quo and moving toward critical praxis.
11. Bilge (2010) argues that intersectional analyses can help pave a path forward for analyzing Muslim women's agency and resistance beyond oppressed versus liberated perspectives. Bilge argues that an intersectional analysis can lend itself to examining the pious experiences of Muslim women.
12. Foucault (1978) has famously argued: "Where there is power, there is resistance and yet, or rather consequently, this resistance is never in a position of exteriority in relation to power" (95).

References

Ahmed, Sara. 2006. *Queer Phenomenology: Orientations, Objects, Others*. Durham: Duke University Press.

Ahmed, Sara. 2011. "Problematic Proximities: Or Why Critiques of Gay Imperialism Matter." *Feminist Legal Studies* 19 (2): 119-132. https://doi.org/10.1007/s10691-011-9180-7.

Al-Sayyad, Ayisha A. 2010. "'You're What?': Engaging Narratives from Diasporic Muslim Women on Identity and Gay Liberation." In *Islam and Homosexuality*, vol. 2, edited by Samar Habib, 373-394. Santa Barbara: Greenwood Publishing.

Alvi, Shahid, and Arshia Zaidi. 2021. "'My Existence Is Not Haram': Intersectional Lives in LGBTQ Muslims Living in Canada." *Journal of Homosexuality* 68 (6): 993-1014. https://doi.org/10.1080/00918369.2019.1695422.

Bilge, Sirma. 2010. "Beyond Subordination vs. Resistance: An Intersectional Approach to the Agency of Veiled Muslim Women." *Journal of Intercultural Studies* 31 (1): 9–28. https://doi.org/10.1080/07256860903477662.

Collins, Patricia Hill. 2009. *Black Feminist Thought*. New York: Routledge Classics.

Collins, Patricia Hill, and Sirma Bilge. 2016. *Intersectionality*. Malden: Polity Press.

Cyrus, Kali. 2017. "Multiple Minorities as Multiply Marginalized: Applying the Minority Stress Theory to LGBTQ People of Color." *Journal of Gay and Lesbian Mental Health* 21 (3): 194–202.

El-Tayeb, Fatima. 2011. *European Others: Queering Ethnicity in Postnational Europe*. Minneapolis: University of Minnesota Press.

El-Tayeb, Fatima. 2012. "'Gays Who Cannot Properly Be Gay': Queer Muslims in the Neoliberal European City." *European Journal of Women's Studies* 19 (1): 79–95. https://doi.org/10.1177/1350506811426388.

Esack, Farid. 2018. "Progressive Islam—A Rose by Any Name? American Soft Power in the War for the Hearts and Minds of Muslims." *ReOrient* 4 (1): 78–106. https://doi.org/10.13169/reorient.4.1.0078.

Foucault, Michel. 1972. *The Archaeology of Knowledge*. Translated by Alan Sheridan. New York: Pantheon Books.

Foucault, Michel. 1978. *The History of Sexuality. Volume 1: An Introduction*. Translated by Robert Hurley. New York: Pantheon Books.

Ghosh, Sutama. 2012. "'Am I a South Asian, Really?' Constructing 'South Asians' in Canada and Being South Asian in Toronto." *South Asian Diaspora* 5 (1): 35–55. doi:10.1080/19438192.2013.724913.

Gopinath, Gayatri. 2005. *Impossible Desires: Queer Diasporas and South Asian Public Cultures*. Durham: Duke University Press.

Gualtieri, Antonio. 2004. *The Ahmadis: Community, Gender, and Politics in a Muslim Society*. Montreal and Kingston: McGill-Queen's University Press.

Hall, Stuart. 1973. *Encoding and Decoding in the Television Discourse*. Birmingham: University of Birmingham.

Hall, Stuart. 1991. "Old and New Identities, Old and New Ethnicities." In *Culture, Globalization and the World-System*, edited by Anthony King, 41–68. London: Macmillan.

Hall, Stuart. 1992. "New Ethnicities." In *"Race," Culture and Difference*, edited by James Donald and Ali Rattansi, 252–260. London: Sage.

Hall, Stuart. 2005. "New Ethnicities." In *Stuart Hall: Critical Dialogues in Cultural Studies*, edited by David Morley and Kuan-Hsing Chen, 442–451. London: Routledge.

Hunter, Margaret. 2002. "Rethinking Epistemology, Methodology, and Racism: Or, Is White Sociology Really Dead?" *Journal of Race and Society* 5 (2): 119–138. https://doi.org/10.1016/j.racsoc.2004.01.002.

Jaspal, Rusi. 2012. "'I Never Faced Up to Being Gay': Sexual, Religious and Ethnic Identities Among British Indian and British Pakistani Gay Men." *Culture, Health and Sexuality* 14 (7): 767–780.

Jaspal, Rusi, and Asifa Siraj. 2011. "Perceptions of 'Coming Out' Among British Muslim Gay Men." *Psychology and Sexuality* 2 (3): 183–197.

Jha, Sonora, and Alka Kurian, eds. 2018. *New Feminisms in South Asia: Disrupting the Discourse Through Social Media, Film, and Literature.* New York: Routledge. https://doi.org/10.4324/9781315618388.

Khan, Maryam, and Nick J. Mulé. 2021. "Voices of Resistance and Agency: LBTQ Muslim Women Living out Lives in North America and Navigating Hegemonic Discourses." *Journal of Homosexuality* 68 (7): 1144–1168. https://doi.org/10.1080/00918369.2021.1888583.

Krishnamurti, Sailaja V. 2021. "Grounded Religiosities: Women Navigating Hindu Identity and Social Justice." In *Relation and Resistance: Racialized Women, Religion and Diaspora*, edited by Becky R. Lee and Sailaja Krishnamurti, 19–44. Montreal and Kingston: McGill-Queen's University Press.

Kugle, Scott. 2002. "Sultan Mahmud's Makeover: Colonial Homophobia and the Persian-Urdu Literary Tradition." In *Queering India: Same-Sex Love and Eroticism in Indian Culture and Society*, edited by Ruth Vanita, 30–46. New York: Routledge.

Kugle, Scott. 2014. *Living Out Islam: Voices of Gay, Lesbian, and Transgender Muslims*. New York: New York University Press.

Lee, Becky R., and Sailaja Krishnamurti, eds. 2021. *Relation and Resistance: Racialized Women, Religion and Diaspora*. Montreal and Kingston: McGill-Queen's University Press.

Liinason, Mia. 2020. "Challenging the Visibility Paradigm: Tracing Ambivalences in Lesbian Migrant Women's Negotiations of Sexual Identity." *Journal of Lesbian Studies* 24 (2): 110–125. https://doi.org/10.1080/10894160.2019.1623602.

Loomba, Ania, and Ritty A. Lukose, eds. 2012. *South Asian Feminisms*. Durham: Duke University Press. https://doi.org/10.2307/j.ctv11g96jz.

Mohanty, Chandra. 1988. "Under Western Eyes: Feminist Scholarship and Colonial Discourses." *Feminist Review* 30 (1): 61–88. https://doi.org/10.1057/fr.1988.42.

Patel, Sonali. 2019. "'Brown Girls Can't Be Gay': Racism Experienced by Queer South Asian Women in the Toronto LGBTQ Community." *Journal of Lesbian Studies* 23 (3): 410–423. https://doi.org/10.1080/10894160.2019.1585174.

Rahman, Momin, and Ayesha Valliani. 2016. "Challenging the Opposition of LGBT Identities and Muslim Cultures: Initial Research on the Experiences of LGBT Muslims in Canada." *Theology and Sexuality* 22 (1–2): 73–88. https://doi.org/10.1080/13558358.2017.1296689.

Roy, Srila, ed. 2012. *New South Asian Feminisms: Paradoxes and Possibilities*. London: Zed Books. http://dx.doi.org/10.5040/9781350221505.

Said, Edward. 1978. *Orientalism*. New York: Vintage Books.

Siraj, Asifa. 2011. "Isolated, Invisible, and in the Closet: The Life Story of a Scottish Muslim Lesbian." *Journal of Lesbian Studies* 15 (1): 99–121. https://doi.org/10.1080/10894160.2010.490503.

Siraj, Asifa. 2012. "'I Don't Want to Taint the Name of Islam' The Influence of Religion on the Lives of Muslim Lesbians." *Journal of Lesbian Studies* 16 (4): 449–467. http://dx.doi.org/10.1080/10894160.2012.681268.

Siraj, Asifa. 2016a. "Alternative Realities: Queer Muslims and the Qur'an." *Theology and Sexuality* 22 (1–2): 89–101. https://doi.org/10.1080/13558358.2017.1296690.

Siraj, Asifa. 2016b. "British Muslim Lesbians: Reclaiming Islam and Reconfiguring Religious Identity." *Contemporary Islam* 10 (2): 185–200. https://doi.org/10.1007/s11562-015-0348-9.

Siraj, Asifa. 2018a. "British Pakistani Lesbians Existing Within the Confines of the Closet." *Culture, Health and Sexuality* 20 (1): 28–39. https://doi.org/10.1080/13691058.2017.1323349.

Siraj, Asifa. 2018b. "Sexuality in the Shadows of a Friendship: An Intimate Portrayal of Friendship Between Two British Pakistani Lesbians." *Journal of Lesbian Studies* 22 (1): 43–53. https://doi.org/10.1080/ 10894160.2017.1303284.

Tanveer, Rana. 2020. "Ahmadiyya and Secularism: Religious Persecution at Home Affects Endorsement for Secular Values in Canada." *Religion and Culture Major Research Papers* 3. https://scholars.wlu.ca/rlc_mrp/3.

Van Dijk, Teun A. 1997. "The Study of Discourse." *Discourse as Structure and Process* 1 (34): 703–752.

Vanita, Ruth. 2002. "Introduction." In *Queering India: Same-Sex Love and Eroticism in Indian Culture and Society*, edited by Ruth Vanita, 1–11. New York: Routledge.

Van Leeuwen, Theo. 1993. "Genre and Field in Critical Discourse Analysis: A Synopsis." *Discourse and Society* 4 (2): 193–223.

Wadud, Amina. 1999. *Qur'an and Woman: Rereading the Sacred Text from a Woman's Perspective*. Oxford: Oxford University Press.

Yazdannik, Ahmadreza, Alireza Yousefy, and Sepideh Mohammadi. 2017. "Discourse Analysis: A Useful Methodology for Health-Care System Research." *Journal of Education and Health Promotion* 4 (6): 1–7. https://doi.org/10.4103/jehp.jehp_124_15.

Yip, Andrew K.T. 2005. "Queering Religious Texts: An Exploration of British Non-Heterosexual Christians' and Muslims' Strategy of Constructing Sexuality Affirming Hermeneutics." *Sociology* 39 (1): 47–65. https://doi.org/10.1177/0038038505049000.

Yip, Andrew K.T. 2008. "The Quest for Intimate/Sexual Citizenship: Lived Experiences of Lesbian and Bisexual Muslim Women." *Contemporary Islam* 2 (2): 99–117. https://doi.org/10.1007/s11562-008-0046-y.

Yip, Andrew K.T., and Amna Khalid. 2010. "Looking for Allah: Spiritual Quests of Queer Muslims." In *Queer Spiritual Spaces: Sexuality and Sacred Places*, edited by Kath Browne, Sally R. Munt, and Andrew K.T. Yip, 81–110. London: Ashgate.

IV

Anti-Racist Feminism and Settler Colonialisms

Solidarities, Activism, and Futures

12

On Wings of Fire

Parsi Women's Life Stories

FARAH MAHRUKH COOMI SHROFF

Introduction

The Parsi community has survived in the motherlands of modern-day Iran, in the diasporas of South Asia, and beyond. Zoroastrianism is considered to be the earliest monotheistic religion.[1] It was the predominant religion of the ancient Persian empires, and the state religion of Iran until the Arabo-Islamic conquest in the seventh century CE. To escape religious persecution in Persia, Zoroastrians migrated to India in the eighth and tenth centuries, becoming known as Parsis (Mehri 2010). The community has remained very small to the present day, and is known for being eccentric and fun-loving. It has also gained notoriety from traditional death practices within the community, specifically sky burial, or the placing of corpses on a tower for birds to eat the flesh.

Parsi women, while known for being highly educated and strong, are not as represented as Parsi men, who include public iconic figures such as Freddie Mercury, Zubin Mehta, J.R.D. and Ratan Tata, Homi Bhabha, and Sam Manekshaw. Studies about the community—notable among them Rohinton F. Nariman's (2016) *The Inner Fire: Faith, Choice, and Modern-Day Living in Zoroastrianism*—tend to be theological in nature, as divinity scholars find the religion unique and historically important. Cultural studies such as A.M. Shah and Lancy Lobo's (2021) *An Ethnography of the Parsees of India: 1886-1936* are limited, and much of the research has been conducted by academics who are outside the community. There is a paucity of studies on Parsi women's lives.

This chapter attempts to close this gap by documenting the oral herstory of Parsi women,[2] making this the first study by and about Canadian Parsi women. This insider oral herstory study was conducted by a research team comprised of this chapter's author, Dr Farah Mahrukh Coomi Shroff, Vera Minwalla, Nazneen Kasad, and Dario Dharsi, with the assistance of Dr Manpreet Basi. This study builds on an oral history study in the US profiling new Zoroastrian immigrants (FIRES 2025), and a four-volume series highlighting the work of Parsis by profession (Desai et al. 2017). One of our objectives as insiders was to examine life stories from inside the Parsi community, to understand identity, values, the role of education and faith, and other such questions. This study does not attempt to advance theory or compare our community to others.

Methods

Using a community-based insider participatory approach, where research team members are also reflexive participants, this study explores and celebrates the lives of those who identify as Parsi women, including transgender, non-binary, and other gender non-conforming people. Data collection was done in video format, an easily accessible medium for non-scholars and those outside the community, and was posted on the ZXX research team's website (Zarthusti Women's Herstories, n.d.).

This project was initiated by Parsi women to showcase the lives of other Parsi women. In the tradition of participatory action research (PAR), as conceptualized by Orlando Fals Borda (1997), the project aims to combine scholarly pursuits of knowledge creation with community wisdom. It is a tribute to the Parsi community, with a focus on listening to women's stories in their own words, unedited, in the tradition of feminist PAR (Maguire 1987). When communities tell their *own* stories as evidence of how they relate to the world, their narratives become known to a wider audience. Applying feminist oral history techniques was determined to be the most logical method for this study, given that oral history methods offer participants opportunities to speak in a relatively safe environment where they will be heard (Leclair, Nicholson, and Hartley 2012).

Recruitment

Twenty-four Parsi women in the lower mainland of British Columbia, Canada, and in Mumbai and Pune in Maharashtra, India, were recruited through communications sent out by community organizations and members via email or WhatsApp. The participants were all 19 years of age or older and self-identified as women, including transgender, non-binary, and other gender non-conforming people.[3] They had wide-ranging careers and talents, in research, law, film, education, and other areas. All but three participants consented to publicly sharing their life stories with no anonymity or confidentiality. The recorded interviews of those who gave their consent were posted on the university's website. The stories of the three participants who elected to remain anonymous are included in the analysis, but their videos have not been posted on the website.

Data Analysis

We recorded and partially transcribed each interview. Each recording and transcription was reviewed by three members of the research team, to ascribe meaning to each interview and to identify common themes. These themes were discussed by research members over multiple meetings.

Research Team

This insider oral herstory project was carried out by Parsis residing in British Columbia,[4] to foster knowledge creation through shared social and cultural contexts. All interviews were carried out by the author of this chapter. As insiders, our team members have a high level of expertise and advanced knowledge through shared experiences and unique perspectives (Vass 2015), as well as greater sensitivity in terms of presenting participant realities and honouring their words (Saidin and Yaacob 2016). We also included a non-Parsi research team member as an outside investigator. This was done to prevent the insider investigators from overlooking issues prevalent in the data that they might not have otherwise considered as important, and to allow for fresh perspectives.

Limitations

The interviews followed a free-form conversational style, without prompting around areas of experience that participants would be hesitant to publicize on video, such as sexual violence or incest. The public nature of the study potentially limited the amount of personal information that participants were willing to disclose, and they may have omitted painful or confidential issues. We were also limited by the lack of participants who identified as Iranian Zoroastrian, despite our recruitment efforts, possibly due to geopolitical and national political issues that made it challenging for Iranian Zoroastrian women to participate and publicize their life stories. Furthermore, we are aware that a significant percentage of the Parsi community is not heterosexual, yet none of our participants disclosed a queer identity.

Results and Discussion

Three main themes emerged from our data: social support, the role of religion, and support for women's rights.

Social Support

Our participants discussed social support in two main ways: as mitigating migrational malaise, and as sustained continuous social sustenance.

> The solidness of love I had as a child has made me a strong woman now.
>
> —Anonymous study participant

Like this participant, most participants underscored the importance of their early years, which were filled with love, followed by tremendous social support in their adult years. Scholarly literature is unequivocal about the benefits of social support for bolstering mental and social well-being (Glanz, Rimer, and Viswanath 2015). Social support—provided by spouses, parents, children, friends, and teachers—was the strongest theme in the study.

One participant, Sherna, spoke about the struggle of immigrating to Canada. Her family had emigrated from Kenya due to political instability and limited educational opportunities. Post-immigration life was difficult, but the support Sherna and her family received from a Parsi friend had made the transition easier.

Sherna's daughter, Nazneen, described the difficulty of migrating to a new country at the age of 6. Moving to an unfamiliar environment meant she had to adapt to a new school and make new friends. She spoke of how she started working when she was 14 years old because she wanted to be financially self-sufficient. Nazneen and her family were actively involved in the Zoroastrian community, which had allowed her to make close friends who provided a valuable emotional and social support system and shared her Zoroastrian background: "A lot of my closest friends are actually Zoroastrian...I interact with them on a level I don't with a lot of my other friends because our parents are friends, our grandparents are friends...we have shared values and culture that we can all relate to."

Another participant, Vera, had moved from Pakistan to Canada when she was only 10 months old. Vera described the struggles her family faced when adjusting to life in Canada. At first, her parents had a newspaper route to provide for Vera and her two siblings. Then, her father secured a job through friends back in Pakistan. Her mother got a job at a movie theatre, and the children would head there after school because childcare was too expensive, which her mother's Zoroastrian manager had understood. Vera expressed gratitude for the sacrifices that she and her family made over the years, and for the Parsi friends she met some years after migration:

"I never really had Parsi friends before...I was never really part of ZSBC [Zoroastrian Society of British Columbia], so I didn't really know Parsis other than our own family...Everyone knew each other and had close-knit friendships. I'm able to share so much more with those who are Parsi."

Another North American participant, Freya, mentioned how the Parsi community in her city was strong and supportive. Visiting Mumbai had reinforced for Freya the notion of support through roots and culture, which had helped her express her identity as a Parsi. She talked about being the first generation in her family to be born outside South Asia, and her yearning to fit in and be like a "blonde, blue-eyed cheerleader." Freya expressed her appreciation for her upbringing as she grew older: "I'm darn lucky to have two really good parents who prioritized my sister and I and just brought us up well. As we get older, we realize their struggles...but we had a nice life."

Sustained and Continuous Social Sustenance

Nargis Wadia had a supportive family who provided her with kindness and material assistance. She recalled a childhood full of reading, biking, and playing games. As she grew older, Nargis followed her parents' advice and created a successful international advertising career. She credited her parents for her achievements. After her first child was born, Nargis stayed home to take care of him, as there were no other family members available to help. Notably, Nargis's husband encouraged her to get back into advertising, and she eventually started her own agency: "When Roy [her son] was very young, I started this ad agency, not realizing how time-consuming it would be. It grew so fast...In five years, it became the tenth largest ad agency in India, and I was always traveling and working. Without the help of my family, especially my mother-in-law, I don't know how I would have done it."

Unusual for many Parsi women was Nargis's appreciation of her mother-in-law. Sooni also described how she had a great deal of family support in pursuing her career as a filmmaker, photographer, and writer, even after having children: "I had grown up with women who worked. I was a mother who worked as well. Luckily, I had a very good and extensive support system which helped me raise my children...I'm very lucky to have a supportive husband."

Likewise, Arnie recounted the support and guidance she had received from her grandfather, as well as her friends: "I had a wonderful childhood...My life has been a wonderful exposure to so many things and so many people. I've been very fortunate in always having friends, always having some support in all the things I did." She recalled one difficult instance where she spoke about her religion at her college in England. Her speech had sparked uproar and resentment from her classmates, but, she said, explaining her feelings to her friend had made her feel less isolated and misunderstood. Many years later, when her husband died, Arnie's friends and family had taken her on a trip to console and soothe her during the grieving process. Another participant, Armene, spoke of the extensive support she had received from family and friends who helped her through her divorce at 39 years of age, with two children to look after by herself.

Our participants spoke about kindness and caring in various ways. Songwriters, lovers, and poets, such as the poet Shamlu, who wrote the poem below, highlight kindness and compassion as a form of social support, and remind us there is nothing more important than open-hearted connections with others:

> Bright Horizon
> That day, when you will come,
> you will come forever, and
> kindness and beauty will become equal.
> (as quoted in Khorrami 1999)

The support provided to our participants allowed them to gain an education, pursue successful careers, raise children, and generally have a high quality of life, nourishing their lives on many levels.

The Role of Religion

The Zoroastrian religion is based on the principles of *Humata*, *Hukhta*, and *Huvarshta*—good thoughts, good words, and good deeds. Purity of thought, word, and deed are symbolized through fire. The *ashofarao* (a winged figure that signifies a guardian angel) often symbolizes the community. This chapter's title, "On Wings of Fire," thus speaks to the iconography in these combined classic images.

Our participants, like many members of the community, had varying relationships with the Zoroastrian faith. Zenobia Karkaria, whose father was a *mobed* (priest), spoke enthusiastically about being raised in a family where religious ritual was part of daily life, but where, like others, religion did not play a harsh role in her life: "I escaped boarding school, being the youngest, and cherished every minute being with my parents. My father, being a priest, was not at all orthodox. He gave us our space; he let us do what we wanted."

One of our anonymous Canadian participants, on the other hand, recalled her childhood as harshly punctuated by her father's insistence on following religious rules. As a result, she was still debating the merits and demerits of inducting her children into the faith.

There is a difference in the societal contexts of India and Canada. Expressions of religious faith are common in India. Temples, mosques, and other places of worship are all around, and most Indians participate in ritualistic religious practices regularly. Within this context, Parsis also feel comfortable expressing themselves as members of a religious community. Our participants, like most Parsis, were raised to be open-minded. Most were highly educated and practiced Zoroastrianism in ways that spoke to them personally, without pressure to prove their religiosity to others.

In contrast, while Canada is a predominantly Christian society, most Canadians do not outwardly follow religious practices

(Cornelissen 2021), and do not regularly attend church or practice other aspects of their faith. Agnosticism and atheism are commonly held beliefs and, overall, the country is secular (Lipka 2019). With this backdrop, our Canadian participants navigated Zoroastrianism as part of a culture that includes religion.

Most participants spoke about following the Zoroastrian motto of "good words, good thoughts, and good deeds." They enjoyed their religious identity in a relaxed fashion, applying these tenets as a life philosophy that may not include ritualistic elements.

Many participants celebrated their good fortune in being born into a community that offered so many opportunities and little by way of prescriptive diktat, as illustrated by Nerges Mistry: "The other thing that makes me very proud in being a Parsi is the attributes which we are recognized for and that's basically honesty and integrity and a sense of doing what's best for one's society...People in India recognize us for that...it makes you very proud to be a Parsi." She alluded to Parsis being appreciated for their strong ethical foundations, and often working in the field of banking and financial administration because other Indians trust Parsis to manage money. Most Parsi children are raised with the ethical Zoroastrian notion of *asha* (truth/righteousness) as a guiding principle.

Many participants noted that they would pick and choose the tenets of the religion that suited them the most and blend them with their own ideas. Vera, for example, had created her personal belief system based on the aspects of the religion that meant the most to her. Sherna spoke about the deeply significant religious practices that she incorporated into her daily life. She started and ended her day with "*Ahura Mazda*," a gender-neutral Zoroastrian term for higher power that means "Wise Spirit." Nazneen had her own way of expressing religious devotion, and did not feel forced to conform to the same level of commitment to religious practice as her mother, Sherna.

Arnie expressed her devotion to the tenets of Zoroastrianism and the deep comfort her nightly prayers brought her:

Arnie: "I think our simple prayers of *Ashem Vohu* and *Yatha Ahu Vairyo* are so powerful that in any situation, and whenever things bother us, if we can just trust in the Lord and pray to them with ultimate faith, help is always available."

FMCS: "Do you say your prayers every day?"

Arnie: "I'm not a great religious person, but there is never a time when I can go to sleep without saying my [prayers]. They support me through the night and for that, I am so grateful for being a Zoroastrian because it is something I can truly believe in."

Despite Arnie's love of her Zoroastrian identity, she, like Sherna, felt no compunction to enforce doctrinaire practices when it came to her children. Arnie mentioned that it was more important for her children to have a good moral character as opposed to rigid religious beliefs.

Like Arnie, many Parsis are raised with the idea that religion emphasizes fighting for what's right. Their expression of faith does not extend to daily visits to a place of worship or lengthy periods devoted to religious activities. None of our participants expressed that they would classify themselves as extremely religious, and in no way did they describe themselves as "fundamentalist" Zoroastrians. The majority of Parsis, like our participants, consider religion to be a quietly important part of life.

Most participants expressed their connection to Zoroastrianism as being close to their hearts, but not in a way requiring consistent outward demonstrations of worship. Zenobia Daruwala, for example, believed that, "All religions say: be a good human. It's just man-made—this religion part is man-made. I always feel that the world is just one."

Similarly, Nina mentioned that all religions are interconnected: "It boils down to: all are one; all religions are one...I have more knowledge about the Hindu religion than the Zoroastrian religion... [my kids] were never exposed to Zoroastrianism because I myself didn't know what it was. I didn't know the language, and no one explained it to us when growing up. So, they just followed the general path of being a good human being."

One of our anonymous participants in India had married a Hindu, and they had held a *navjote* (ceremony of initiation into the Zoroastrian religion) for their children at home instead of in an *agyari*, a Zoroastrian temple. While she experienced a great deal of anguish because she had decided to marry outside of the community, she vividly expressed how both the *Yatha Ahu Vairyo* and *Gayatri mantra* (a sacred Sanskrit chant) were woven into their family's religious tapestry.

In addition to their personalization of the religion, our participants seemed to truly resonate with the core values of Zoroastrianism. As Nargis Wadia said, "I think what moves me into being proud as a Parsi is not the rituals or prayers, but it's the practising of the religion—the practicality and the simplicity of that religion and the message it gives. Good thoughts, good words, and good deeds is such a simple, practicable tenet that our religion gives us."

Similarly, Shazneen echoed the idea of Zoroastrianism as a simple, guiding principle that encourages goodness from within, saying that in addition to "being good citizens...we try to focus on what is positive, and there is a certain focus on excellence."

Zenobia stated that having to continuously explain the religion to Canadians became frustrating, but she was able to turn this into a positive educational experience by spreading awareness about the religion. Similarly, Dubs stated: "What really gave Minu and me—Minu being my husband—a Parsi identity, is our stays abroad, where we had to explain who we were and our identity."

Some participants considered prayer to be a vital part of their everyday lives, whereas others believed that living as a good individual was the best way they could embody the tenets of the religion. The participants generally loved who they were, and religion and faith were one part of their identity. As there is no missionary aspect to Zoroastrianism, none of our participants mentioned a zeal for converting others.

Support for Women's Rights

Most women in our study, remarkably, did not mention that patriarchal norms had shaped their upbringing. Given that some of our participants were born seventy to one hundred years ago in India, this is noteworthy.

Parsi legal traditions reflect the community's relatively progressive views toward gender parity. For example, Parsi matrimonial laws from the mid-1880s banned polygamy (Sharafi 2017). Other Parsi laws have followed this pattern. The Parsi Marriage and Divorce Act (1936) stated that divorce could be granted, at the discretion of the court, on the grounds of grievous hurt or infection with venereal disease. Legal traditions such as these have given Parsi women a wellspring of human rights not experienced by others.

The Parsi community is held up as a "model minority" in India because of its industriousness, honesty, prosperity, and generosity to India (Hinnells 2005), as well as its gender parity. Our participants were questioned, on and off camera, about their experiences as girls and women, within their families and in the larger society. They had all felt empowered to make their own decisions from girlhood into their adult years, specifically pertaining to education, around which they received significant support. Shazneen told us, "My mom brought us up to be passionate about education," while Armene said, "My mother...raised us all, and today all of us are highly educated, doing well."

Education and career are of utmost importance in the Parsi community, so most participants, of all ages, noted that their parents had prohibited marriage before they completed their university studies. This enduring importance of educating girls has led to high achievements for Parsi women in postsecondary education (Misra 1966; Mory 2007), and to approximately 100 percent literacy rates among the Parsi community (Dadrawala 2019).

Off camera, participants expressed their experiences of sexism in other aspects of their lives. Those with brothers stated that they had experienced less freedom: their brothers were permitted to stay out late, and had no curfew or other restrictions, while they were told to be home earlier and received more surveillance. Others noted that patriarchal notions of femininity prevailed within their families, pressuring them to care for sick and aging family members. One participant mentioned that she had been shunned by her family as an adult because she did not devote herself to caring for her aging parents.

Evidently, sexism exists within the Parsi community, but is not expressed as vehemently as in other communities. Additionally, menstruation is stigmatized in many religions, including Zoroastrianism. Armene described her mandated isolation during her menses: "One of the rituals I was very, very upset about was [when] my mother made me sit separately during my periods." Up until recently, menstrual taboos within the community have prevented women from becoming *dasturs* (high priests), but they are now being accepted as *mobedyars* (assistant priests), which is a significant step forward for the community.

Insider/Outsider Status

One of the most contentious issues relating to women's rights in the Parsi community is who is considered "in" and who is considered "out." Designation of insider status is dependent upon at least the father being identified as a Zoroastrian, meaning that women who marry "out" of the community are excluded in some settings in India. This designation has been met with resistance and does not represent the thoughts of the majority of the community, as demonstrated by this anonymous participant's opinion: "That's one thing that never bodes well with me, that it's a patriarchal religion. But I understand that back then, that's how it was...It's beautiful now that women can do it [have navjotes for their children even if they've married non-Zoroastrians]." This participant spoke positively about her father's Zoroastrianism, and made a point of explaining that she had chosen her mother's Christian religious affiliation despite having had a navjote. She attended church regularly and considered her faith community to be an important part of her life in Canada.

In summary, the Parsi community is exceptionally progressive in many aspects of women's equity issues, particularly education. Overwhelmingly, our participants spoke in enthusiastic tones about the support they had received from their families to "shine out" in their education and other achievements. Yet sexism is still prevalent in the Zoroastrian community, especially regarding outsider marriage, particularly in India.

Conclusions

This is the first published study about Parsi women in Canada. Our interviews showcase Parsi women as happy and strong, and as leading fulfilling lives, despite significant challenges posed by migration, financial stress, and illness. Each story was illuminating for me, as the deep connections between community members made it feel like a small piece of myself was illuminated. Many key trends were noted in participants' narratives. These Parsi women had typically received significant support from childhood to adulthood, particularly around postsecondary education. Women spoke in glowing terms about both their parents and often their fathers, noting that there was little, if any, difference in the treatment they had received regarding their education when compared to their brothers.

Participants spoke about having a non-sexist upbringing, which does not negate the sexism that does exist in the community—up to and including violence against Parsi women. It is reasonable to assume that they did not reveal secrets or personal struggles for fear of embarrassing themselves or outing their families, given that they consented to publicizing their stories.

For most participants, religion played a small but significant role in their lives. Almost all of the women mentioned "good thoughts, good words, and good deeds" as important guiding principles in their lives. Many participants considered themselves to be nominally engaged with religious rituals; daily prayers were not something that most of our participants took part in.

Many participants voiced an open-minded spirit of acceptance, tolerance, and love for all members of the community, regardless of their choice of spouse or sexual orientation. Interestingly, this trend was seen among participants of all ages, and this did not differ between geographic locations; those in India were just as likely to hold this outlook as participants in Canada. One participant specifically brought up 2SLGBTQ+ issues because both her sons were gay. Her journey toward peacefully embracing this reality was an important part of her life, and she now advocated for 2SLGBTQ+ rights. This could be an area of further study.

Besides practicing the Zoroastrian faith, some of our participants also followed different spiritual traditions. For example, some of our participants followed the teachings of Meher Baba (1894-1969), a Zoroastrian born as Merwan Irani and an international spiritual leader (Shepherd 1988). Many of our participants practiced Zoroastrianism alongside other spiritual belief systems, such as yoga, meditation, and other South Asian spiritual practices.

The Parsi community is often perceived as a bright example of powerful and supported women in South Asia. Indeed, Parsi women are typically educated, strong, and confident members of our communities in South Asia and Canada. Raised to feel proud of who they are and to live up to their full potential, most Parsi women have been encouraged to shine. Our community, for most participants, provides a nest of love, encouragement, and support.

Notes

1. Judaism has also been typified as the world's first monotheistic religion. The members of the research team are not theological scholars, and this point is tangential to our study.
2. We have changed oral *his*tory to oral *her*story, as we are telling the stories of those who identify as women only.
3. For the purposes of this study, "women" are defined as those people who self-identify as women, regardless of their gender assignment at birth. Trans women, non-binary women, and other gender non-conforming people who self-identified as women were welcome to partipate.
4. The study team was comprised of Dr Farah Mahrukh Coomi Shroff, Vera Minwalla, Nazneen Kasad, and Dario Dharsi, with the assistance of Dr Manpreet Basi.

References

Cornelissen, Louis. 2021. "Religiosity in Canada and Its Evolution from 1985 to 2019." *Insights on Canadian Society.* October 28. Statistics Canada catalogue no. 75-006. https://www150.statcan.gc.ca/n1/pub/75-006-x/2021001/article/00010/citation-eng.htm.

Dadrawala, Noshir H. 2019. "Parsis and Education in India—Part I." *Parsi Times*, January 5. https://parsi-times.com/2019/01/parsis-and-education-in-india-part-i/.

Desai, Armaity S., Shalini Bharat, Lata Narayan, and S. Siva Raju. 2017. *The Parsis of India: Continuing at the Crossroads*. Los Angeles: Sage.

Fals Borda, Orlando. 1997. "Participatory Action Research." *Development* 40 (1): 92-92.

Fezana Information Research Education System (FIRES). 2023. Home page. https://fires-fezana.org/.

Glanz, Karen, Barbara K. Rimer, and K. Viswanath. 2015. *Health Behavior: Theory, Research, and Practice*. New York: John Wiley and Sons.

Hinnells, John R. 2005. *The Zoroastrian Diaspora: Religion and Migration*. Oxford: Oxford University Press.

Khorrami, Mohammad Mehdi. 1999. "Ahmad Shamlu (1925–2000)." *Iranian Studies* 32 (4): 633–637.

Leclair, Carole, Lynn Nicholson, and Elize Hartley. 2012. "From the Stories that Women Tell: The Metis Women's Circle." In *Strong Women Stories: Native Vision and Community Survival*, edited by Kim Anderson and Bonita Lawrence, 55–69. Toronto: Sumach Press.

Lipka, Michael. 2019. "5 Facts About Religion in Canada." *Pew Research Center*, July 1. https://www.pewresearch.org/fact-tank/2019/07/01/5-facts-about-religion-in-canada/.

Maguire, Patricia. 1987. *Doing Participatory Research: A Feminist Approach.* Amherst: Center for International Education.

Mehri, Rastin. 2010. "Zoroastrians in British Columbia." In *Asian Religions in British Columbia*, edited by Larry DeVries, Don Baker, and Dan Overmeyer, 85–104. Vancouver: UBC Press.

Misra, Lakshmi. 1966. *Education of Women in India, 1921–66*. Bombay: Macmillan and Co.

Mory, Dilnaz. 2007. "Parsi Demographic Statistics." *Parsi Khabar*, March 20. https://parsikhabar.net/bombay/parsi-demographic-statistics/634/.

Nariman, Rohinton F. 2016. *The Inner Fire: Faith, Choice, and Modern-Day Living in Zoroastrianism*. New York: Hay House.

Parsi Marriage and Divorce Act. 1936. "Section IV: Matrimonial Suits. 32 Grounds for Divorce." https://www.indiacode.nic.in/bitstream/123456789/2476/1/a1936_____3.pdf.

Saidin, Khaliza, and Aizan Yaacob. 2016. "Insider Researchers: Challenges and Opportunities." Paper presented at the International Seminar on Generating Knowledge Through Research, Universiti Utara Malaysia, Malaysia.

Shah, A.M., and Lancy Lobo, eds. 2021. *An Ethnography of the Parsees of India: 1886–1936*. New York: Routledge.

Sharafi, Mitra. 2017. "Many Think Parsis Are a Model Minority. Are They?" *Times of India*, September 20. https://timesofindia.indiatimes.com/india/many-think-parsis-are-a-model-minority-are-they/articleshow/60759044.cms.

Shepherd, Kevin R.D. 1988. *Meher Baba: An Iranian Liberal*. Cambridge: Anthropographia Publications.

Vass, Greg. 2015. "Getting Inside the Insider Researcher: Does Race-Symmetry Help or Hinder Research?" *International Journal of Research and Method in Education* 40 (2): 137–153.

13

Claiming Physical Space in a Settler Colonial Context

A Scalar Analysis of Gendered Islamophobia in Canada from Nation to Body

AALIYA KHAN

AS A SOUTH ASIAN MUSLIM WOMAN who lives in the intersections of race, religion, and gender, what does it mean for me to belong in Canada? In the following chapter, I examine the ways in which belonging is constructed through highly spatialized legal and administrative processes, blurring the boundaries between public and private space and ultimately demonstrating that Islamophobia is as much a geographic project as it is a political one. The body becomes implicated in this analysis as a continued target of these legal and administrative processes. However, the body also proves itself to be a force for agency on account of its ability to challenge geographical boundaries and the enforcement thereof. Is belonging important? What avenues can South Asian feminism offer me to situate myself as a racialized and gendered body?

I start this chapter by locating myself in this work. Next, beginning at the broadest geographical scale, I examine some of the ways in which Muslims are banished from "Canadian" sovereign spaces, through the formal and informal mobilization of violence on their bodies, at the national and transnational scales, and in racialized and gendered ways. I then narrow down my scale to the institutional level and look at some of the specific challenges Muslim women face in institutional and community spaces. Finally, I examine some of the ways that they can resituate belonging and agency by reclaiming space in embodied ways. In summary, this chapter is an appeal for a scalar analysis of Muslim women's spatialized experiences of belonging and dis/belonging.

Starting at the Self

This chapter is the natural progression of my own research on challenges faced by mosque builders in Peel, Ontario, a major research project that I completed at Toronto Metropolitan University in 2018. In my master's research paper, I argued that when Muslim communities attempt to build mosques, they are faced with exceptional challenges at every step of the process, reinforcing the findings of a 2002 chapter by urban geographer Engin Isin (Isin and Siemiatycki 1999). I am interested in this work because it helps me understand my own relationship with the Canadian nation-state in relation to multiculturalism in the post-9/11 era, and it enables me to think of the ways in which I can be an agent of insurgency, disruption, and social justice as a Muslim woman, researcher, teacher, friend, and ally.

Like many South Asian immigrants from East Africa, my relationship with "South Asian-ness" is complicated. Like many racialized immigrants with an ambivalent relationship with "home," I turn to "Muslim-ness" as a more cohesive point of reference for identity formation. The history of East African South Asian immigrants in Western nations is an important piece of the story of mosque building in Canada, and what it means for Muslims to belong in Canada. Many South Asians from East Africa transitioned from the middle class in East Africa to the middle class in Canada, affording them a level of sociopolitical and economic mobility that migrants and refugees fleeing global violence and ecological disasters have never been afforded. While there is little scholarship about the history of South Asian immigrants in Kenya, historian Sana Aiyar (2015) notes: "Between 1887 and 1968 the number of Indians resident in Kenya increased from approximately 6,878 to 176,613. The majority of these were traders, skilled workers, and their families who settled in Kenya during British colonial rule. At independence in 1963 Indians constituted 2 percent of the nation's population and formed its petty bourgeoisie" (2).

Second and third-generation South Asians from East Africa get absorbed into a broader "South Asian" category in the Canadian census (Buchignani 2010). In my personal experience, ethnic, cultural, and linguistic proximity to Indian and Pakistani immigrants has afforded them acceptance and integration at the community level as well. As middle-class transplants, they are afforded a presumed level of cultural competency that allows them to navigate Canadian respectability politics. Yet, even with the bureaucratic know-how and resources at hand, in their attempts to build mosques, South Asian Muslims across the Greater Toronto Area in Ontario have been stalled by bureaucratic red tape through land-use policies and practices (Khan 2018). These bureaucratic measures have been supported by vocal unfriendly neighbours in both formal and informal capacities. Accounting for my positionality as a gendered and racialized minority on the one hand, but as a privileged settler with middle-class parents on the other, I start my analysis of gendered Islamophobia at the national and transnational scales.

I turn to South Asian feminists in my political and academic pursuits because they have sought answers for the same questions I ask in these very transnational contexts. For example, Gayatri Spivak (2023) asks whether the subaltern can speak; I initially embarked on this project to respond to the oversaturation of white academic voices in studies about Muslim women's experiences. Scholars like Ash Amin (2013) examine Muslim immigrants' experiences in Western contexts, broadening the scope of what it means to be South Asian from a political and geographical perspective. Scholars like Sadia Toor (2011) look at Muslim women's specific experiences of inclusion and exclusion within South Asian communities during the post-9/11 era. These scholars broaden the horizons of South Asian feminisms in terms of geographical scale and extend analyses about colonial power into the present. The purpose of this chapter is to continue to extend and expand this rich tradition, acknowledge synergies, and introduce even more nuance into the study of not only South Asians and Muslims, but also racialized and gendered people more broadly.

Islamophobia, Settler Colonialism, and the Canadian State

Within the current historical juncture, having proximity to a Muslim identity in Canada carries the embodied and discursive heaviness of Islamophobia. This study examines policies and politics after September 11, 2001, a period where Islamophobia snowballed into a widespread phenomenon across the West (Razack 2004). Canada brands itself as a multicultural state, a space where, at least theoretically, difference is celebrated (Brosseau and Dewing 2018). However, this premise has been contested by multiple scholars, including linguist Eve Haque (2012), who argues that the imposition of the official languages as a universal site for community cohesion is incompatible with openness in a racially differentiated landscape. In particular, the imposition of French and English prompts ethnically and linguistically diverse peoples to assimilate to the hegemonic Canadian culture. This facilitates an "us versus them" framework that positions non-anglophones and non-francophones as "others." Indigenous scholar Glen Coulthard (2014) contextualizes Canadian multiculturalism within a broader "politics of recognition," asserting that a multicultural framework simply seeks to neutralize Indigenous claims to nationhood. Coulthard argues that Canadian multiculturalism presents Indigenous Peoples with a rebranded version of settler-state sovereignty that acknowledges Indigenous identities on paper, but not in practice, effectively continuing the Canadian history of erasing legacies of injustice and ignoring the ongoing marginalization of Indigenous Peoples.

In the context of this chapter, the geographical specificity of Haque's (2012) and Coulthard's (2014) analyses are important, and the guise of inclusion and progress presented by multiculturalism and a politics of recognition are important because these politics advance some of the more sinister racial violence that is operating in Canada by masking it. Muslims in Canada like myself occupy

Indigenous land and actively benefit from legacies of colonialism on the one hand, and experience racialization and exclusion on the other.

Exceptional Policies and the Politics of the War on Terror

Criminologists Baljit Nagra and Paula Marutto (2016) have characterized Canadian borders as "states of exception" for Muslims, where they have been identified, singled out, patted down, strip-searched, and interrogated. Within the bounds of these borders, the endless hamster wheel of policies targeting Muslims in Canada—including the 2015 Anti-Terrorism Act, the 2015 Zero Tolerance for Barbaric Cultural Practices Act, and the 2017 National Security Act[1]—reinforce to Canadians the "us versus them" dichotomy, positioning Muslims, and especially Muslim women, as outsiders. In Quebec, Muslim women's bodies have become sites of political violence through the enactment of policies that specifically target their clothing choices. The 2011 Bill 94 and the more recent 2021 Bill C-21 both require that public sector employees remove "religious symbols" at work, including headscarves and facial coverings.[2] These policies have been critiqued widely for compromising the human rights of Muslim women by creating thinly disguised legal exceptions out of them (Syed 2013). Canada's role in the War on Terror is one example of the importance of an even broader transnational lens interrogating the ways in which Canadian identity and belonging are reinforced through foreign occupation and invasion. For example, the invasion of Afghanistan and Iraq and continued support of the occupation of Palestine were all justified with propaganda that suggested that women "over there" could only be saved from barbaric Muslim men through violent military interventions that are characteristically Canadian (Jiwani 2021). On the flip side, many Muslim families in Canada fled these invasions to start a new life here as refugees and migrants, and they continue to face challenges in gaining and maintaining the security of citizenship (Nagra and Maurutto 2016). The invasion of Muslim countries abroad and the exodus of Muslim refugees from their homes are some examples of the ways in which racialized identities in Canada are constructed through justifications of brutal violence, as Muslim identity is viewed as fundamentally oppositional to Canadian identity.

Gendering the State of Exception

Gender is always an important point of reference for these oppositional constructions. However, critical race scholars like Robyn Maynard (2017) and Grace-Edward Galabuzi (2006) have also highlighted some of the ways in which race is weaponized against populations within the bounds of the Canadian state. While Galabuzi (2006) focuses on the underemployment of immigrant populations, resulting in "economic apartheid," Maynard (2017) critiques the over-policing and incarceration of Black and Indigenous people. Read in conversation, the two scholars offer a comprehensive look into the ways in which unemployment produces vulnerability, which then results in carceral and punitive approaches to social ills. I pull from scholarship about Indigenous, Black, racialized, and gendered identities in this analysis, prompting me to emphasize the critical importance of thinking about the ways in which bodies experience state-based violence in complex, layered, and nuanced ways. I do this in conversation with South Asian feminists because the settler colonial and anti-Black context does not get lost in a Muslim environment, where Arab-ness and South Asian-ness are put on a pedestal at the expense of Blackness and Indigeneity. This is particularly important to recognize when we acknowledge that the post-9/11 "terrorism" framework used to scrutinize and punish Muslims in the West was developed in reference to the ways in which Black American Muslims were represented during the era of the civil rights movement (Chan-Malik 2018).

Gender studies scholar Sherene Razack (2008) makes sense of policies targeting Muslims in Canada, arguing that following September 11th, the normalization of representations of "terrorists" in the media included defining them as "Muslims" with "brown skin" (12). These representations did not remain contained in media and became part of Western foreign and domestic policies (5). Razack (2004) notes that "dangerous Muslim men" and "imperiled Muslim women in need of saving" tropes were used to characterize Muslim communities as populations incompatible with "civilized European" (settler) populations. In the post-9/11 context, Razack argues that Muslims have become legal exceptions in Western states in the interest of "national security" (130-131).

The legal construction of exceptions becomes an ongoing theme in a scalar analysis of the relationships Muslim women have with belonging in Canada, and so I turn to Giorgio Agamben's (2004) *State of Exception* to understand the banishment of Muslim women from Canadian law and society. Agamben argues that the state of exception is either defined by the suspension of the constitution or the discretionary power of law enforcers. While Agamben's work has been critiqued for neglecting to specify race and gender as distinguishers of target populations for states of exception (Whitley 2017)—a particularly concerning claim given that he analyzes the Holocaust and the invasion of Afghanistan in particular—his text offers us a framework to think of the ways in which policies and strategies are mobilized to target the racialized other. Ultimately, target populations' experiences of belonging or dis-belonging are undoubtedly influenced by the state-sanctioned use of violence and death.

Agamben references geographically specific states of various scales, refering to the scale of state in reference to Germany, the US, and Afghanistan, among other examples. He also mentions institutions as states of exception; for example, he categorizes Guantanamo Bay as a state of exception. He argues that in these environments, laws and administrative powers are mobilized against populations such that target populations are no longer guaranteed the security of legal personhood. Further, once the rule of law is suspended, it remains so for an unconstrained time moving forward.

While this chapter might reinforce problematic assumptions like the male-female gender binary and the definition of a settler colonial nation-state through borders—of which scholars like Jasbir Puar (2018), Nishant Upadhyay (2020), and Harsha Walia (2014) offer important critiques—I offer South Asian feminism an interdisciplinary approach that helps us visualize the effects of racial projects in concrete, physical, and embodied ways by implicating the concept of space. In conversation with the aforementioned critiques, this approach translates theory into day-to-day experiences and appeals to scholars to think about how we can capture racialization and gendering through a scalar analysis that can be captured through the use of mapping.

The Mosque as the State of Exception

Narrowing my analysis down to the institutional scale, I am interested in contextualizing the mosque as a site of exception. It would be disingenuous to compare Afghanistan, for example, to Canada when it comes to the experiences of the general population and marginalized peoples, but mosques can still be understood as sites of exception using Agamben's technical definition, and race becomes the identifying factor that helps the Canadian state distinguish whether these sites should exist at all. Geographer Engin Isin (2002) argues that "the presence of significant Muslim groups challenges established norms of citizenship through symbolic struggles such as women wearing the veil and burka and the construction of mosques" (192). Isin fundamentally argues that the presence of Muslims in Canada challenges normative conceptions of who belongs and who does not. Mosques are the most recognizable feature of communities with a significant Muslim population—they often take on the form of architectural masterpieces that represent a concession to the claims to space that a marginalized population has made. However, while there is a growing number of mosques in communities across Canada, mosque builders are faced with restrictive policies that are disproportionately applied to them, backed by the apprehensions of unfriendly neighbours that hinder or limit mosque building projects (Khan 2018). Mosques thus become sites of exception in Canada in the sense that they are spaces where the rule of law does not apply, or where discretionary power is weaponized against members of the community.

The Untethered State of Exception

While Agamben's examples were more dire, the red tape faced by Muslim communities when attempting to secure approvals for proposed mosques and the requirements that mosques should be scaled down are symptoms of a general sense that Muslims should not exist in Canada, especially when viewed in conversation with some of the more violent military interventions previously mentioned. However, even after a mosque building project is completed, communities are hounded with ongoing battles over parking that their Jewish and Christian counterparts do not experience (Isin 2002), and in instances where Muslims congregate in the absence of a built form establishing their claim to space, there is a strong police presence, a continual reminder that if the community steps out of line, state violence will be mobilized to put them in place. Eid prayers and cultural festivals like Muslimfest are just two examples (Wang 2021).

The 2021 murder of the Afzaal family in London, Ontario is another example of an incident where Muslim bodies, untethered to any formal institutions, are turned into exceptions. On June 6, 2021, a white man named Nathaniel Veltmann drove a truck into a family of five who were taking a walk in their neighbourhood, killing four and leaving nine-year-old Fayez Afzaal critically injured and traumatized for life (Faheid 2021). It is highly likely that this family was targeted because at least one member of the family, Madiha Afzaal, was wearing a headscarf. A 2020 UK-based study by political scientists Najib and Hopkins (2020) observed that up to 80 percent of hate crime targets are Muslim women who wear some sort of head or facial covering (Fahed 2021). While Veltmann was not acting upon the instructions of the state, his actions were very much in line with what public discourses and policies tell us about who belongs and who does not, especially in the wake of the rise of the far right (Bello 2019). But if a built form does not need to exist to distinguish who is occupying a given space at a given time, it is necessary to narrow down the scale of this analysis even further to the scale of the body.

Body as Scale

While mosques represent a physical manifestation of the presence, acceptance, and assimilation of a diverse and vibrant but "othered" community, Canadian mosques fall short in terms of meeting the needs of Muslims within the margins of the community. It is worth mentioning here that while I do not explore the experiences of queer and trans Muslims in this chapter, I recognize that the issues I raise here related to Muslim women's experiences are exacerbated for Muslims in Canada who hold these identities, as they challenge the long-standing gender binary and respectability politics within the Muslim community, even more so than straight and/or cisgender Muslim women. Nevertheless, the mosque remains a space where women are an afterthought, if they are even allowed entry. This exclusionary attitude is highlighted by Australian scholar Nafiseh Ghafournia (2020), who comments:

> Women's attendance is dependent on the availability of a gender segregated space separated entirely from the main prayer room and a separate entrance (Shannahan 2014). Mosques that are open to women usually allocate women worse physical spaces compared to those provided for men which reveals 'an overall prioritization of male space and needs' (2014, 15). When women go to mosques, they are peripheral, separate, and invisible. (2)

The bodily scale becomes important, then, because Muslim women represent the racialized other to Canadian society on the one hand, and the gendered other to Muslim communities on the other. Sociologist Jasmin Zine (2008) provides us with the term "gendered Islamophobia" to understand this very experience among Muslim girls in Islamic schools in Canada. Thus, in this convoluted space of binaries, the distinction between the public and the private becomes blurred through the one demand that is consistently made of these Muslim girls: to make themselves invisible.

Mis-Categories and Marginalized Bodies

Geographers Sweet and Escalante (2015) argue that the distinction between the public and the private is a mis-categorization of bodies who exist at the margins of gender, race, sexuality, and citizenship. These bodies experience violence and fear on multiple sites along the false public-private dichotomy, and thus urban planners "must understand how bodies as geographic spaces experience violence and fear" (1827).

It is worth mentioning that in response to policies targeting Muslim women, there is no shortage of virtue signalling and public outrage about headscarf bans by publicly platformed Muslim men. Symbolically, hijab-wearing Muslim women represent a departure from a more "liberal," "neutral," and "unmarked" Canadian identity, and some men feel empowered by the idea that women who don the headscarf can only reveal their hair to their husbands, fathers, sons, and brothers. On public platforms, Muslim men's critiques of hijab and niqab bans are rooted in maintaining the appearance of autonomy in Canadian society, rather than about the actual bodily autonomy of Muslim women in general.

If this outrage was about women's bodily autonomy, perhaps men would raise their voices in opposition to mandatory veiling requirements in Saudi Arabia and Iran, and to the mobilization of brutal state violence against those who do not comply, like Kurdish Iranian woman, Mahsa Amini (Associated Press 2022). If this uproar was about choice, perhaps when Queer Egyptian activist Sara Hegazy died by suicide in Toronto after raising a pride flag at a concert in Egypt (Boisvert 2020), outrage would have emerged. If this performative public outrage was about choice, perhaps women in the community who chose not to veil would not experience slut-shaming and stigma at multiple points within the private and public sectors.

While embodied acts of violence such as hate crimes, carceral violence, and policies dictating what Muslim women can wear are examples of some of the ways in which bodies experience violence, Muslim women are actively challenging exclusion at every scale. In thinking about the body as space, a scalar analysis allows us to view the body as a state of exception. While borders demarcating nations, cities, and institutions are frequently moved and disrupted, often by human bodies themselves, bodies are the core targets of state- and community-based practices dictating who belongs and who does not. Conceptualizing the body as a site of exception is the final landing point for this analysis, because doing so demystifies and focuses on the violence that racialized and gendered bodies experience.

Muslim Women's Explicit and Implicit Resistance

Many of the sources cited in this chapter were produced by Muslim women in academic and non-academic environments, including South Asian feminists like Sherene Razack, Jasmine Zine, and Sadia Toor. Muslim women are organizers, reformists, and agents of revolutionary and quotidian resistance in their day-to-day lives. But I want to focus here on what it means for Muslim women to simply take up physical space in an environment that is designed to space them out.

In an environment that is characterized by contradictions and violence, Muslim women challenge attempts at making them invisible in multiple ways. In *The Politics of Piety*, anthropologist Sabah Mahmood (2012) analyzed members of the women's movement in Egypt, noting that their acts of worship qualified as articulations of their individual and collective agency. I hesitate to state the obvious here and repeat a soundbite that Muslim women are often forced to regurgitate, but very often, Muslim women make the active choice to wear the headscarf as an act of worship.

In her analysis of the role of organizers' bodies in the 2011 Egyptian revolution at Tahrir Square, international relations expert Mona Lilja (2017) argues that "resisting bodies, whether they are individual or in assemblies, signify something more than what is expressed." They "indicate agency and a mode of resistance, subversive standpoints and eruptive views, thereby challenging the logic and technologies of governing bodies" (347). Further, within the context of revolution, "linguistic and bodily representations support each other, thereby clarifying and strengthening the political message" (Pourmokhtari 2020). In their physicality, bodies can barricade and disperse and transport large objects, amplify sound, and—as Lilja (2017) emphasizes in her analysis—represent subversion, resistance, and insubordination. While Lilja's analysis is providing commentary on the specific context of organized resistance, these principles still apply to Muslim women in Canada: her article focuses on what bodies *represent.* In hospitals, schools, mosques, and homes, the presence of Muslim women signifies something more than what is expressed, indicating agency, resistance, "subversive standpoints and eruptive views," simply by occupying physical space (347).

Within a context of gendered repression, political scientist Navid Pourmokhtari (2020) offers us the "presence-as-resistance" framework, which became even more interesting in the wake of the uproar in Iran following the murder of Kurdish Iranian Mahsa Amini in prison after her arrest by the morality police (Associated Press 2022). Presence-as-resistance refers to the everyday, public, and visible mode of resistance that women participate in to make their existence felt, by participating in everyday life practices that are considered "normatively, and hence governmentally reserved for the private sphere of the home," such as singing, performing music, and engaging in sports. According to Pourmokhtari (2020), presence-as-resistance works to de-subordinate governmentalized bodies by transforming them into agents who undermine the state's ability to control the public domain. He argues that "presence-as-resistance can create and/or make visible 'an immense new field of possibility for resistance'...by fostering among resisting subjugated bodies a new awareness of their civic rights." Both Lilja and Pourmokhtari offer us analyses about interventions in public space that are active, but these analyses are translatable in the passive. After all, even when Muslim women partake in everyday, mundane activities that are unrelated to protest, the presence of their bodies challenges agreed-upon norms about who belongs in public, private, and in-between spaces, which are enforced by state violence not only in Egypt and Iran, but in Canadian society as well.

Conclusion

My study of Muslim women's experiences in Canada argues that beyond geopolitics, a scalar analysis can demonstrate some of the ways in which state and community violence are experienced by target populations. Policing, interpersonal violence, and social isolation are innately geographical phenomena, and a scalar analysis that accounts for the body as space is important to this analysis because it demonstrates some of the ways that violence is experienced by human bodies, as well as some of the ways these very bodies can challenge this violence at multiple scales.

Notes

1. Zero Tolerance for Barbaric Cultural Practices Act, S.C. 2015, c. 29, https://laws-lois.justice.gc.ca/eng/annualstatutes/2015_29/; Anti-terrorism Act, S.C. 2001, c. 41, https://laws-lois.justice.gc.ca/eng/acts/a-11.7/page-1.html; National Security Act, S.C. 2019, c. 13, https://laws-lois.justice.gc.ca/eng/annualstatutes/2019_13/FullText.html.
2. Bill C-21, An Act Respecting the Laicity of the State, 1st Sess., 42nd Leg., Quebec (assented to on 16 June, 2019), SO 2019; Bill 94, An Act to Establish Guidelines Governing Accommodations Requests Within the Administration and Certain Institutions, 1st Sess., 39th Leg., Quebec, SO 2010.

References

Agamben, Giorgio. 2004. *State of Exception*. Translated by Kevin Attell. Chicago: University of Chicago Press.

Aiyar, Sana. 2015. *Indians in Kenya: The Politics of Diaspora.* Cambridge: Harvard University Press.

Amin, Ash. 2013. "Land of Strangers." *Identities* 20 (1): 1–8.

Associated Press. 2022. "'Iranian Women Are Furious' Over Death of Mahsa Amini, Dissidents Say." *Global News*, September 24. https://globalnews.ca/news/9153506/iranian-women-furious-death-mahsa-amini/.

Bello, Walden F. 2019. *Counterrevolution: The Global Rise of the Far Right.* Black Point: Fernwood.

Boisvert, Nick. 2020. "LGBTQ Activist Sara Hegazy Exiled in Canada After Torture in Egypt, Dead at 30." *CBC News*, June 17. https://www.cbc.ca/news/canada/toronto/sarah-hegazi-death-1.5614698.

Brosseau, Laurence, and Michael Dewing. 2018. "Canadian Multiculturalism, Background Paper." *Canadian Multiculturalism*, January 1. Publication no. 2009-20-E. Ottawa: Library of Parliament.

Buchignani, Norman. 2010. "South Asian Canadians." *The Canadian Encyclopedia*, May 12.

Chan-Malik, Sylvia. 2018. *Being Muslim: A Cultural History of Women of Color in American Islam*. New York: New York University Press.

Coulthard, Glen Sean. 2014. *Red Skin, White Masks: Rejecting the Colonial Politics of Recognition*. Minneapolis: Minnesota University Press.

Faheid, Dalia. 2021. "Hate Wiped Away a Muslim Canadian Family. Here's How Friends Want Them Remembered." *NPR*, June 12. https://www.npr.org/2021/06/12/1005268914/hate-wiped-away-a-muslim-canadian-family-heres-how-friends-want-them-remembered.

Galabuzi, Grace-Edward. 2006. *Canada's Economic Apartheid: The Social Exclusion of Racialized Groups in the New Century.* Toronto: Canadian Scholars' Press.

Ghafournia, Nafiseh. 2020. "Negotiating Gendered Religious Space: Australian Muslim Women and the Mosque." *Religions* 11 (686): 1-17.

Haque, Eve. 2012. *Multiculturalism Within a Bilingual Framework: Language, Race, and Belonging in Canada.* Toronto: University in Toronto Press.

Isin, Engin F., and Myer Siemiatycki. 1999. *Fate and Faith: Claiming Urban Citizenship in Immigrant Toronto.* Toronto: Joint Centre of Excellence for Research on Immigration and Settlement.

Isin, Engin F., and Myer Siemiatycki. 2002. "Making Space for Mosques: Claiming Urban Citizenship." In *Race, Space and the Law: The Making of a White Settler Society*, edited by Sherene H. Razack, 185-209. Toronto: Between the Lines.

Jiwani, Yasmin. 2021. "Gendered Islamophobia in the Case of the Returning ISIS Women: A Canadian Narrative." *Islamophobia Studies Journal* 6 (1): 52-77.

Khan, Aaliya. 2018. "Exploring Islamophobia in Land Use Regulations: The Case of the City of Mississauga." Master's thesis, Ryerson University.

Lilja, Mona. 2017. "Dangerous Bodies, Matter and Emotions: Public Assemblies and Embodied Resistance." *Journal of Political Power* 10 (3): 342-352.

Mahmood, Saba. 2012. *Politics of Piety: The Islamic Revival and the Feminist Subject.* Princeton: Princeton University Press.

Maynard, Robyn. 2017. *Policing Black Lives: State Violence in Canada from Slavery to the Present.* Black Point: Fernwood Publishing.

Nagra, Baljit, and Paula Maurutto. 2016. "Crossing Borders and Managing Racialized Identities: Experiences of Security and Surveillance Among Young Canadian Muslims." *Canadian Journal of Sociology* 41 (2): 165-194.

Najib, Kawtar, and Peter Hopkins. 2020. "Where Does Islamophobia Take Place and Who Is Involved? Reflections from Paris and London." *Social and Cultural Geography* 21 (4): 458-478.

Pourmokhtari, Navid. 2020. "Presence-as-Resistance: Iranian Women and the Politics of Social Contestation." *Informed Comment*, March 31. https://www.juancole.com/2020/03/presence-resistance-contestation.html.

Puar, Jasbir K. 2018. *Terrorist Assemblages: Homonationalism in Queer Times*. Durham: Duke University Press.

Razack, Sherene H. 2004. "Imperiled Muslim Women, Dangerous Muslim Men and Civilised Europeans: Legal and Social Responses to Forced Marriages." *Feminist Legal Studies* 12 (October): 129-174. https://doi.org/10.1023/B:FEST.0000043305.66172.92.

Razack, Sherene. 2008. *Casting Out: The Eviction of Muslims from Western Law and Politics.* Toronto: University of Toronto Press.

Spivak, Gayatri Chakravorty. 2023. "Can the Subaltern Speak?" In *Imperialism*, Critical Concepts in Historical Studies Series, vol. III, edited by Peter H. Cain and Mark Harrison, 171-219. London: Routledge.

Sweet, Elizabeth L., and Sara Ortiz Escalante. 2015. "Bringing Bodies Into Planning: Visceral Methods, Fear and Gender Violence." *Urban Studies* 52 (10): 1826-1845.

Syed, Iffath. 2013. "Forced Assimilation Is an Unhealthy Policy Intervention: The Case of the Hijab Ban in France and Quebec, Canada." *The International Journal of Human Rights* 17 (3): 428-440.

Toor, Saadia. 2011. *The State of Islam: Culture and Cold War Politics in Pakistan.* London: Pluto Press.

Upadhyay, Nishant. 2020. "Hindu Nation and its Queers: Caste, Islamophobia, and De/Coloniality in India." *Interventions* 22 (4): 464-480.

Walia, Harsha. 2014. *Undoing Border Imperialism.* Chico: AK Press.

Wang, Kelly. 2021. "Muslimfest Returning to London, Ont. Following Tragic Vehicle Attack." *Global News*, August 14. https://globalnews.ca/news/8112547/muslimfest-london-2021/.

Whitley, Leila. 2017. "The Disappearance of Race: A Critique of the Use of Agamben in Border and Migration Scholarship." *Borderlands E-journal* 16 (1): 1-23.

Zine, Jasmin. 2008. *Canadian Islamic Schools: Unravelling the Politics of Faith, Gender, Knowledge and Identity.* Toronto: University of Toronto Press.

14

Translating Chinese Indian Nationalism as the Site of Political Intervention

JANE KU

Rememorying Chinese Indian Belonging

"South Asia" is a place where I have lived and a memory and history that shape how I interpret and speak about and against various oppressions, to intervene in current events shaped by geopolitical turmoil, Euro-American imperialism, and reconsolidated hegemonies around nation, class, gender, and race. It is also a place of speech and politics that is inflected by the experience of being born and raised in India and negotiated through my diasporic Hakka Chinese experience and Western indoctrination. My cultural and political memories and social networks built through this diasporic experience offer a specific South Asian sensibility that engages with multiple hegemonies, including the essentialism of South Asian identification. I appeal to a transnational feminism (Grewal and Kaplan 1994; Mohanty 2003) to reframe this South Asian attachment, and call for a South Asian feminism that goes beyond binaries and reductive notions of gender to interrupt imperial violence, oppressive nationalism, racism, and economic exploitation. South Asian feminism becomes a political home, rather than simply an identity for questioning the binary imperialist limits of either celebrating the greatness of our diasporic homes or attesting to Western benevolence. This chapter opens up the political and intellectual space to develop a more nuanced analysis of contemporary issues to create a transnational anti-colonial future that is built on grounding my reflection in a South Asian feminist methodology of "translation" (Fuchs 2009; Sakai 2006; Niranjana 1992), politics, and difference. It is also a way to communicate across different histories and oppressions, as part of what we must do to create and decolonize transnational solidarity. Finally, this chapter is about building a community of resistance around South Asian feminism and constructing histories of other kinds of South Asian-ness.

Reports of India-China border clashes in Ladakh in 2020 (Anbarasan 2021; Sharma 2020; Tarapore 2021) were accompanied by pictures circulated in my online communities of an Indian Chinese demonstration in Tangra, my hometown in Calcutta (Kolkata), with demonstrators protesting against Chinese incursion and showing their support and loyalty to India (Indian Express 2020). As Chinese Indians re-lived the fears of the 1962 Sino-Indian war, when many Chinese in India were incarcerated in Deoli, Rajasthan (Ghosh 2020; Xing 2017, 2009), this demonstration called attention to slogans like "We are Indians" and "We support Indian army" that emphasized Indian Chinese distance from China, and perhaps even from Chineseness, and reclaimed their Indian belonging. Masked Chinese Indian men (no Chinese Indian women) held up these slogans, signalling the pandemic by wearing masks, which also served to blur the identity of the demonstrators. These pictures are the distillation of the complex histories and diasporic belongings of the Chinese, wrapped up in a spectacle of patriotic nationalism to their generationally naturalized homeland.

The images speak to "Chinese Indian" as a failed identity, arising from the contradictions and difficulties we have in talking about multiple, different, and shifting histories and experiences shaping affective ties and oppressions. The photographs and accompanying news stories are an occasion for marking, deconstructing, and reconstructing Indian Hakka Chinese history, both oral and documented, personal and public. I explore these photographs as traces of personal and social history, and as ways to recall memories, in the service of accounting for both continuities and discontinuities resulting from colonialism, imperialism, migration, assimilation, and integration into modern nation-states.

The photographs could be thought of as rememories (Morrison 1987; Rhee 2021), our own and others' memories, which have lives of their own outside ourselves while they trigger different perceptions and negotiations. Although they are an element of individual experiences, they are a dimension of collective experience. These photographs remind me of my past and my relationship to India, but more particularly this place called Tangra, where the Hakka Chinese lived in Kolkata. In engaging with these photographs that represent the time-space of Tangra, I attempt to translate some of the meaningful elements by creating a gateway to interpreting being Chinese Indian or Indian Chinese in Tangra. This reflection articulates difference as a relationality, a process of knowing self and others, a fluidity that cannot be easily bordered, and as a practice of translation—what we must do to engage across difference. Through articulating this rememory, I advocate for a method of living with difference that borrows from and validates colonized and oppressed communities' work of reading their everyday world as a perpetual act of moving across different epistemes and outlooks (Collins 1990; Du Bois 2007; Fanon 1986; Smith 1987). It also involves exploring contemporary politics and diasporic conditions that are at once global and local, or "glocal" (Grewal and Caplan 1994; Robertson 2012). In doing so, this methodology transcends the language of identity and citizenship that restricts us to questions of nation-states—race, ethnicity, nationality, and diasporic territoriality with an imagined geographic centre (China, India, or Canada, in my case).

Postcolonial Translation of Difference

In postcolonial scholarship, translation is an epistemic violence whereby the colonized can either be seen as unintelligible or fully translatable by the Western and/or Westernized interlocutor; she is the "native informant" who has the privilege of speech but is not necessarily heard (Asad 1986; Bhabha 1994; Chow 1993; Ivekovic 2010; Kothari 2016; Orsini and Srivastava 2013; Spivak 2001). The colonial and imperial practice of translation renders the translated subject opaque. It is precisely this opacity that should be acknowledged and mobilized to remodel translation, not so much to strive for fuller intelligibility as to see translation as an ongoing process of interacting and engaging with the foreigner and stranger, who is allowed to keep the space of unintelligibility. I favour conceptualizing translation as a practice of our everyday world and an essential dimension of social life, precisely because it is representational and interactional, involving a whole range of activities and exchanges and interconnections across multiple contexts (Bowman 2010; Fuchs 2009).

Through the interconnection, interaction, and relationship-building process, translation, then, is a "long term epistemological revolution" (Ivekovic 2010, 47) that builds upon multiple entry points, where actors move from one episteme to another, from one location to another, and take the opportunity to become fully immersed in a foreign culture and another's lifeworld (Asad 1986; Mignolo 2011). Bielsa and Aguilera (2017) argue that we have all had practice integrating the stranger's world into our own, and, borrowing from Derrida (1998) and Benjamin (1996), that there is an "ineradicable strangeness" (19) within us that comes from the fact that our language is the language of the other. As newborns, we begin to enter the world of language and the social world by turning strangeness into our own world. In this way, Bielsa and Aguilera (2017) argue that it is possible to see how we have the capacity to create a space for being hospitable to unassimilable strangeness, and how translation becomes imperfect copies of the original rather than the exact replica (see Chow 1993).

Estranging ourselves has been a subjective mode demanded of the oppressed and one that the privileged may have a harder time with. The oppressed move deftly across multiple perspectives *à la* Black double consciousness (Du Bois 2007), and women's bifurcated knowledge (Smith 1987). As we de-ontologize subjectivity through the questioning of histories and identities, we are more open to exploring connections and disconnections among our diverse experiences, making possible different points of assembling, dissembling, and engaging with each other across our differences, and seeing how multiple histories intersect in ways that are rhizomatic rather than singular genealogies. Our intersectionalities are confronted as fluid temporal and spatial imaginations of ourselves and our world. They are a space where we can intentionally envision a futurity with a re-imagined past that reconstructs not just our place in the world but also the very history that ontologizes who we are (Ku 2019). Identity and spatial and temporal borders become porous as we open ourselves to multiple histories and knowledges (Evans and Ringrow 2017). Or as Niranjana (1992) argues, translating our intersectionalities can be reclaimed as a strategy of resistance and intervention.

This understanding of translation highlights intercultural contact and how subjects are constituted in and by their relations to each other. It treats relations among colonizers and co-colonized, travellers and those who stay put, and cosmopolitan subjects in diasporic spaces not in terms of separateness or apartheid, but in terms of co-presence and interaction, often within radically asymmetrical relations of power that shape a reciprocity that can be diffusionist and hegemonic, but also creative and transformative, even liberating, in building new knowledge and culture (Pratt 1992; Robertson 2021). Consequently, I argue here that translation is or should be treated as an ongoing and intentional exchange and interconnection that seeks to build relationalities (not just relationships) that accept and acknowledge unintelligibility, and that moves toward fluid and less-than-perfect understanding. It is an impulse rather than an achieved and fully comprehended text. It is an open process and unfinished business, where we seek to continuously encounter and understand each other and find points of intersection. In sum, translation is a politic of living with difference, as well as a method to question and challenge colonial frameworks and epistemology in producing knowledges, subjectivities, and oppressions.

"There's a Place Where the Chinese Live..."

Tangra is now known for its restaurants, since the leather industry that fostered its growth has mostly disappeared (Bhattacharjee 2021). During the lunar Chinese New Year, it draws large crowds of both tourists and Indian Chinese who have emigrated overseas, with its dragon/tiger dance troupes and firecrackers, its special homage to the goddess Guanyin, and the Earth and Wealth deities, and its night market and restaurants. For me, it is a place of nostalgia, a place that made me who I am, with all of the contradictions. It is certainly not simply another "Chinatown." It is the time-space that produced the Indian Chinese demonstration of nationalism.

Some of the media photographs show reporters and other Indian bystanders watching the public spectacle, repeating a familiar act of reproducing "Chinatowns" as public spaces of consumption, entertainment, and tourism, even as they are private living quarters of Chinese denizens (Moufakkir 2019; Anderson 1995). However, there are also photographs where both Indians and Chinese Indians stand together in a show of solidarity. Seeing from the experience of Chinese discourse and fears over the "China Virus" and reports of discrimination against Indian Chinese, it is not clear who the target is of the messages: "Stop abusing us" and "We are Indians." Is it China or fellow Indians? Translating this demonstration is not a one-time event; it involves conversations about the history of migration, making a living, economic marginalization and upward mobility, pure childhood joy, family celebrations, and fears of being outsiders and of violence. From a modernist gaze, it is a place of tourism and consumption—designated easily as a "Chinatown," its roots and routes easily told in one accounting. Rememories include prior knowledge and stories, as well as my re-interpretation and re-experiencing of this time-space that both recalls and fills in the gaps of fuzzy memories, the longing, sweet, as well as unpleasant ties, joys, and sorrows that tether a part of me always to that place, even as I clamoured to leave. It involves a rememory that confronts my own strangeness and the impossibility of a fully translated original experience.

When I was a child, I described myself mainly as *"tang ren"* or *"tong gnin"* (Hakka pronunciation), which simply mean the people of "tang." "Chinese" did not become part of my vocabulary until I spoke English. "Cheena" was what Indians called us. "Chin chong man chong" was also thrown at us sometimes, but I never paid it undue attention. We were protected by having this enclave of Hakka Chinese where we belonged. Looking back, identifying myself in English as "Chinese" represents a break in my family biography, and a new suturing of my history to the postcolonial Westernized modern invention of "China" and "Chineseness," as well as "India" and "Indianness." "Indian Chinese" became more important to differentiate myself from other diasporic Chinese once in Canada. My biography is framed through these constructed categories—the newer ones becoming more familiar, and the ones closer to birth becoming estranged and private.

Before becoming a Chinatown where tourists visit, Tangra was merely a reclaimed swamp, a site of pollution, foul smells, and unassumed roads that lacked public utilities and that cab drivers hesitated to enter. The Indian Chinese built their wealth through their family-owned tanneries there, and could afford to send their children to boarding schools to become Western-educated. Tangra was a place where we didn't care enough about the rest of the world to ensure that our dates of birth or names were recorded accurately in the official imperial language. As a result, my brother and I do not have the same last name (in English). It was a place where we played with neighbourhood children near the pond—lost our slippers to it but not our lives, thankfully—climbed to the rooftop, and got caned by teachers, but had a blast generally. Modern aversions to any risk were not in our repertoire. My mother also referred to many dates by the Chinese lunar calendar, so we had to often think in dual temporal modes. I was already considered 2 Chinese years old by the time of my first Gregorian calendar birthday. We had three dogs who were our guards rather than pets—we didn't give them special food, and they mostly ate what we had left over. We lived in the midst of all the machinery and leather at different stages of production.

All this had become very confusing and shameful by the time I went to boarding school, which turned me into a stranger. I was already learning to translate by suppressing the "irrelevant" information. I learned to align my age with the "proper" calendar system, to minimize the complexities of having multiple ways of being, to make my experience equivalent to what the English system could allow. This included, for example, explaining my living space in terms of modern living. This did not always work smoothly, because our rooms were multi-purposed. The master bedroom was a misnomer because, at one time, we all slept in the same room out of necessity. Once I left to go to boarding school, I became very proper and stopped hanging out with the other neighbourhood kids whenever I went home during school breaks. Becoming a respectable young woman also involved this cocooning of oneself from one's past and community. My friends were from the boarding school, and mainly Indian, rather than folks in Tangra. The increasing distance from this place was set in motion.

Tangra became a Chinatown rather than a place where I lived, despite its difficult history of Chinese internment in the 1960s, with the Indian-Chinese border conflict in 1962. The forcible departure of my aunt, who had taught in a pro-Communist Chinese school, and the stigma attached to being Chinese from Tangra existed in the background. Our family experienced an upward mobility that many Indians did not. My father recounts as an adventure his brief detention for flouting the Chinese curfew. Hakka Chinese strategically took up the niche of leather tanning precisely because this was work prohibited for the high-caste Hindus, leaving the industry wide open for Chinese, Muslims, and other minorities to succeed in. The Tangra Hakka Chinese knew our place in the society; the young men grew up to work in the leather businesses, and young women grew up to support this enterprise (although not everyone accepted this as their destiny). Members of less wealthy families also found work in other tanneries or related businesses, Chinese operated restaurants, shoe shops, dry cleaners, and hair salons (Liang 2007). If this did not work, they did what the earlier generations of Hakkas did: migrate elsewhere in India or to other countries for opportunities (Oxfeld 1993).

Western episteme was inculcated in the boarding school, where I read English books voraciously. Tangra had become a place where I wanted to both improve and leave. As a Western-educated student, I knew I had places to go beyond the prospect of getting married. Learning about "women's liberation" and Sandra Day O'Connor—the first woman in the US Supreme Court—further oriented me to the West. Even before I moved to Canada, America and Britain were the source of culture for us. With this new cultural framework, we became very critical of our community—for the scandals, (lack of) secrets, illicit affairs, gossipy neighbours, and elaborate rituals, among other things. What also became pronounced was the critique of the lack of civility and uncouth denizens, and the village-bumpkin-meets-the-city jokes. My desire to leave was cemented by bloody violence that impacted not only my family but the whole community with a botched robbery, during which my uncle, grandfather and a neighbour died, while my father was seriously injured. This was an exceptional event that stamped the psyche of the whole community with violence, deep inside Tangra.

Leaving Tangra physically was foreshadowed by my leaving it many years before—symbolically, ideologically, and culturally. The relationship itself was a rupture brought about by modernization, Western colonial education, and imperialism. Reflecting on my estrangement—both the forcible one and the expedient one—helps me recover both the familiarity and the alien-ness that became a part of me at different times, with different meaning and significance. If the estrangement has been imposed on us, we can also embrace it and deploy it strategically. We can direct our learnings to immersing ourselves in other minority cultures, rather than the hegemonic Western ones. The translational problematic I face is that I could never capture Tangra in the way I really want to; this requires an immersive experience, which not everyone can do. We can develop a habit of relating to ourselves and others through multiple gazes and entry points. We can use multiple epistemes to build novel and more engaged cultural encounters and exchanges among lateral groups. Our own experience tells us that this is possible—I have walked the path being strange and being familiar. "Chinatown" is how I now describe Tangra at a distance. But I am re-living it by exploring it as "a place where the Chinese/I lived..."

Chinese Indian Nationalism as the Site of South Asian Feminist Intervention

My first reaction to the public demonstration was to highlight Chinese Indian nationalism as a performance as opposed to authentic, recalling pictures of South Asians in the US draping American flags as a demonstration of their American loyalty right after the 9/11 event (Grewal 2005). My questioning of its authenticity is both problematic and revealing of my hyper-vigilance over discrimination and the contradictory position of diasporic Chinese in Westernized spaces. When an Indian Canadian friend unquestionably accepted this performance of Indian Chinese nationalism, with their authenticity arising from simply having lived there many generations, I had to stop and reflect on why I questioned their nationalism as authentic. I thought about the 180-degree turn I took during my university years in Toronto, when I wanted to return to India and really get to know it in the way I never did before, as I rebelled against the West as the only path for us. While getting decolonized internally and embracing anti-racist feminist networks and scholarship, I romanticized India as a place where I never experienced racism, and where I was in an equal and lateral relationship and partnership with Indians against Western imperialism and white supremacy. I thought we were on the same boat, regardless of whether I was "Indian Indian" or "Chinese Indian." Re-embracing Indian culture and becoming a neoliberal cosmopolitan consumer of Bollywood culture in the 1990s was part of this move, implicated by the global capitalism and consumerism that reshaped diasporic relations. "Back in India" and "back home" became my synonyms; but increasingly salient is the connection I am making between geopolitically driven Sinophobic discourse and anti-Asian violence, which is reorienting diasporic Chinese relations to nation-states, and particularly to China as the homeland.

There is not only a change in my biography; there is an ongoing reflection and re-evaluation of the experience and the knowledge context from which we make our interpretation. This reflexive exploration stops us from accepting easy answers and reductive representations of our experiences. This reflection attends to Indian Chinese negotiation with and the making of the Chinese Indian community through colonialism, migration, and anti-Chinese policies and practices, as well as the validating experiences of family, friendships, and networks, and economic capacity building. My interpretation also arises from my current Western positioning shaped by recent geopolitics, neoimperialism, racial hierarchy, anti-Chinese ideologies that position India and China as geopolitical rivals, and local experiences of difference making in Canada. I do not feel I have a say in Indian politics because I do not consciously follow them (nor Chinese politics), and I no longer hold Indian citizenship. Still, I watch with glee as Asian, African, and Middle Eastern nations are increasingly aligned with each other in their critique of American imperialism with respect to NATO and American actions in geopolitical conflict. These developments compel me to look for a more anti-imperial and transnational way of approaching how we understand contemporary issues and how we communicate with each other.

Chinese Indian nationalism is a complicated negotiation of these geopolitics, which are glocally (both locally and globally) experienced by Indian Chinese living inside or outside of Tangra. Those identifying as South Asian feminists do not necessarily need to share memories, but we can strategically deploy the translation of our rememories to find an intersection for working across differences. South Asian or Indian feminism has offered here an entry point to address these complex issues and interrupt both personal and political experiences, and perhaps offer a different perspective. This space aligns with a transnational feminist vision of glocalism, as well as global solidarity to challenge the neoliberal, imperial, and heteropatriarchal order (Mohanty 2013). This lends itself well to translation as a process of revising our essentialisms and working with multiple epistemes through a transnational feminist intersectional lens. A South Asian feminist framing of translation allows me to wear my Chinese Indian identity lightly, to reference my South Asian history and rememory without calcifying them. As my affective experience becomes more activated and centred around the imagined homeland of China, a place I only visited for the first time very recently, South Asian feminism is still a useful space to speak to the anti-China ideology being promoted across the American hegemonized world. It brings into focus the commonalities within which we make denials: "I am Asian, not Chinese," "I am anti-CCP, not anti-Chinese," or "I am Indian Chinese, and not Chinese from China." South Asian feminism is a space to stop and reflect on how feminists can gather and speak against the troubling developments in our times, while acknowledging our intersectionalities, differences, and estrangement from ourselves and from each other.

South Asian Feminism as a Methodology of Living With and Speaking to Difference

Critical South Asian feminism has opened up a space for documenting and creating alternative histories that can be the basis for doing cultural exchanges differently. While my claim to speak as "Indian," "Chinese," "Chinese Indian," or "Indian Chinese" is precarious (and should be), this reconstruction of history makes it possible to speak to world politics, to speak beyond the national identity we are saddled with, to the ways our glocal contexts are being shaped by geopolitics that are distinctly understood and interpreted in different parts of the world. I speak to those who experience similar contradictions in their lives, of having their experiences spill over the categories of our language—nation, diaspora, identity, ethnicity, or even gender. I speak to those who are Westernized by our histories and who see the need to forge different alliances and intersectionalities to counter the hegemonies that prevent us from speaking, or being recognized as subjects of specific politics. I also speak to the divisions created through the gaslighting of our social realities, which are deeply embedded in the imperial, neoliberal, and neocolonial order. My re-encounter with my own and public memories is an interaction with the selves of my past, with other Others, and offers ways for us to see our own and others' strangeness as a method of encountering others—so that we do not stop at centring ourselves, but instead can find new intersections of political organizing and imagining.

We make our and other people's strangeness our own. Strangeness moves between an exception as a point of exploration and a mundanity that we take for granted or challenge. Instead of speaking as native informants, a role designated for Westernized diasporic actors as translators, we ought to challenge the history that has been written for us, as well as the imperial definitions of our times, issues, experiences, communities, and identities. We question ruptures to re-forge and re-suture our histories strategically, with a clear-eyed intention for building solidarity. Our differences are places to speak to each other and to situate a shared context where differences can become the basis for accepting strangeness. Rememorying can be the basis for challenging hegemonies in South Asia, North America, and elsewhere. This helps me reclaim my right to critique, and forge a strategic place to question Indian nationalism as a foil for various forms of essentialisms, tyrannies, and amnesias. Questioning South Asian-ness further allows me to question American imperialism and militarism, which are just as responsible for displacements, destruction, violence, and death everywhere (especially in the Muslim and Arab world), for the related anti-China and anti-Communist tactics and ideologies, and for the suppression of grassroots movements against neoliberalisms everywhere. From this space, I speak in solidarity with those struggling against Islamophobia, casteism, and displacements of the marginalized in India and across the world, and work with them by forging a community of belonging toward a shared future.

References

Anbarasan, Ethirajan. 2021. "China-India Clashes: No Change a Year After Ladakh Stand-Off." *BBC News*, June 1. https://www.bbc.com/news/world-asia-57234024.

Anderson, Kay. 1995. *Vancouver's Chinatown*. Montreal and Kingston: McGill Queen's University Press.

Asad, Talal. 1986. "The Concept of Cultural Translation in British Social Anthropology." In *Writing Culture: The Poetics and Politics of Ethnography*, edited by James Clifford and George E. Marcus, 141–164. Berkeley: University of California Press.

Benjamin, Walter. 1996. *Gesammelte* Schriften, vol. I, 3. Frankfurt: Suhrkamp.

Bhabha, Homi. 1994. *The Location of Culture*. London: Routledge.

Bhattacharjee, Gopal. 2021. "Where Have Tangra's Chinese Tanneries Gone?" *Get Bengal*, April 6. https://www.getbengal.com/details/where-have-tangras-chinese-tanneries-gone.

Bielsa, Esperanca, and Antonio Aguilera. 2017. "Politics of Translation: A Cosmopolitan Approach." *European Journal of Cultural and Political Sociology* 4 (1): 7–24.

Bowman, Paul. 2010. "Sick Man of Transl-Asia: Bruce Lee and Rey Chow's Queer Cultural Translation." *Social Semiotics* 20 (4): 393–409.

Chow, Rey. 1993. *Writing Diaspora: Tactics of Intervention in Contemporary Cultural Studies*. Bloomington: Indiana University Press.

Collins, Patricia. 1990. *Black Feminist Thought: Knowledge, Consciousness and the Politics of Empowerment*. New York: Routledge.

Derrida, Jacques. 1998. *Monolingualism of the Other: Or, The Prosthesis of Origin*. Translated by Patrick Mensah. Stanford: Stanford University Press.

Du Bois, W.E.B. 2007 [1903]. *The Souls of Black Folk*. Oxford: Oxford University Press.

Evans, Jonathan, and Helen Ringrow. 2017. "Introduction: Borders in Translation and Intercultural Communication." *TranscUlturAl* 9 (2): 1–12.

Fanon, Franz. 1986 [1967]. *Black Skin, White Masks*. London: Pluto Press.

Fuchs, Martin. 2009. "Reaching Out; Or, Nobody Exists in One Context Only: Society as Translation." *Translation Studies* 2 (1): 21–40.

Ghosh, Bishwanath. 2020. "Shadow of LAC Tensions Over Indian-Chinese Community." *The Hindu*, June 19. https://www.thehindu.com/news/cities/kolkata/shadow-of-lac-tensions-over-indian-chinese-community/article31870590.ece.

Grewal, Inderpal. 2005. *Transnational America: Feminisms, Diasporas, Neoliberalisms*. Durham: Duke University Press.

Grewal, Inderpal, and Karen Caplan. 1994. *Scattered Hegemonies: Postmodernity and Transntional Feminist Practices*. Minneapolis: University of Minnesota Press.

Indian Express. 2020. "India-China Border Row: People Stage Protest, Shout Anti-China Slogans in Kolkata." June 20. https://indianexpress.com/photos/india-news/india-china-lac-border-kolkata-protest-6468434/.

Ivekovic, Rada. 2010. "The Watershed of Modernity: Translation and the Epistemological Revolution." *Inter-Asia Cultural Studies* 11 (1): 45–63.

Kothari, Rita. 2016. "Translation, Language, Anthropology: Notes from the Field." *Interventions* 18 (1): 43–59.

Ku, Jane. 2019. "Intentional Solidarity as a Decolonizing Practice." *Intermédialités / Intermediality* 34 (Fall). https://doi.org/10.7202/1070870ar.

Liang, Jennifer. 2007. "Migration Patterns and Occupational Specializations of Kolkata Chinese: An Insider's History." *China Report* 43 (4): 397–410.

Mignolo, Walter. 2011. "I Am Where I Think: Remapping the Order of Knowing." In *The Creolization of Theory*, edited by Francoise Lionnet and Shumei Shih, 159–192. Durham: Duke University Press.

Mohanty, Chandra Talpade. 2003. *Feminism Without Borders: Decolonizing Theory, Practicing Solidarity*. Durham: Duke University Press.

Mohanty, Chandra Talpade. 2013. "Transnational Feminist Crossings: On Neoliberalism and Radical Critique." *Signs: Journal of Women and Culture* 38 (4): 967–991.

Morrison, Toni. 1987. *Beloved*. New York: Random House.

Moufakkir, Omar. 2019. "The Liminal Gaze: Chinese Restaurant Workers Gazing Upon Chinese Tourists Dining in London's Chinatown." *Tourist Studies* 19 (1): 89–109.

Niranjana, Tejaswini. 1992. *Siting Translation: History, Post-Structuralism and the Colonial Context*. Berkeley: University of California Press.

Orsini, Francesa, and Neelam Srivastava. 2013. "Translation and the Postcolonial." *Interventions* 15 (3): 323–331.

Oxfeld, Ellen. 1993. *Blood, Sweat and Mahjong*. Ithaca: Cornell University Press.

Pratt, Mary. 1992. *Imperial Eyes: Travel Writing and Transculturalization*. New York: Routledge.

Rhee, Jeong-Eun. 2021. *Decolonial Feminist Research: Haunting, Rememory and Mothers*. New York: Routledge.

Robertson, Roland. 2012. "Globalization or Glocalization?" *Journal of International Communication* 18 (2): 191–208.

Sakai, Naoki. 2006. "Translation." *Theory, Culture and Society* 23 (2/3): 71–78.

Sharma, Ashok. 2020. "India, China Agree to Disengage Thousands of Troops at Border, Easing Standoff." *Global News*, September 11. https://globalnews.ca/news/7328539/india-china-dispute-agreement/.

Smith, Dorothy. 1987. *Everyday World a Problematic: A Feminist Sociology*. Toronto: University of Toronto Press.

Spivak, Gayatri. 2001. "Questioned on Translation: Adrift." *Public Culture* 13 (1): 13–22.

Tarapore, Arzan. 2021. "The Crisis after the Crisis: How Ladakh Will Shape India's Competition With China." Lowy Institute, May 5. https://www.lowyinstitute.org/publications/crisis-after-crisis-how-ladakh-will-shape-india-s-competition-china.

Xing, Zhang. 2009. "Creating a New Cultural Identity: India-Related Religious Practices as the Chinese Community in Kolkata." *China Report* 45 (1): 53–63.

Xing, Zhang. 2017. "Study on the Cultural Identity of the Chinese-Indians in Kolkata, Sihui and Toronto." *Identities: Global Studies in Culture and Power* 24 (3): 237–253.

15

Queering Islam to Root Us in Our Lived Experiences

AMEERA SULTANA KHAN

NEOCONSERVATIVE NARRATIVES in Islamic culture often invoke Islamic concepts to justify heteronormativity and cisnormativity.[1] However, many traditional and modern theologies suggest that these neoconservative efforts are incongruent with Islam itself in both spirit and law. In this chapter, I will make a case for adopting Islamic liberation theology as a lens through which to cultivate social and theological acceptance of queerness. Drawing from contemporary Islamic theories, as well as personal experiences of 2SLGBTQ+ and progressive Muslims, I intend to reconstruct the line between our past and present to invest in our future as Muslims. By refuting aspects of neoconservative Muslim thought and cultural stigmas from both Muslims and non-Muslim South Asians toward 2SLGBTQ+ Muslims, I will point to the dangers of adopting ahistorical and amoral approaches and show the deeply powerful, transformative, and communally liberatory concepts that Islam can sustain. In doing so, I will make a case for an Islam that is inclusive, progressive, and better equipped to take our *Ummah* (the community of Muslims worldwide, transcending all barriers of race, gender, economics, and sect) into the future.

What Is Islamic Liberation Theology and Why Is It an Important Alternative?

Islamic liberation theology (hereafter referred to as ILT) is defined broadly in Scott Kugle's (2010) book *Homosexuality in Islam: Critical Reflection on Gay, Lesbian, and Transgender Muslims* as an approach to interacting with Islamic theology and the Qur'an by centring the principles of justice and protest against oppression. He writes: "Liberation theology argues that the existential condition of those who interpret shapes their interpretation...[Oppressed communities] have a privileged position as interpreters of scripture precisely because they are in a disempowered position, because they are oppressed within their society" (Kugle 2010, 7). Kugle draws attention to the work of many contemporary scholars who are engaged in contributing to this area, and emphasizes the insights of Farid Esack (1997), a pioneer of modern Islamic liberation theology in the context of the South African fight against apartheid. Esack's liberation theology views "the Qur'an [as] both liberating and in need of liberation. To fulfill its promise of liberation, Muslims must first free the Qur'an from partial, limited, and corrupted interpretations that enshrine injustice" (Kugle 2010, 38).

My view is that ILT, by centring these principles, becomes a more accurate version of Islam that incorporates historical, sociological, political, and academic knowledge from experts in how it shapes theology, in addition to keeping true to the spirit of Islam as a form of divinely inspired protest against injustice. ILT considers the knowledge of marginalized people such as the 2SLGBTQ+ community and understands and attempts to correct the pitfalls of so-called "traditional" Islam in fulfilling the intended goals of Islam. It does this by by creating inclusive communities, which more and more North American and diasporic Muslims are seeking after leaving their traditional communities.

As an aside, I will refer to followers of ILT as followers of "an Islam," as there are many "Islams" when considering the vast diversity of theology and ritual within Islam.

The Unmosqued and Their Future in the *Ummah*

Many North American Muslims are not attending the masjid frequently, for reasons similar to why many Christians don't attend church: what is preached is not what is practiced. The Pew Research Center (2011) reports that there are more Muslims who either do not attend the masjid or attend infrequently than there are Muslims who attend the masjid regularly. And while many masjids still have imams railing against the evils of homosexuality, most Muslims in the US believe homosexuality should be accepted (Pew Research Center 2017). Brianna Dee, a self-reported "unmosqued" Muslim, said of her experience as an ex-Pentecostal queer and transgender Muslim woman that it "expanded upon the lessons [she] learned while growing up under devout Apostolic Pentecostal parents and obliterated biases [she] didn't even know [she] had. Devout exclusionary traditionalists exist in every form, practice, and sect of religion, just like [they do] in Christianity" (interview with the author, January 13, 2022). She had experienced judgmental cliques of people who attended the mosque or church more frequently, judging and excluding outsiders while ignoring her valid critiques of their theology.

Despite these critiques, the masjid also has the potential to be a place of empowerment for youth and marginalized communities, as is the case for many attendees of inclusive churches (Predelli 2008). It can be a healthy outlet for women and youth to engage proactively in political discourse and action while also building community and faith (Jamal 2005). It does not have to be yet another place of oppressive theology and alienation.

While many espouse culture and religion as separate, it is undeniable that the two have a profound and often subtle influence on each other. One example Michael Muhammad Knight (2013) examines in his book *Tripping with Allah: Islam, Drugs, and Writing* is the story of how coffee became widely accepted as halal. Initially some muftis considered it haram, calling it a "mind altering substance" like alcohol, while others said that it didn't induce a drunken state, so it was halal. Due to the influence of coffee growers on the Caliphate, coffee eventually "became halal" and remains so in most Muslim spaces today. While seemingly trivial today, this example shows us that changing cultural ideas around what is socially acceptable can also change the theology of what is halal, giving us hope for Islams adapting to the growing acceptance of 2SLGBTQ+ identities in the West.

Historical Revisionism and Queer Erasure

While it is widely publicized in mainstream Muslim spaces that the Muslim world brought a Golden Age to civilization by spreading medicine, technology, and ideas that sparked the Renaissance across the world, there are also historical examples of oppression during these times, for example bloody struggles for succession. Knowledge of this multifaceted history prevents us from romanticizing this past, but it also allows us to see pre-colonial queerness reflected in it. Ali Olomi (2021a) notes that bisexuality was practiced and actually encouraged by the upper class, and *mukhannathūn* were allowed to marry people of any gender.[2] These were considered perfectly normal and socially acceptable practices. Doctors would even prescribe same-sex relations for patients experiencing same-sex desires, and several *khulafa* of the Muslim empires like al-Amin and Mansur were known to have had male lovers (Olomi 2021a; Joubin 2020). Even during the lifetime of the Prophet, and with his knowledge, mukhannathūn married people of any gender, and it was considered halal and socially acceptable (Olomi 2021a). Many, if not all, reported narrations of the Prophet explicitly condemning homosexuality are likely fabricated or otherwise have unreliable chains of narration (Zahed 2020).

To see our history accurately and with nuance is to repudiate the historical romanticizing that engages the imagination of many Muslims. Those who claim that Islam's history shuns 2SLGBTQ+ Muslims must recognize that they are crafting a cherry-picked image of Islamic history by selectively filtering out many of these complex and queer identities[3]—adding more products of colonization to further the marginalization of 2SLGBTQ+ people (Velte 2020).

Subject Matter Experts and Deferring to Them in *Fiqḥ*

The Prophet Muhammad ﷺ once said, "Being a student of knowledge is an obligation upon every Muslim" (Ibn Majah 1952). In alignment with this Prophetic principle, a general tenet of ILT is that one's theology and religion are grounded in a true and current material analysis of the world, and thus one should not look at scripture in a vacuum of either historical context or "spirit of the law" (Wikipedia 2023).[4] To this end, I assert that Islam must be updated with new knowledge via feedback loops, bringing it back into the Islamic corpus of knowledge, where Islamic scholars can reference that knowledge and use it to champion a more nuanced and progressive Islam.

Indeed, *'Uqūd rasm al-muftī*, a treatise by Ibn 'Ābidīn (Calder 2000) specifically advising muftis,[5] says that for subject areas that one does not have specific expertise in, they must refer to the professional opinion of a subject matter expert (hereafter referred to as SME). For example, if a mufti gives a fatwā on a medical issue as it relates to fasting, they must consult a doctor who specializes in that specific medical issue and consider their opinion (often above even their own) when making a fatwā around it (Dudgeon 2018). This principle can be taken from the Holy Qur'an itself in verses 21:7 and 16:43, where it instructs: "So ask the people of remembrance if you do not know" (author's translation). While there does exist specific context referring to Jews and Christians for these verses, that does not abrogate the general meaning of the Arabic, where scholars interpret "people of remembrance" as SMEs (Rahman 2019). This ability for the Qur'an to hold dual meanings is part of its divine wisdom and complexity (Saeed 2006).

There are many experts who speak on how 2SLGBTQ+ identities are a natural subset of the broader population; how they have existed throughout all history and cultures despite historical erasure; and how their inherent worth as humans tell us, as followers of a religion that considers itself universally applicable, that they should be fully included and accepted in public life (Hoel and Henderson-Espinoza 2016). Yet, when many mainstream Muslims talk about 2SLGBTQ+ people, they often claim that their identity is too Western and incompatible with Islam if "acted upon" (i.e., having same-sex sexual relations). The problem with many of these voices is that they are not grounded in the realities that 2SLGBTQ+ people live, nor are they supported by evidence for differentiating between having same-sex desires and having sexual relations. As queer Muslim organizer Ramish Nadeem (personal communication, 2022) says, "it doesn't matter whether or not we have sex, because sex is just a small part of the experience of being queer and Muslim."

Another reality of the 2SLGBTQ+ community that Muslims often overlook is the impact that acceptance can have on mental health, social outcomes, and even life expectancy. This must be considered in discussing ILT, the central tenet of which is centring the lived oppression of marginalized Muslims to create an Islam that is liberatory for all and that follows the spirit of the law. Research has shown that familial acceptance of a transgender child is often lifesaving (Ryan et al. 2010), and that providing gender-affirming care is one of the most cost-effective treatments—in terms of cost per quality-adjusted life year, a measure of health outcomes—provided in the entire medical field (Padula, Heru, and Campbell 2016). On the flip side, 2SLGBTQ+ youth are overrepresented within the homeless youth population due to familial/community rejection and suffer in terms of social and health outcomes because of it (Abramovich 2012).

As Muslims, we are told repeatedly to take care of those in need. The Qur'an's verses 107:2–3 are one example, and the Prophet ﷺ famously said, "I have only been sent to perfect righteous character" (Ibn Ḥanbal 1990). Many Muslims might believe that treating those in need well is a good thing, but then rescind that behaviour when they find out a person is part of the 2SLGBTQ+ community, exhibiting hypocritical and un-Islamic behaviour. This rejection of 2SLGBTQ+ Muslims is commonplace in mainstream Muslim spaces and results in 2SLGBTQ+ Muslims being further marginalized, often encouraging them to leave the faith and the community entirely (Lundqvist 2020).

Speaking of SMEs on 2SLGBTQ+ Muslim experiences, Kugle's (2010) *Homosexuality in Islam* both examines and contextualizes the specific Qur'anic verses and *aḥādīth* (plural of hadith) that homophobic and transphobic Muslims cite to justify anti-2SLGBTQ+ theology. Kugle concludes that there is no clear argument in the Qur'an or hadith to justify these positions. From the Qur'anic story of the people of Lut, he concludes that their sin was not their consensual same-sex relationships, but rather that they were perpetrators of sexual violence and rape in addition to their "infidelity and rejection" of God's Prophet and his message. Kugle also states that a major reason the homophobic interpretation became so widespread was due to the endorsement given to it by the exegesis of the tenth-century Islamic scholar and historian Abu Jaafar Al Tabari. His interpretation was based on the fallacious strategy of "replacement and substitution," substituting the word *fāḥisha* (literally "immorality") with the specific act and associated legal concept of *liwāṭ* (the insertion of a penis into a man's anus), a strategy that the eleventh-century jurist Ibn Hazm called out as an improper use of Qur'anic analysis and fiqḥ legislation.

As for the hadith cursing "men who imitate women," Kugle (2010) interprets this as a socially progressive command, arguing that the imitation in question refers to a specific type of mocking of the opposite sex. This is akin to the way transphobic or misogynistic male comedians often use a falsetto voice to caricature women, even though most women do not naturally speak in such tones (Olomi 2021b). Another progressive interpretation of this hadith, argued by Yasmin Chanel (2018), is that it refers to a specific incident with the mukhannath Hit. Hit was banished by the Prophet from the city of Madina, but only after Hit began to speak inappropriately of the Prophet's wife. Hit's story, interestingly, is also a Prophetic example in favour of queer and transgender people being allowed in the spaces of their choosing, as Hit was allowed in private, "hijab-less" spaces with the wife of the Prophet before this incident without rebuke, even though Hit was assigned male at birth. In either case, Chanel (2018) argues, this hadith is not applicable to people experimenting with their gender, nor should it be used for delegitimizing a 2SLGBTQ+ person's existence.

These interpretations provide necessary textual and historical context to the narrations, pointing to the unavoidable conclusion: 2SLGBTQ+ Muslims are oppressed in Islam due to selective interpretations and improperly informed theology, and they should be fully accepted as per the Prophetic example. Islam should not be a static mindset clinging to a selectively curated past, but an evolving way of life that adapts with cultures and social situations, complete with systemic and material analyses of power and the social justice activism around it. As Muslims, we have a duty to ensure that our faith and our communities are properly informed on all topics, including the lived realities and professional opinions around 2SLGBTQ+ identities. And while some muftis in the modern era have made *fatāwā* pushing for the inclusion of 2SLGBTQ+ Muslims in public life, there will not be a truly liberatory progressiveness in the institution of Islamic scholarship across the world until the voices of those with lived experience as part of the 2SLGBTQ+ community take up scholarship equal to or greater than the voices supporting the status quo (Zaharin and Pallotta-Chiarolli 2020).

'Urf: Political and Social Realities

The *sharʿī* principle of *'urf*, often translated to accommodations based on "custom" or "culture," is important to ILT because Islam falls short of its purpose of serving all of humanity if it does not accommodate the lived realities of people, especially the marginalized. 'Urf has historically been used as a legal basis to accommodate local practices, instead of "converting" them to the more hegemonic version of Islam practiced in a society; thus, it enables the fusing of subjective experience with sharʿī principles and justifications (Khan 2016). Even though classical Islamic theology maintains that Islam is "complete," as inscribed in Qur'an 5:3, it has always been implemented through the filter of interpretation and applicability to different communities. This is in part why Islam has such a variety of diverse practices and theologies unique to particular places or cultures. Since 'urf is tied to the lived realities experienced by a community, it is important to talk about the lived realities of 2SLGBTQ+ Muslims, and how they tie into the politics of oppression. Much of progressive and liberation-oriented political action is a fight for justice, which is a central goal of ILT. Progressive Muslim scholars, such as Omid Safi, have explored the concept of anti-racism as a "spiritual practice" (Encyclopedia Britannica 2016; Safi and Singh 2021). Allah commands us in Qur'an 4:135 to "be [of] those who stand up firmly for justice, as a witness to God, even if against yourselves or your parents or those close to you, and whether it be against rich or poor" (author's translation). This is one of the reasons why even conservative Muslims today express support for causes like the freedom of Palestine and the state of Uyghur Muslims and Rohingya refugees. If we embrace this politico-religious awareness fully, we can understand that, in its spirit, Islam has always had the capacity for progressive political good and uplifting other marginalized communities. Most notable is the prophetic example of participating in the Hiful Fadool, a pre-Islamic agreement to give marginalized people due process in seeking justice, and later the inception of the Madina Charter, which is one of the first documented examples of a human rights charter aimed at enabling interfaith communities to live peacefully together. What all these prophetic examples have in common is that they centre the lived realities of marginalized communities and create systems of protection for them within a religious and political context. The two realms are intertwined; the advocacy for the rights of the marginalized is not just theological, but also material and legal. Both the principle of 'urf and the prophetic example show us different ways of considering the lived realities of marginalized people and fighting on their behalf, as well as advocating for 2SLGBTQ+ Muslims based on their lived realities as part of a marginalized community. Indeed, this is essential to keeping the religion true to its goals in the modern sociopolitical context of the Global North.

Ijtihād as Reclaiming Islam

Acknowledging the individual agency of 2SLGBTQ+ and progressive Muslims in redefining faith, community, and religion gives us the power to interact with Islam and Muslims on our own terms. This principle of using deductive reasoning to come up with

Islamic conclusions using fundamental Islamic and scholarly principles like this is called ijtihād, and more progressive Muslims are espousing it as a way of understanding our own lives and making definite assertions based on it. Indeed, Asra Q. Nomani, an Islamic feminist organizer, argues that "Islam was originally a dynamic and progressive tradition, and ijtihad allows contemporary Muslims to recover that dynamism and progressivism" (Cervantes-Altamirano 2011, 7). As an example, Amina Wadud (1999) utilizes ijtihād in her feminist *tafsīr* (lexical and contextual interpretation) of the Qur'an, interpreting the verse of Qur'an 4:34 as referring to marital discord instead of "a woman's disobedience," as a means of reducing the excessive use of force practiced in pre-Islamic Arabia. Acknowledging every Muslim's right to engage with Islam on their own level and make their own ijtihād, especially Muslims marginalized in their own community, moves the locus of control back into the hands of these marginalized Muslims, who have a far more intimate and nuanced understanding of their own needs and how Muslim spaces can meet them. This is, in turn, aligned with the core tenet of ILT that the interpretations and shaping of theology by the most marginalized people should be privileged over other interpretations, and is more salient to the ultimate liberatory goals of Islam.

Many Salafis warn that only highly qualified Islamic scholars are capable of doing ijtihād properly,[6] and state that the only option for lay people is *taqlīd*, or a near-unquestioning acceptance of the decisions that scholars have already made (Sharif 2009). Those who dare to do ijtihād anyway are labeled as *ahlul bid'ah*, or the people of innovation in the religion. However, mainstream Islamic scholars have been utilizing ijtihād since the early days of Islam to interpret the Qur'an and Sunnah (Cervantes-Altamirano 2011). Claiming that those who use ijtihād to make decisions are practicing bid'ah is therefore an invalid interpretation of Islamic law (Lucas 2006). It is also important to note that these interpretations are no less valid than other classical approaches, and "rely on [their] own 'correctness' just as patriarchal or literal interpretations [of the Qur'an and Sunnah] do" (Cervantes-Altamirano 2011). As long as we make our own ijtihād centring progressive values, Islamic principles, and the goals of Islamic law, we are making our best-informed guess at what a truer Islam looks like today. And as the Prophet ﷺ said, "If a judge makes a ruling, striving to apply his reasoning and he is correct, he will have two rewards. If a judge makes a ruling, striving to apply his reasoning and he is mistaken, he will have one reward" (Bukhārī 1966).

So how do we reconcile the concepts of ijtihād and listening to experts? Is Islam subjective or is it objective? In truth, when we give a platform to and are informed by the needs of the most marginalized Muslims, we are in fact listening to SMES, as they are the experts when it comes to knowledge of their own marginalization. The expressed needs and hopes of marginalized communities as a whole allow us to interpret Islam from an informed lens of liberation and anti-oppression politics. Progressive Muslims, Islamic feminists, many Sufis, and Islamic liberation theologists have all been laying the groundwork to create this growing, living theology to address the needs of marginalized groups for decades.

Relevance for the South Asian Diasporic Identity

As a Bengali American Muslim transgender woman born and raised in the American Midwest, I affirm this theology based on my personal experiences. I have experienced forced removal from masjid spaces meant to build my connection with Allah and my Muslim community, along with a sort of "social death," in that nearly all of those who I called my dearest friends cut themselves off from me, effectively leaving me without a community. Spirituality is always practiced and reinforced in a social context, and in this case society's intended context was that after coming out as transgender, I no longer belonged in a masjid at all. My experience is not unique among 2SLGBTQ+ Muslims, many of whom come from South Asian backgrounds, who thus seek to build spaces where they can feel safe and affirmed in being themselves.

Progressive South Asians celebrated the decriminalization of homosexuality in India in 2018, after much fighting by activists to repeal a colonial law that criminalized homosexuality. South Asian Muslims often borrow the homophobic interpretation of the greater conservative Muslim community in their claims of what is haram (forbidden) and halal (permitted), without necessarily caring about the veracity of those claims from an authentic and theologically sound viewpoint. While the conservative theology they use might be either Arab or South Asian in origin, many of the associated legal and social measures of enforcement, for example, relegating 2SLGBTQ+ identities to the shadows, are left over from European colonization (see Vanita and Kidwai 2000). However, while transgender people can now mark their IDs with "X" to indicate their identification as non-binary or hijra, they still face the material conditions of oppression, which were codified under British rule and remain to this day. Indians and South Asians generally tend to ignore the presence of homonationalism, where the "good queers" uphold ideas of caste-based discrimination and anti-Muslim tendencies to justify their acceptance into wider Indian society (Bachetta 2019). While accepting 2SLGBTQ+ identities is essential, doing it at the cost of other marginalized communities such as members of lower castes and Muslims justifies their past and ongoing oppression, and stands in the way of solidarity with the oppressed and social progress for all (Zahed 2020). 2SLGBTQ+ Muslim activists like Mubina Qureshi have often brought this to the attention of the wider South Asian community, with mixed reception. As the director of SEWA-AIFW (Asian Indian Family Wellness), a non-profit that works with South Asians in Minnesota, she has seen Hindus who continue to uphold notions of caste that engender Islamophobia, as well as those who are open to understanding their shared oppression and how to create Muslim-Hindu solidarity. In a conversation with the author, Qureshi stated: "Even queer South Asian spaces can be tainted by homonationalism. So the need for us to centre Muslim experiences and shared oppression in those spaces is crucial. This is why praying in LGBTQ+ inclusive masjids is extraordinarily powerful" (September 2022).

Conclusion

If we want to embody our progressive values as an extension of our Islamic values, we can intentionally centre these deeply powerful, transformative, and communally liberatory concepts in our interpretations and understandings of Islam. In doing so, we are not "bending Islam to our personal will" or creating haram innovation in Islam by "Westernizing" our faith; rather, we are acting with a deep politico-religious awareness and set of values that centre real material and communal needs, without cherry-picking from our history to build that community. We can follow the prophetic tradition to inspire a progressive Islamic community that is inclusive of all marginalized people and that is deeply committed to social justice, while simultaneously being academically and intellectually rigorous. Adopting ILT and including with it 2SLGBTQ+ Muslims as co-creators in the shaping of theology, are crucial steps in creating community and fighting for our collective liberation.

Notes

1. By neoconservative, I refer to contemporary projects of reform that claim to return to a pure tradition but that are in fact political ideological attempts to reinstate precepts from conservative exegesis produced during the ninth to thirteenth centuries AD.
2. *Mukhannathūn* is the plural of *mukhannath*. A group of people in pre-Islamic Arabia that existed outside of the gender binary, considered a cross between modern homosexual males, transgender females, and *hijras* from the South Asian subcontinent.
3. Referring to identities that are "non-heteronormative," as these people did not identify with labels of queer, bisexuality, homosexuality, and so on as the modern Western 2SLGBTQ+ community does. Furthermore, imposing Western lenses of identity onto historical societies that do not ascribe to that framework is also an example of selective filtering.
4. A dichotomy adapted into theological applications following its use in law when discussing "the Letter of the Law" (laws as written) and "the Spirit of the Law" (laws as intended).
5. An Islamic scholar qualified to make an Islamic legal verdict, or fatwā.
6. Muslims who claim to emulate the *salaf* or companions of the Prophet Muhammed and commit themselves to a singly correct interpretation of Sunni Islam, thereby removing much of the cultural diversity that inherently exists in Islam via the negative label of bid'ah, or "innovation in religion."

References

Abramovich, Ilona Alex. 2012. "No Safe Place to Go—LGBTQ Youth Homelessness in Canada: Reviewing the Literature." *Canadian Journal of Family and Youth* 4 (1): 29–51. https://doi.org/10.29173/cjfy16579.

Bacchetta, Paola. 2019. "Queer Presence in/and Hindu Nationalism." In *Majoritarian State: How Hindu Nationalism is Changing India*, edited by Angana P. Chatterji, Thomas Blom Hansen, and Christophe Jaffrelot. Oxford: Oxford University Press.

Bukhārī, Muḥammad ibn Ismāʿīl. 1966. *Sahih Bukhari*, no. 7352. Karachi: Muhammad Sarid.

Calder, Norman. 2010. "The "Uqūd rasm al-muftī' of Ibn 'Ābidīn." *Bulletin of the School of Oriental and African Studies, University of London* 63 (2): 215–228. http://www.jstor.org/stable/1559538.

Cervantes-Altamirano, Eréndira. 2011. "Recovering the Progressive Spirit of Islam: Ijtihad and Its Transformative Possibilities in Islamic Feminism." *Axis Mundi* 7. https://journals.library.ualberta.ca/axismundi/index.php/axismundi/issue/view/28.

Chanel, Yasmine E. 2018. "Addressing Arguments Regarding the Station of LGBT+ In Islam." Unpublished research paper.

Dudgeon, Hamza A. 2018. "Iftā & the Science of Transgenderism." https://www.academia.edu/36810439/Ift%C4%81.

Esack, Farid. 1997. *Qur'ān, Liberation and Pluralism: An Islamic Perspective of Interreligious Solidarity Against Oppression*. London: Oneworld.

Hoel, Nina, and Robyn Henderson-Espinoza. 2016. "Approaching Islam Queerly." *Theology and Sexuality* 22 (1-2): 1-8. https://doi.org/10.1080/13558358.2017.1296701.

Ibn Mājah, Muḥammad ibn Yazīd. 1952. *Sunan Ibn Majah*, no. 224. Karachi: Vali Muhammad.

Jamal, Amaney. 2005. "Mosques, Collective Identity, and Gender Differences Among Arab American Muslims." *Journal of Middle East Women's Studies* 1 (1): 53–78.

Ibn Ḥanbal, 'Alī Muḥammad, and Aḥmad ibn Muḥammad Jamāz. 1990. *Musnad al-Shāmīyīn min Musnad al-Imām Aḥmad ibn Ḥanbal*, no. 8729. al-Dawḥah, Qatar: Dār al-Thaqāfah.

Joubin, Rebecca. 2020. "The Multifarious Lives of the Sixth 'Abbasid Caliph Muhammad Al-Amin: Collective Memory Construction, Queer Spaces, and Historical Television Drama in Egypt and Syria." *International Journal of Middle East Studies* 52 (4): 643–663. https://doi.org/10.1017/S0020743820000793.

Khan, Zara. 2016. "Refractions Through the Secular: Islam, Human Rights and Universality." PHD diss., City University of New York. https://academicworks.cuny.edu/gc_etds/1618.

Knight, Michael Muhammad. 2013. *Tripping with Allah: Islam, Drugs, and Writing*. New York: Catapult.

Kugle, Scott Siraj al-Haqq. 2010. *Homosexuality in Islam: Critical Reflection on Gay, Lesbian, and Transgender Muslims*. London: Oneworld Publications.

Lucas, Scott C. 2006. "Legal Principles of Muhammad B. Isma'il Al-Bukhari." *Islamic Law and Society* 13 (3): 289–324.

Lundqvist, Erica Li. 2020. "Leaving Islam from a Queer Perspective." In *Handbook of Leaving Religion*, edited by Daniel Enstedt, Göran Larsson, and Teemu T. Mantsinen, 220–230. Leiden: Brill. https://doi.org/10.1163/9789004331471_019.

Olomi, Ali. 2021a. "Homosexuality and Gay Love in Islamic History." *Currently Nerdy*, June 29. Podcast audio, 30:54. http://www.currentlynerdy.com/homosexuality-and-gay-love-in-islamic-history/.

Olomi, Ali. 2021b. "Transgender and Non Binary in Islamic History." *Currently Nerdy*, July 13. Podcast audio, 32:50. http://www.currentlynerdy.com/transgender-and-non-binary-in-islamic-history/.

Padula, William V., Shiona Heru, and Jonathan D. Campbell. 2016. "Societal Implications of Health Insurance Coverage for Medically Necessary Services in the U.S. Transgender Population: A Cost-Effectiveness Analysis." *Journal of General Internal Medicine* 31 (4): 394–401. https://doi.org/10.1007/s11606-015-3529-6.

Pew Research Center. 2011. *Muslim Americans: No Signs of Growth in Alienation or Support for Extremism*. August 30. https://www.pewresearch.org/wp-content/uploads/sites/4/legacy-pdf/Muslim-American-Report-10-02-12-fix.pdf.

Pew Research Centre. 2017. "Like Americans Overall, Muslims Now More Accepting of Homosexuality." Accessed June 26, 2022. https://www.pewresearch.org/religion/2017/07/26/political-and-social-views/pf_2017-06-26_muslimamericans-04new-06/.

Predelli, Line Nyhagen. 2008. "Religion, Citizenship and Participation: A Case Study of Immigrant Muslim Women in Norwegian Mosques." *European Journal of Women's Studies* 15 (3): 241–260. https://doi.org/10.1177/1350506808091506.

Rahman, Abdur. 2019. "Ask the People of Remembrance." *Abdur Rahman's Corner*, January 31. https://thecorner.wordpress.com/2019/01/31/ask-the-people-of-remembrance/.

Ryan, Caitlin, Stephen T. Russel, David Huebner, Rafael Diez, and Jorge Sanchez. 2010. "Family Acceptance in Adolescence and the Health of LGBT Young Adults." *Journal of Child and Adolescent Psychiatric Nursing* 23 (4): 205–213. https://doi.org/10.1111/j.1744-6171.2010.00246.x.

Saeed, Abdullah. 2006. *Interpreting the Qur'an: Towards a Contemporary Approach*. London: Routledge.

Safi, Omid, and Simran Singh. 2021. "Omid Safi, 'Anti-Racism as a Spiritual Practice.'" *Religion News Service*, March 10. Podcast audio, 47:20. https://religionnews.com/2021/03/10/omid-safi-anti-racism-as-a-spiritual-practice/.

Sharif, Surkheel. 2009. *The Truth About Taqlid (Part I)*. London: The Jawziyyah Institute. https://web.archive.org/web/20090306022617/http://web.mac.com/jawziyyah/The_Jawziyyah_Institute/Home_files/Taqlid%201.pdf.

Vanita, Ruth, and Saleem Kidwai, eds. 2000. *Same-Sex Love in India: Readings from Literature and History*. New York: St. Martin's Press.

Velte, Kyle C. 2020. "Straightwashing the Census." *Boston College Law Review* 61 (1): 69–128. https://bclawreview.bc.edu/articles/174.

Wadud, Amina. 1999. *Qur'an and Woman: Rereading the Sacred Text from a Woman's Perspective*. Oxford: Oxford University Press.

Wikipedia. 2023. "Letter and Spirit of the Law." Last updated November 10. https://en.wikipedia.org/wiki/Letter_and_spirit_of_the_law.

Zaharin, Aisya Aymanee M., and Maria Pallotta-Chiarolli. 2020. "Countering Islamic Conservatism on Being Transgender: Clarifying Tantawi's and Khomeini's Fatwas from the Progressive Muslim Standpoint." *International Journal of Transgender Health* 21 (3): 235–241. https://doi.org/10.1080/26895269.2020.1778238.

Zahed, Ludovic-Mohamed. 2020. *Homosexuality, Transidentity, and Islam*. Amsterdam: Amsterdam University Press.

Afterword

Reflections on Critical Diasporic South Asian Feminisms

SUNERA THOBANI

Introduction

Identifications, like identities, are enacted by "external" as well as "internal" factors and processes which are shaped by the histories that flow into the making of contemporary social worlds and their specific forms of (un)socialities. The taking up of identifications and identities hence comes with relations of oppression and affirmation, with exploitation as well as expectation. Invaluable work has been undertaken on the interrogation of identity and identifications (including Fanon 1986; Hall 1996; Nandy 2009; Ahmed 2000; Bannerji 1993); however, it is not my intention to revisit this scholarship here. Rather, my objective in this afterword is more modest; it is driven by an urgent concern to draw attention to some of the dangers that inhere within specific identifications and identities at this perilous juncture, rife as it is with the potential destruction of societies, life worlds, ecosystems, and indeed, the planet as we have known it. It is in this spirit that I interrogate the "identifications" and "identities" that are animated by, and at, this symposium on critical South Asian diasporic feminisms. Far too often, such identificatory representations tend to be taken as laudable in and of themselves, progressive, even liberatory. Yet each element of this naming is contested; none of its terms of reference are transparent, and even less so are they "innocent" in their embedded investments.

In the context of Canada, research and scholarship on the status and experiences of diasporic South Asian communities, including their gendered, sexual, and class formation, have a long history. These communities' forms of struggles, political mobilizations, and cultural production have an even longer history. Yet the present moment calls for an urgent rethinking of the trajectories of this scholarly, intellectual, and cultural body of work, as well as its related forms of political expressions and objectives. For this moment is shaped by the confluence of a number of catastrophes that have been building momentum for some time—state repression, militarization, war, and intra-imperialist rivalry; neoliberalism, deregulation, and privatization; colonialism, genocide, and white supremacy; a pandemic that is feeding off the erosion in public spending on health and social welfare to intensify socioeconomic inequality and food insecurity; and environmental devastation and a climate crisis that are leading to unprecedented refugee and migration flows, among many others. These catastrophes are deeply interlinked, and taken together, they are driving the planet and its peoples to a point of no return. Their combined effects are remaking national, regional, and global politics and societies, including in North America and South Asia.

As we witness daily, the liberal-democratic order that has been in place since World War II is in a process of rapid disintegration, and xenophobic nationalisms and fascisms loom large on the horizon. In Canada, the recent discovery of mass graves of Indigenous children on the grounds of residential schools, even as Indigenous girls and women go missing or are murdered, graphically demonstrates the ongoing colonial violence that structures the foundations of this nation-state. The directing of this violence against Indigenous women (highlighted in what is now known as the issue of Murdered and Missing Indigenous Women) and children (the apprehension of Indigenous children through the child welfare system) speaks to the genocidal logic of power that informs Canadian state and nation formation. This is a logic of power that keeps repeating itself at different historical moments (Thobani 2007), and the present juncture is no exception.

If the mass graves point to one form of violence enacted by the settler state, the global support mobilized by the Black Lives Matter movement against police and vigilante violence shows how the anti-Black racism that was a bedrock of slavery, vital to the emergence of capitalism as a global system, remains an entrenched feature of the Canadian nation-state. Anti-Asian racism also erupted with the emergence of the SARS-COV-2 virus, as the historical association of Asians with disease and contagion that shaped early Western imaginaries came to the fore yet again. This racism is also an entrenched feature of settler society, with the earlier migrations of Asians, including as indentured labour, having been vital to the development of these states' "national" economies, even as these communities were simultaneously hated by nationals. In my work on Canada, I have described this nation-state as a triangulated racial formation: the British and French, later joined by other Europeans, have been exalted in its bilingualism and biculturalism as national subjects; the genocide and dispossession of Indigenous Peoples remain ongoing, notwithstanding the emergence of reconciliation as a state project; and Black, Asian, and other enslaved and colonized peoples are racialized as "immigrants" and "newcomers" against whom the borders of the nation have to be policed (Thobani 2007). In addition to their racialization, these borders are gendered, classed, and sexualized, and they have been reproduced and manifested in the many forms of hatred, alienation, and traumas that have been widely documented (Simpson 2022; Thobani 2007; Bolaria and Li 1988; Bannerji 1995; Dua 2007; Razack 1998). The surveillance and reinforcement of these borders, including the overt political sanction of and public support for racial profiling, intensified with Canada's participation in the US-led global War on Terror. Anti-Muslim rhetoric and violence directly targeted Muslim communities within the US, Canada, and Europe, as well as across Afghanistan, the Middle East, and North Africa, and soon enough, this extended across South Asia. With Islamophobia becoming a potent force in geopolitics, its effects on South Asia have been devastating.

It is in this context that I am addressing the work done by "critical diasporic South Asian Canadian feminisms." What traditions of knowledge production and activism does this work actually engage? How do these intersect with the colonial and postcolonial histories that shape the present juncture? What does this theory/praxis offer in the face of the catastrophes of this particular moment? What challenges does one face in working within this intellectual-political formation? What are its objectives, and what do these mean for the communities of its concern? These are the questions that inform the discussion presented in the following sections.

What Is Critical About Critique?

"Critical" is undoubtedly an approach that remains indispensable to any project seeking to engage dominant ideologies, hegemonies, and discourses in order to advance social transformation, whether this is at the epistemological, political, or social level. What is it that is "critical" about critical South Asian feminisms? Where is this "critical" approach directed? To what end? Asking these questions would not be an insignificant matter at any moment, and it is particularly pertinent now given the extent to which Westernity continues to dominate the global political imaginary. In other words, what are the critical traditions upon which one draws when one contests hegemonic practices from the project of critical South Asian feminism? This is no academic question, for where our critical projects take us has serious consequences.

In the provocatively titled post "Can Non-Europeans Think?" Hamid Dabashi (2013) takes a salutary article on Slavoj Zizek, the Slovenian philosopher, to task for including only European—read white—theorists in his identification of the "important" and "active" philosophers of the early twenty-first century (Zabala 2012). As Dabashi notes, this list amounts to a proprietary European claim over "philosophy today." Philosophy—that tradition most closely tied to, and the platform for, the "thinking" of and from modernity—was, of course, historically premised on the rupture between reason and unreason, such that "reason" (the West) worked to emancipate humanity from irrationality and superstition (the rest). Modernity is characterized by rationality, by objectivity and science, not tradition, religion, or faith—hence goes the popular narrative even now. Admittedly, this is to put the matter somewhat crudely, but the astute reader will get the point being made.

Dabashi's (2013) essay is an attempt to disrupt this Eurocentric construction of "philosophy," the capacity to "reason," and the terms that define "critique," by raising the following question: "Do the constellation of thinkers from South Asia...come together to form a nucleus of thinking that is conscious of itself? Would that constellation perhaps merit the word 'thinking' in a manner that would qualify one of them—as a South Asian—to the term 'philosopher' or public 'intellectuals'?" Putting aside for the moment the question of canon building with regard to "South Asian philosophy," the issue of who gets to be recognized—and by who—as a "thinker" worthy of engagement in this globalizing, "decolonial," and postcolonial era is clearly not insignificant. The compilation of this list of the "most importants" is what enables western philosophers to claim the authority to serve as the rightful adjudicators of such matters.

Dabashi's further contention is that the "thinking" of non-Europeans "is more the subject of Western European and North American anthropological fieldwork and investigation." There is, of course, a long history to such classificatory practices, one that has been vigorously challenged by "thinkers" from the Global South (Asad et al. 2009; Fanon 1986). To fully comprehend how Euro-American philosophy—and by extension, rationality and critical thinking—become instituted as "philosophy" and as "critical theory" by reducing non-European thinkers to the space of "ethnos" and "culture," one cannot overlook the role of feminist theory and praxis in deepening these relations of domination and subjugation.

The feminist philosophers Wendy Brown and Judith Butler (Asad et al. 2009) have taken up this issue of what counts as critique in the present juncture, that is, what can be taken as "critical," in a discussion that examines the question of secularism and blasphemy as raised by the publication of the cartoons that linked Islam's Prophet to terrorism. They do so in an exchange with Saba

Mahmood and Talal Asad, in which the latter discuss the experiences and perspectives of Muslim communities in their responses to the publication of these cartoons, and to the larger War on Terror (Asad et al. 2009). I have written about this exchange at some length (Thobani 2020), and can only present a brief recap of this here. Mahmood and Asad expand the discussion by focusing on Muslims' embodied experience of Islam, of European racism, and the problems entailed in applying Christian notions of blasphemy to Islamic praxis (in Mahmood's case), and the relationship between colonialism, secular modernity, and the historical emergence of the idea of "freedom of speech" as a key bourgeois demand that protects private property rights while banning specific forms of speech, including censorship and protection of intellectual property (in the case of Asad). In response, Brown and Butler go to great lengths to reiterate the Eurocentric narrative that secularism and free speech are foundational to modernity, reason, and critique. As they do so, the two feminist philosophers reduce Mahmood's critique of "blasphemy" to the genre of "cultural information" regarding Muslim peculiarities; they treat Asad's historically informed critique of colonialism and the development of bourgeois rights as arising from a failure to comprehend the difference between "critique" and "criticism." Critique, the feminists explain to their interlocutors, comes from the distinction made by Marx between this term (entailing interrogation of the conditions that give rise to the object of critique) and mere "criticism" (primarily a judgemental response).

Ethno-philosophy is how the intellectual traditions of non-Europeans are treated by Western academia, Dabashi (2013) argues. In the exchange I cite above, Mahmood's and Asad's critiques are likewise dismissed as "culture talk" and apologetics by the feminist philosophers.

If the philosophies and intellectual traditions of the peoples and worlds colonized by Euro-America are denied by their reduction to ethno-cultural affairs, one might make the case that a similar practice is to also be found in the field of feminist theory. That is, diasporic and South Asian feminisms continue to be treated as forms of "ethno-feminisms," or to be more accurate, as "women of colour feminisms," "multicultural feminisms," or "transnational feminisms." In this manner, feminism itself remains staunchly Western, staunchly white.

How then do diasporic South Asian feminists engage in the practice of critique, of being "critical"? By critiquing the concept of critique itself? Or by reinstating the coloniality of the practice of critique? What critical traditions actually inform diasporic South Asian feminisms' critical approaches? Are these to be directed toward gender equality and "inclusion" in a system that is daily showing itself to be incapable of responding to the multiple crises of our times? In a system that is the cause of these crises? What does inclusion—even equality—mean within a system that thrives on violence, death, and destruction? If not "inclusion" and "equality," where is this diasporic critical project headed? These questions, I believe, cannot be evaded, whatever stance one may decide to take on them.

Diaspora: Here or There? Everywhere or Nowhere?

Like "critical," the term "diaspora" demands deeper reflection that accounts for its historicity. Is "diaspora" to be defined as an "in-between" place, one that exists between "here" and "there," which creates multi-generational disorientation, as some theorists have argued (Poulsen 2009)? Is it a "third space," a hybrid location that moves beyond "here" and "there" (Bhabha 1994)? The term, of course, gestures to both "here" and "there"; the important question is how to conceive of the "here" and the "there," and how to rechart these spaces. For in that space are to be found many worlds that evade becoming encompassed by these terms. What is the approach of diasporic South Asian feminists to the "here" and to the "there"? What specific meaning is given to the space, to the time, of the "here" and "there," the "then" and the "now"? Can the complexities that give meaning to the "here" and to the "there" of these dynamic, always changing spaces be flattened out? Can one traverse that space via the concept of transnationalism, a short cut overpassing the vexing conundrums of the new/old "here" and the new/old "there"?

It is instructive here to turn to Avtar Brah (1996), who has theorized "diasporic space" as a new configuration of both here and there. Pointing out that the crossing of borders remains central to the making of diaspora, she raises the question of when it is that one's site of location becomes "home." Brah underscores how central personal biography and experience are to shaping one's understanding of the here and the there. As she examines her own, and her family's, experience of migrations from South Asia to East Africa and back, followed by travel to the US and displacement from East Africa to the UK, she unpacks how deeply contested identity, home, and belonging have been for her, and for those of us who have histories of "voluntary" and "forced" migrations, of unreturnable leavings, expulsions, rejections, and beckonings.

Yet Brah is quick to point out that such is also the case for those who have "stayed put," who believe their identities to be securely located. Brah's point is that those who have not been compelled to cross borders, to uproot themselves, to relocate, unsettle, and resettle themselves, who remain "here" as well as "there," are likewise changed by their interactions, relationships with, welcoming of, and resentments toward those who cross borders. As "immigrants," "migrants," "refugees"—all racially coded terms that override history, citizenship, and birthright—"diasporic" South Asian subjects continue to be constructed as interlopers into the whiteness of the worlds of white British, Canadian, and American subjects, including in the imaginaries of white working classes and of women. In the case of Canada, "newcomers" and "visible minorities" are among the more polite terms used in its liberal forms of exclusion.

The concept of diaspora space thus speaks to the interlinking of the politics of dislocation and the politics of location. This is a space that brings together those who move across borders, those who stay put in the source of their migrations, and those who are already there in the new locations of migration/destination. This expansive conceptualization is applicable to the contemporary politics of the "diasporic South Asia/n" feminist. The globalization of the 1990s tied South Asian diasporas around the world—dating from the nineteenth and twentieth centuries—more closely to South Asia. The opportunities offered by relatively easy travel, growing international trade relations, economic restructuring, and the Bollywoodization of cultural industries have immensely strengthened the linkages between "home" and "diaspora" in economic, political, and social terms. It is no longer possible to study "South Asia" in isolation of the impact of these diasporas on the region, nor can one adequately study these diasporas without attending to the solidification of the presence of the "homeland" in the daily life of these communities across North America, the UK, or indeed elsewhere in the world.

Migration patterns from South Asia, and from within South Asian diasporas, have changed profoundly during the last few decades, such that the class composition of these communities has been utterly transformed, cross cutting with relations of caste, gender, religion, region, nation, language, ethnicity, and so on. The post-World War II migrations into Western countries were largely of working and peasant classes, which built on the earlier trade, labour, and indentured migrations of the nineteenth and early twentieth centuries. Certainly there was an elite sector emergent in these migrations, but these were relatively small minorities. In North America, for example, these diasporic communities were established in the context of the transcontinental British empire as they sought to escape the socioeconomic effects of, or to directly contest, the imperial policies of British colonization. These migrants had to contend with the full force of the racializations and violence of the settler societies to which they migrated, founded on the genocides and dispossessions of Indigenous Peoples.

With the neoliberalization of the 1990s, migration patterns from South Asia have since seen the rising numbers of middle and upper-middle classes overtaking those of the disenfranchised working classes and the rise of undocumented migration. Family reunification policies, the technological revolution, the internationalization of Western educational institutions, which rely heavily on international student fees, and the deeper integration of the South Asian bourgeoisie into the international circuits of capitalism have remade these diasporic communities, such that their earlier anti-imperialist/capitalist, anti-racist, and working-class politics are no longer dominant. The upward mobility of sectors of the earlier diasporic communities has also contributed to the sea change that has taken place in diasporic political alignments. Elite and middle-class, assimilationist, and neoliberal consumerist values now shape the most vocal and visible political expressions and aspirations of these communities. In the context of the rise of the violent nationalisms in South Asia, which have intensified with the coming to power of Hindu extremism in India, powerful sectors of the newly reconfigured diasporic communities are now heavily involved in funding, legitimizing, and defending these political shifts, both "here" and "there."

Hence the urgency of the question: what is the relation of contemporary diasporic subjects, of their political commitments, to "there" and to "here"? Interrogation of the changing nature of the ties that bind the "here" and the "there" is crucial.

Although now commonly normalized as a term that is primarily geographical in reference, the more recently coined name "South Asia" is heavily weighted with investments that are political-economic and international-imperialist in scope. The subcontinent to which this term refers has been known by different names, with different meanings for different purposes; "South Asia" is a term that builds upon, encapsulates, and refines the colonial term "British India" in the post-independence period. Emerging from the field of international relations, the term speaks to the post-World War II rearrangement of the international order as the end of the direct rule of European empires gave way to US domination over the global economy as its foremost capitalist power. This term became institutionalized in US foreign policy, where it functioned to organize and expand US strategic interests in this region. The integration of this term into the emerging academic field of area studies was an essential avenue for the extension of these imperialist interests and the epistemologies that served them.

In the decades following Partition and independence, India grew into the uncontested regional power. And to cut a long story short, Indian national politics have now shifted from the Nehruvian vision of a secular social democracy with its pro-Third Worldism commitment to a neoliberal, globalizing "New" India that has been significantly remade by the political ideology of Hindu nationalism that sees India as a Hindu Rashtra. With the 1971 Bangladesh War of Independence, Pakistan was further subdivided, with both states subsequently caught between Islamization and secularization as a result of both national and geopolitical conflicts and their shifting conditions, to put it somewhat crudely. Sri Lanka was torn apart by the Tamil struggle for independence and the ensuing civil war, which ended in a bloodbath carried out by the state. South Asia's geographical location made it a key battlefield in the Cold War and the wars that have erupted in its aftermath, but it is beyond the scope of this chapter to delve further into the region's complex political histories and the contemporary conflicts in which it is now engulfed. It will suffice for me to underscore the point that the term "South Asia" obfuscates at least as much as it reveals about the challenges that have besieged these and other nation-states in the region, at the national, transnational, and geopolitical levels.

With regard to the diasporic communities that migrated—whether involuntarily or voluntarily—from the region, the issue of identification has long been a fraught matter. In Canada, for example, the early migrants from "British India" at the turn of the twentieth century were classified by the Canadian state as "non-preferred races," "Hindoos," or "East Indians" until well into the mid-twentieth century. These designations organized as well as reflected the racialization accomplished by colonial policies across the British empire and in the settler-colonial dominions. Upon the liberalization of the Canadian state in the 1970s, which entailed the introduction of the point system in immigration policy and the adoption of official multiculturalism, immigrants from South Asia were re-designated variously as "Indo-Canadians," "East Indians," "immigrants," and "visible minorities." At this time, "Indo-Canadian" was the term that became commonly used by these communities, but these classifications shifted yet again with the neoliberalization of the last decade of the twentieth century. The term "Indo-Canadian" was now replaced by "South Asian Canadian," with the latter considered a more inclusive term that recognized the heterogeneity and changing demographics that were the result of the then increasing immigration from the region. "Visible minorities" also gave way to the label "newcomers," which was no less an exclusionary and racially coded term. The idea that these communities were recent arrivals continued to racialize them and to undermine their claims to citizenship and belonging. Yet even as "South Asian Canadian" was being taken up as the preferable designation, especially among the more progressive and activist sectors within these communities, the global War on Terror instigated an internal splitting of the category, so that Muslim South Asian Canadians were now set apart by the state as well as within diasporic communities and classified simply as "Muslim," an identity now explicitly associated with terrorism, misogyny, and "cultural barbarism." The point being made here is that identity making remains a contentious process for diasporas in the West, this being informed as much by Canadian state categories, practices, and policies as by "internal" factors arising from within communities themselves—as much by the "national" political shifts in Canada as in the various South Asian post-independence nation-states and in "international" shifts in geopolitics.

In another useful example, no less illustrative of the changing nature of identity as well as identification, South Asians in the UK included themselves in the designation "Black" during the 1970s and 1980s (Ahmed 2000; Mirza 1997). This was a political self-naming based on anti-racist solidarities among communities of African and South Asian descent in their collective struggles against the discriminations and violence of the British state, a racism that was most charged in its immigration and deportation policies; social welfare, housing, education, and employment programs; and legal and policing practices. Black feminists were at the forefront of these struggles, and of building coalitional politics, alliances, and solidarities. These solidarities were soon undermined by British state practice and their implicit use of multiculturalism, with its divide and rule tactics, as well as by the neoliberalization of the British economy and related social values during the 1990s, which escalated class divisions within and among these communities.

Such solidarities would henceforth become difficult to sustain, as upwardly mobile sectors of South Asian diasporic communities became integrated into neoliberalism's turn to political conservatism. The name "British-Asian" replaced the identity "Black British," with the term undergoing yet another transformation as the War on Terror siloed off "British Muslims" to further erode their status, citizenship, and entitlements.

This very cursory discussion of the politics of naming among South Asian diasporas in Canada and the UK calls for constant vigilance about what these shifts in designations actually accomplish in their particular national as well as diasporic settings, and in the national, regional, and global contexts of their deployment. Changing migration patterns from South Asia, with elite classes increasingly migrating to join elite institutions in the West, and with disenfranchised and working classes and undocumented migrants becoming subjected to greater violence, surveillance, and exclusion, call for increased interrogation of these politics of naming. Taking these politics for granted only serves to further entrench economic as well as sociopolitical divides within these communities, and shields from view their growing involvement in, and support for, the extremist politics of violent nationalisms in their countries of migration and in South Asia. Diasporic South Asian feminists, like South Asian feminists, are situated squarely within these divisive conditions and politics, whether they are located "here" or "there."

If identity, like identification, remains unstable and constantly in flux, examining its shifts and turns remains indispensable to confronting the catastrophes of the present, and to building community and relations of affinity that are based in deep and lasting exchange, dialogue, and alliance. The conflation and flattening out of hierarchies and asymmetries of power that shape relationalities in and between identities, and their communities of identification, only feed these catastrophes.

Feminism(s), "South Asian," or What?

In the preceding sections, I discussed how the proclamation of specific identities and identifications has been of profound importance to "South Asians" as well as to "diasporic South Asians," who, as colonized peoples—with all the richness and deprivations of their heterogeneous experiences—have been racialized in specific kinds of ways. In this final section, I discuss how this is no less the case with "diasporic South Asian feminisms." As I have implicitly pointed out, the "feminisms" associated with the terms "South Asia" and "diaspora" have undergone considerable transformations "here," "there," and "in-between" that are specific to their temporal and spatial contexts of articulation.

The influence of Western feminism on South Asian feminisms has been a contentious issue. This is receiving greater attention as the effects of the entrenchment of class, caste, and national and religious relations among women in the region are deepening (Loomba and Lukose 2012; Rege 1998; Hasan 2016). The hold of elite and upper-middle-class, upper caste, urban, and Westernized communities of women over "South Asian feminisms" has too often replicated the hierarchies and practices of power that characterize feminist movements in the West, and these hierarchies have been challenged by women of colour (hooks 1981; Davis 1983; Bannerji 1995). The development of what is presently termed "diasporic South Asian feminism" has been shaped by its own trajectories of migration and relocation, as well as the specificity of its more direct engagement with Western feminism in diasporic space. The complex histories of these various South Asian feminisms are not something I can take up in this chapter. What I will make note of here is how deeply the experience of encountering and confronting gendered whiteness in hegemonic feminist politics has shaped the theorizing of the intersections of race, class, and sexuality with gender and nation central to the activism and knowledge production of diasporic/women of colour feminists.

Among the early concerns of feminists in the South Asian diasporas—the examples I will use are from the UK and Canada—were immigration policy and citizenship, family reunification, access to education and employment, state and national racisms, and violence against women (Amos and Parmar 1984; Mirza 1997; Dua 2007; Bannerji 1995). Notably also is that addressing race, class, and imperialism were central to their feminist politics and activism. In the UK of the 1970s and 1980s, and into the early 1990s, this women's activism was developed in solidarity with Black women of African descent (Amos and Parmer 1984; Mirza 1997), such that Black British feminism became the overarching frame for the struggles they waged, which were grounded in the experiences of working-class diasporic African, Caribbean, and South Asian communities. In the US and Canada of that period, this diasporic feminism developed under the rubric of "women of colour" and "anti-racist" feminisms, which included a conscious critique of borderlands, settler colonialism, anti-Black racism, and global imperialism in coalitional politics with the larger communities of diasporic women (Brah 1996; Loomba and Lukose 2012; Bannerji 1995; Dua 2007; Thobani 2020). As was the case in the UK, anti-race, class, and anti-colonial/imperialist politics shaped these feminisms in the US and Canada. Indeed, feminists of South Asian diasporas were central to the development of critical race theory in Canada (among others, see Razack 1998; Thobani 2007; Dua 2007; Bannerji 1995).

No less significantly, the feminisms of these diasporic communities in the different national sites (the UK, the US, and Canada) did not articulate their politics as being in tandem, or parallel, with the feminism of white/Western women. Instead, these "Black" and "woman of colour" feminisms were developed as a contestation of Western feminism, of its conflation of elite/middle-class white women with the category "woman" and its universalization of the experience of this particular group of women. Exposing the racial-colonial and national-imperial investments of white feminism was a key characteristic of these diasporic feminisms. In other words, the feminism of Black/South Asian women in their respective diasporic contexts did not develop a pluralist approach to feminist politics (by adding the "s" to feminisms), but centred the positionality as well as the relationality of specific communities of women to explicitly challenge the politics of whiteness articulated within Western feminism, as well as to confront its colonial moorings.

This is not a claim one can readily make about contemporary iterations of diasporic South Asian feminisms. The class composition of immigration from South Asia changed dramatically from the early 1960s through the 1970s and 1980s, so that much of this migration was that of the middle and upper classes, including women, from South Asia. Among the impact of these changes was the reshaping of diasporic South Asian communities' political focus to the objective of equality and inclusion, and this on the grounds of multiculturalism. In North America, for example, "transnationalism" became the overarching frame for the articulation of feminist politics, which often dovetailed with the values dominant within neoliberalism, especially on the question of choice and individual rights. Confronting imperialism, the global hierarchy of race, settler colonialism, and growing class divides within the diaspora cannot be identified, with few exceptions, as key concerns in this formation of feminism, nor can building anti-capitalist solidarities with other communities of disenfranchised and dispossessed women of colour be taken as central to its key objectives. In the case of Canada, for example, it was only after the Indigenous resurgence that had been ongoing since the Oka Crisis gained increased visibility in national politics with the appointment of the Truth and Reconciliation Commission that settler colonialism came to be identified as a major concern in the casting of "diasporic South Asian feminisms." The on-the-ground solidarities built with Indigenous women by anti-racist and anti-colonial South Asian diasporic feminists during the preceding decades on the issues of residential schools and the ongoing murders and disappearances of Indigenous women and girls are made invisible in the new inward-looking formation of South Asian diasporic feminism. Likewise, it was not until the international support mobilized by Black Lives Matter dominated the news after the police killing of George Floyd in 2020 that building coalitions against anti-Black racism emerged as an area of concern for this feminist formation, which even now continues to evade the issue of anti-Blackness in the diaspora and in South Asia itself. The question of why transnational feminism in the South Asian/diasporic context does not have an explicitly articulated anti-capitalist, anti-imperialist, and pro-working class politics, or why building women of colour solidarity on this basis does not shape its political agenda, requires attention. How to explain why it is the case that the experiences of, and issues of concern to, elite and middle-class South Asian and South Asian diasporic women have so disproportionately shaped this articulation of "transnational feminism"? That women from these classes, whose transnational mobility is read by them as universally accessible, have a stake in the neoliberalization of "there" and "here" is an issue that needs to be confronted. The experiences of South Asian and other migrant workers, farm workers, domestic workers, or indeed—post-pandemic—front-line workers do not figure much in this "transnational" feminist political project.

The War on Terror demonstrated the extent to which feminists from elite and Westernized classes—in the diaspora and in South Asia—dominate feminist politics in their respective locations. Islamophobia was the ideological frame for this global war, and anti-Muslim racism and the demonization of Islam legitimized the invasion of Afghanistan and Iraq, as well as the US-led proxy wars across the Middle East and North Africa. "Saving" Muslim women from their families, communities, and Islam, and incarcerating, torturing, and killing Muslim men in order to do so, became part of the rationale for globalizing the War on Terror. In my work on this topic, I have argued that the gender-sexual politics of the West were being remade through the global War on Terror, and that feminist movements were playing a key role by gendering the Islamophobia of both imperialist and post-independence states (Thobani 2020). The construction of the West and its subjects as "saviours" of Muslim women and Muslim gender and sexual minorities was advanced by feminists, including in their reworkings of South Asian and diasporic South Asian feminisms, as the means to civilize and modernize Muslims. The Islamophobia of this new imperialist phase was thus grounded in feminist theory and praxis. As a result, new political splits were engendered among people of colour communities, as well as within Muslim communities, with the latter being left politically and socially isolated within the diasporas, as elsewhere. The lack of a rigorous feminist critique of imperialism, militarization, invasions, proxy wars, and occupations, and even of the destruction of the third world state and Muslim societies in this moment of crisis was striking.

Engagement with the terrain of feminism in this particular moment remains urgent and necessary. Yet this is not an easy task, for what "feminism" represents today is not entirely self-evident. Approached in an un-self-reflexive manner, proclaiming oneself a feminist can today be read on a spectrum ranging from endorsement of individualism and its signature neoliberal value of "free choice," to support for imperialist wars as the means to "free" Muslim and Third World women, to a commitment to achieving "equality" for women, even if the terms "woman" and "equality" remain unclear. Each one of these terms of engagement is contested.

A reckoning with how the violence of the past forms the present, and a commitment to confronting contemporary forms of violence to build just futures are the tasks of the day. Assimilation into neoliberalism and promises of equality and inclusion are on offer aplenty. Whither, then, critical South Asian diasporic feminisms?

References

Ahmed, Sara. 2000. *Strange Encounters: Embodied Others in Post-Coloniality*. London: Routledge.

Amos, Valerie, and Pratibha Parmar. 1984. "Challenging Imperial Feminism." *Feminist Review* 17 (Autumn): 3–19. https://doi.org/10.2307/1395006.

Asad, Talal, Wendy Brown, Judith Butler, and Saba Mahmood. 2009. *Is Critique Secular? Blasphemy, Injury and Free Speech*. Berkeley: The Townsend Papers in the Humanities.

Bannerji, Himani, ed. 1993. *Returning the Gaze: Essays on Racism, Feminism and Politics*. Toronto: Sister Vision Press.

Bannerji, Himani. 1995. *Thinking Through: Essays on Feminism, Marxism and Anti-Racism*. Toronto: Canadian Scholars Press.

Bhabha, Homi K. 1994. *The Location of Culture*. London: Routledge.

Bolaria, B. Singh, and Peter S. Li. 1988. *Racial Oppression in Canada*. Toronto: Garamond Press.

Brah, Avtar. 1996. *Cartographies of Diaspora: Contesting Identities*. London: Routledge.

Dabashi, Hamid. 2013. "Can Non-Europeans Think?: What Happens with Thinkers Who Operate Outside the European Philosophical 'Pedigree'?" *Al Jazeera*, January 15. https://www.aljazeera.com/opinions/2013/1/15/can-non-europeans-think.

Davis, Angela. 1983. *Women, Race and Class*. New York: Vintage Books.

Dua, Enakshi. 2007. "Exclusion Through Inclusion." *Gender, Place and Culture: A Journal of Feminist Geography* 14 (4): 445–466.

Fanon, Frantz. 1986. *Black Skin, White Masks*. Translated by Charles Lam Markmann. London: Pluto Press.

Hall, Stuart. 1996. "Who Needs Identity?" In *Questions of Cultural Identity*, edited by Stuart Hall and Paul Gay, 1–17. London: Sage.

Hasan, Zoya. 2016. "Democracy and Growing Inequalities in India." *Social Change* 46 (2): 290–301. https://doi.org/10.1177/0049085716635432.

hooks, bell. 1981. *Ain't I a Woman? Black Women and Feminism*. Toronto: Between the Lines.

Loomba, Ania, and Ritty A. Lukose, eds. 2012. *South Asian Feminisms: Contemporary Interventions*. Durham: Duke University Press.

Mirza, Heidi. 1997. *Black British Feminism: A Reader*. London: Routledge.

Nandy, Ashis. 2009. *The Intimate Enemy: Loss and Recovery of Self Under Colonialism*. Oxford: Oxford University Press.

Poulsen, Shruti. 2009. "East Indian Families Raising ABCD Adolescents." *The Family Journal* 17 (2): 168–174.

Razack, Sherene. 1998. *Looking White People in the Eye: Gender, Nation and Culture in Courtrooms and Classes*. Toronto: University of Toronto Press.

Rege, Sharmila. 1998. "Dalit Women Talk Differently: A Critique of Difference and Towards a Dalit Feminist Standpoint Position." *Economic and Political Weekly* 33 (44): WS-39–WS-46.

Simpson, Audra. 2022. "The State Is a Man: Theresa Spence, Loretta Saunders and the Gender of Settler Sovereignty." In *Coloniality and Racial (In)Justice in the University: Counting for Nothing?*, edited by Sunera Thobani, 136–162. Toronto: University of Toronto Press.

Thobani, Sunera. 2007. *Exalted Subjects: Studies in the Making of Race and Nation in Canada*. Toronto: University of Toronto Press.

Thobani, Sunera. 2020. *Contesting Islam, Constructing Race and Sexuality: The Inordinate Desire of the West*. New York: Bloomsbury Academic.

Zabala, Santiogo. 2012. "Slavoj Zizek and the Role of the Philosopher." *Al Jazeera*, December 25. https://www.aljazeera.com/opinions/2012/12/25/slavoj-zizek-and-the-role-of-the-philosopher/.

Contributors

Marshia Akbar is a senior research associate with the Canada Excellence Research Chair (CERC) in the migration and integration program at Ryerson University. She earned a doctorate from York University with a focus on migration and settlement. Her research broadly encompasses how social inequalities and settlement policies shape the labour market integration of migrants, particularly racialized migrant women in Canada. Currently working with settlement agencies in major urban areas, she is assessing policies about eligibility for permanent residency and settlement services and their impacts on the employment outcomes of different categories of temporary and skilled migrants in Canada.

Dolores Chew, originally from Kolkata, India, lives in Tio'tia:ke (Montreal), on the unceded territory of the Kanien'kehà:ka (Mohawk). Dolores teaches history and humanities at Marianopolis College and is the coordinator of its liberal arts program. Her research and writing, with a focus on women, intersects with her activism in the areas of justice for the victims of the Gujarat genocide, Anglo-Indian studies, and migrant justice. She is active in organizing related to India and South Asia, community organizing with the South Asian Women's Community Centre and Women of Diverse Origins, and decolonizing solidarity work. Currently, she also serves on the board of the Fédération des femmes du Québec.

Safiyya Hosein is an instructor in the Faculty of Arts at Toronto Metropolitan University, where she teaches courses in the radio and television arts department as well as in sociology. She has published in the *Popular Culture Studies Journal*, the *Fashion Studies Journal*, and *Feminist Encounters: A Journal of Critical Studies in Culture and Politics*. She was selected by Vice Media's Motherboard for their "Humans of the Year" series in 2017.

Amina Jamal is a professor of sociology at Toronto Metropolitan University. She is presently investigating the dilemmas of feminist and progressive Muslim politics and poetics in South Asia, as these are threatened by diverse hegemonic discourses and multiple forms of violence emanating from local, national, and global interests. Amina is author of the monograph *Jamaat-e-Islami Women in Pakistan: Vanguard of a New Modernity?* She writes in the areas of women, Islam and modernity, transnational and postcolonial feminism, violence against women, and Muslim women's struggles in Pakistan and Canada.

Nayyar S. Javed is a psychologist (MA, Reg.) and anti-racism feminist activist. As a psychologist, she has offered therapy, integrating feminist therapy with an anti-racism approach, taught courses, published articles and book chapters, delivered programs for refugees and immigrants, and presented papers at local and international levels. She has supervised students and been part of a team researching racial disparities in health services and health outcomes. Nayyar has served as steering committee member for the Advanced Institute of Feminist Therapy and as a member of the United Nations' NGO Committee on Mental Health. She has been deeply engaged in local anti-racism and feminist organizations in Saskatchewan, and served in national feminist organizations including the National Action Committee on the Status of Women, Canadian Research Institute for the Advancement of Women (CRIAW), and Feminist Alliance for International Actions.

Peruvemba S. Jaya is an associate professor in the Department of Communication, Faculty of Arts, at the University of Ottawa. Her research interests include the areas of gender diversity and multiculturalism in the workplace, immigrant women, South Asian immigrant women's experience, interpersonal communication, identity formation and construction processes, postcolonial theory, intercultural communication, ethnic media, and qualitative research methodologies. She is currently the regional representative (Canada) of Research Committee 32: Women in Society of the International Sociological Association. She has published in journals such as *Canadian Ethnic Studies*, *Qualitative Report*, and *Journal of Identity and Migration Studies*.

Aaliya Khan is a first-year PHD student at York University who is interested in spatial politics and gendered Islamophobia. She has a bachelor's in political science and a master's in urban and regional planning, in addition to substantive experience working in the gender-based violence sector. She draws from her lived experiences as a hijab-wearing Muslim woman and first-generation immigrant.

Ameera Sultana Khan (she/her) is a Bengali American Muslim whose Islam is informed from a myriad of sources, including the memorization of the Qur'an and studying progressive Muslim perspectives. She is informed by Sunni, Sufi, anti-patriarchal, and liberation theology-oriented traditions within Shariah, Quran, Hadith, and Islamic history. She joined the Muslim Youth Leadership Council in 2018 to come together with empowered Muslims reclaiming their narratives across the country, and has held numerous workshops and given talks on reclaiming queer Islamic history, Muslim identity, and shariah laws. She has also organized conferences, most recently the Muslim Youth Leadership Council's virtual conference, which drew attendees from across the globe. In her professional life, she works as a DevOps engineer for Carrot Health in Minneapolis, Minnesota.

Maryam Khan, PHD, is an associate professor at Wilfred Laurier University's Faculty of Social Work. Maryam has over ten years of clinical experience in mental health and addictions, working with children, queer youth, and adults in various interdisciplinary non-profit settings. As a qualitative and mixed methods researcher, Maryam is passionate about producing critical knowledges and working with racialized 2SLGBTQ+ individuals and communities, religious, spiritual, and sexual minorities, and Muslim women.

Kanwal Khokhar obtained a master's degree in criminal and social justice at Toronto Metropolitan University. Kanwal's research interests include examining the intricacies of crafting evidence-based immigration policies and gendered considerations in terrorism and radicalization research, and investigating the knowledge gaps that exist within Western literature relating to minority populations.

Sailaja V. Krishnamurti, PHD, is an associate professor of religious studies and women and gender studies, and coordinator of the program in Asian studies, at Saint Mary's University, Halifax. Her research takes a critical race feminist approach to religion, migration, and representation in the South Asian diaspora and in transnational cultures. She is the author of several refereed articles and book chapters and co-editor of *Relation and Resistance: Racialized Women, Religion and Diaspora* (McGill-Queen's University Press, 2021). Dr. Krishnamurti co-chairs the Women of Color Scholarship, Teaching, and Activism unit of the American Academy of Religion, and is a founding member of the Intersectional Feminist Hindu Studies Collective.

Jane Ku is an associate professor in sociology and women and gender studies at the University of Windsor. She comes to this project with a scholarly interest and contributions in the transnational and postcolonial feminist interrogation of ethnoracial identity and Canadian multiculturalism. She has been exploring her Chinese and Indian background through an autoethnographic approach. In 2019, she published an article in *Canadian Ethnic*

Studies on being hailed as Chinese and Hakka in Canada, and another on re-narrating one's history as a path to feminist solidarity in *Intermédialités*. She is currently studying the experiences of racism among African, Caribbean, and Black women in Windsor.

Ayesha Mian Akram is a PHD candidate in the University of Windsor's Department of Sociology and Criminology. Her SSHRC-funded doctoral research in the field of sociology/social justice is a participatory project, working with Muslim women activists to investigate how they develop collectives of resistance. She is a community-based educator, researcher, and organizer whose work is rooted in the intersections of anti-racism studies, religion, gender, and subjectivity.

Mandeep Kaur Mucina, MSW, PHD, is an assistant professor in the School of Child and Youth Care at the University of Victoria. Mandeep's research interests include family and gender-based violence in South Asian communities, second-generation immigrant women's and girls' stories of survival and resistance in Canada, and the intersection of racism and bordering practices in the child welfare system.

Sarah Shah (they/them) is an assistant professor at the Department of Sociology, Texas State University, and a lead researcher at the Muslims in Canada Data Initiative (MICDI), Institute of Islamic Studies, University of Toronto. Shah's research unpacks how religion dialectically structures and is structured by gender and family relations, immigration and racialization processes, and mental health. In their current project on Canadian Muslim families, Shah looks at Muslim religious reflexivities, or the critical ways in which diasporic Muslims navigate and negotiate their religious identities and practices.

Farah Mahrukh Coomi Shroff was a Harvard School of Public Health Fellow in International Health from August 2021 to June 2022. She is the principal of Shroff Consulting, a public health, education, and social issues consulting company that focuses on research, writing, facilitation, and more. Dr. Shroff also works in the

Department of Family Practice and the School of Population and Public Health at the University of British Columbia's Faculty of Medicine. The emphasis in her research is on envisioning and developing health for all. Her main areas of research are holistic health and community development within a social justice framework. She has been a womxn's health researcher and educator for many years, focusing on reproduction, midwifery, HIV, sexuality, mental well-being, and so forth. Dr. Shroff is passionate about the health and human rights of womxn. She founded and leads Maternal and Infant Health Canada (MIHCan), a global public health collaborative that focuses on improving the lives of womxn and children through education, research, and innovation.

Sunera Thobani (she/her) is a professor in Asian studies at the University of British Columbia. Her scholarship focuses on critical South Asian, postcolonial, and transnational feminist theory and politics; intersectionality and social movements; colonialism, indigeneity, and racial violence; globalization, citizenship, and migration; Islam, gender, and Muslims in South Asian and Western media; South Asian diasporas; and South Asian women's gender and sexuality studies. She has served as the Ruth Wynn Woodward Endowed Chair in Women's Studies at Simon Fraser University and as president of the National Action Committee on the Status of Women. She is a founding member of the cross-Canada network, Researchers and Academics of Colour for Equity (RACE).

www.ingramcontent.com/pod-product-compliance
Lightning Source LLC
LaVergne TN
LVHW040757070826
844660LV00025B/1179

* 9 7 8 1 7 7 2 1 2 8 2 2 2 *